AQA History

A2
Unit 3

Triumph and Collapse: Russia and the USSR, 1941–91

Exclusively endorsed by AQA

John Laver
Series editor
Sally Waller

Nelson Thornes

Published in 2009 by:
Nelson Thornes Ltd
Delta Place
27 Bath Road
CHELTENHAM
GL53 7TH
United Kingdom

09 10 11 12 13 / 10 9 8 7 6 5 4 3 2 1

A catalogue record for this book is available from the British Library

ISBN 978 1 4085 0316 4

Cover photograph: Russian Look Photo Agency
Illustrations by David Russell Illustration

Page make-up by Thomson Digital

Printed in Croatia by Zrinski

Contents

AQA introduction

Nelson Thornes and AQA

Nelson Thornes has worked in partnership with AQA to ensure this book offers you the best support for your A Level course and helps you to prepare for your exams. All resources have been approved by senior AQA examiners so you can feel assured that they closely match the specification for this subject and provide you with everything you need to prepare successfully for your exams.

How to use this book

This book covers the specification for your course and is arranged in a sequence approved by AQA.

The features in this book include:

Timeline

Key events are outlined at the beginning of the book. The events are colour-coded so you can clearly see the categories of change.

Learning objectives

At the beginning of each section you will find a list of learning objectives that contain targets linked to the requirements of the specification.

Key chronology

A short list of dates usually with a focus on a specific event or legislation.

Key profile

The profile of a key person you should be aware of to fully understand the period in question.

Key terms

A term that you will need to be able to define and understand.

Did you know?

Interesting information to bring the subject under discussion to life.

Exploring the detail

Information to put further context around the subject under discussion.

A closer look

An in-depth look at a theme, person or event to deepen your understanding. Activities around the extra information may be included.

Sources

Sources reinforce topics or themes and may provide fact or opinion. They may be quotations from historical works, contemporaries of the period or photographs.

Cross-reference

Links to related content within the book which may offer more detail on the subject in question.

Activity

Various types of activity to provide you with different challenges and opportunities to demonstrate the content and skills you are learning. Some can be worked on individually, some as part of group work and some are designed to specifically 'stretch and challenge'.

Question

Questions to prompt further discussion on the topic under consideration and to aid revision.

Summary questions

Summary questions at the end of each chapter to test your knowledge and allow you to demonstrate your understanding.

AQA Examiner's tip

Hints from AQA examiners to help you with your study and to prepare for your exam.

AQA Examination-style questions

Questions at the end of each section in the style that you can expect in your exam.

Learning outcomes

Learning outcomes at the end of each section remind you what you should know having completed the chapters in that section.

Web links in the book

As Nelson Thornes is not responsible for third party content online, there may be some changes to this material that are beyond our control. In order for us to ensure that the links referred to in the book are as up-to-date and stable as possible, the web sites provided are usually homepages with supporting instructions on how to reach the relevant pages if necessary.

Please let us know at **kerboodle@nelsonthornes.com** if you find a link that doesn't work and we will do our best to correct this at reprint, or to find an alternative site.

Introduction to the History series

When Bruce Bogtrotter in Roald Dahl's *Matilda* was challenged to eat a huge chocolate cake, he just opened his mouth and ploughed in, taking bite after bite and lump after lump until the cake was gone and he was feeling decidedly sick. The picture is not dissimilar to that of some A Level history students. They are attracted to history because of its inherent appeal but, when faced with a bulging file and a forthcoming examination, their enjoyment evaporates. They try desperately to cram their brains with an assortment of random facts and subsequently prove unable to control the outpouring of their ill-digested material in the examination.

The books in this series are designed to help students and teachers avoid this feeling of overload and examination panic by breaking down the AQA history specification in such a way that it is easily absorbed. Above all, they are designed to retain and promote students' enthusiasm for history by avoiding a dreary rehash of dates and events. Each book is divided into sections, closely matched to those given in the specification, and the content is further broken down into chapters that present the historical material in a lively and attractive form, offering guidance on the key terms, events and issues, and blending thought-provoking activities and questions in a way designed to advance students' understanding. By encouraging students to think for themselves and to share their ideas with others, as well as helping them to develop the knowledge and skills they will need to pass their examination, this book should ensure that students' learning remains a pleasure rather than an endurance test.

To make the most of what this book provides, students will need to develop efficient study skills from the start and it is worth spending some time considering what these involve:

▪ Good organisation of material in a subject-specific file. Organised notes help develop an organised brain and sensible filing ensures time is not wasted hunting for misplaced material. This book uses cross-references to indicate where material in one chapter has relevance to material in another. Students are advised to adopt the same technique.

▪ A sensible approach to note-making. Students are often too ready to copy large chunks of material from printed books or to download sheaves of printouts from the internet. This series is designed to encourage students to think about the notes they collect and to undertake research with a particular purpose in mind. The activities encourage students to pick out information that is relevant to the issue being addressed and to avoid making notes on material that is not properly understood.

▪ Taking time to think, which is by far the most important component of study. By encouraging students to think before they write or speak, be it for a written answer, presentation or class debate, students should learn to form opinions and make judgements based on the accumulation of evidence. These are the skills that the examiner will be looking for in the final examination. The beauty of history is that there is rarely a right or wrong answer so, with sufficient evidence, one student's view will count for as much as the next.

▪ Unit 3

The topics chosen for study in Unit 3 are all concerned with the changing relationship between state and people over a period of around 50 years. These topics enable students to build on the skills acquired at AS Level, combining breadth, by looking at change and continuity over a period of time, with depth, in analysing specific events and developments. The chosen topics offer plentiful opportunities for an understanding of historical processes enabling students to realise that history moves forward through the interaction of many different factors, some of which may change in importance over a period of time. Significant individuals, societies, events, developments and issues are explored in a historical context and developments affecting different groups within the societies studied from a range of historical perspectives. Study at Unit 3 will therefore develop full synoptic awareness and enable students to understand the way a professional historian goes about the task of developing a full historical understanding.

Unit 3 is tested by a 1 hour 30 minute paper containing three essay questions from which students need to select two. Details relating to the style of questions, with additional hints, are given in the accompanying table and helpful tips to enable students to meet the examination demands are given throughout this book. Students should familiarise themselves with both the question demands and the marking criteria which follow before attempting any of the practice examination questions at the end of each section of this book.

Answers will be marked according to a scheme based on 'levels of response'. This means that an essay will be assessed according to which level best matches the

Unit 3 (Three essay questions in total)	Question type	Marks	Question stem	Hints for students
Two essay questions	Standard essay questions addressing a part of the Specification content and seeking a judgement based on debate and evaluation	45	These are not prescriptive but likely stems include: To what extent… How far… A quotation followed by, 'How valid is this assessment/view?'	All answers should convey an argument. Plan before beginning to write and make the argument clear at the outset. The essay should show an awareness of how factors interlink and students should make some judgement between them (synoptic links). All comments should be supported by secure and precise evidence.
One essay question	Standard essay question covering the whole period of the unit or a large part of that period and seeking a judgement based on debate and evaluation	45	As above	Evidence will need to be carefully selected from across the full period to support the argument. It might prove useful to emphasise the situation at the beginning and end of the period, identify key turning points and assess factors promoting change and continuity.

historical skills it displays, taking both knowledge and understanding into account. All students should keep a copy of the marking criteria in their files and need to use them wisely.

Marking criteria

Level 1 Answers will display a limited understanding of the demands of the question. They may either contain some descriptive material which is only loosely linked to the focus of the question or they may address only a part of the question. Alternatively, they may contain some explicit comment but will make few, if any, synoptic links and will have limited accurate and relevant historical support. There will be little, if any, awareness of differing historical interpretations. The response will be limited in development and skills of written communication will be weak. *(0–6 marks)*

Level 2 Answers will show some understanding of the demands of the question. They will either be primarily descriptive with few explicit links to the question or they may contain explicit comment but show limited relevant factual support. They will display limited understanding of differing historical interpretations. Historical debate may be described rather than used to illustrate an argument and any synoptic links will be undeveloped. Answers will be coherent but weakly expressed and/or poorly structured. *(7–15 marks)*

Level 3 Answers will show a good understanding of the demands of the question. They will provide some

assessment, backed by relevant and appropriately selected evidence, which may, however, lack depth. There will be some synoptic links made between the ideas, arguments and information included although these may not be highly developed. There will be some understanding of varying historical interpretations. Answers will be clearly expressed and show reasonable organisation in the presentation of material. *(16–25 marks)*

Level 4 Answers will show a very good understanding of the demands of the question. There will be synoptic links made between the ideas, arguments and information included showing an overall historical understanding. There will be good understanding and use of differing historical interpretations and debate and the answer will show judgement through sustained argument backed by a carefully selected range of precise evidence. Answers will be well-organised and display good skills of written communication. *(26–37 marks)*

Level 5 Answers will show a full understanding of the demands of the question. The ideas, arguments and information included will be wide-ranging, carefully chosen and closely interwoven to produce a sustained and convincing answer with a high level of synopticity. Conceptual depth, independent judgement and a mature historical understanding, informed by a well-developed understanding of historical interpretations and debate, will be displayed. Answers will be well-structured and fluently written. *(38–45 marks)*

Introduction to this book

The USSR, 1917–41

Lenin and the establishment of Communist rule

The Communists, led by Lenin, seized power in the old Russian Empire in 1917. They immediately became involved in a brutal and costly civil war. The Communists, or 'Reds', were fought by those Russians known as 'Whites', who objected to Lenin's seizure of power. The Whites were supported by armies, or given other assistance, from 17 foreign countries, including Britain, France and the USA. Their governments were fighting Germany in the First World War, and Russia was a major ally. However, Lenin wanted nothing to do with the war and made a separate peace with Germany in March 1918. The Western Allies were opposed to Russia's withdrawal from the war, because it put them under more pressure from a German army that no longer had to fight on two fronts. They also feared that the Communists would try to export their revolutionary ideology abroad, directed against them. The Communists were fighting for their very existence and emerged victorious from the war. However, their victory left Russia, particularly its economy, badly damaged.

Lenin ensured that his regime survived by introducing the New Economic Policy in 1921. This allowed peasants and businessmen to work for themselves and make profits. This appeared to go against the spirit of socialism, which was based on the idea of the state owning resources on behalf of the people. However, the new policy helped to stabilise Russia and led to a moderate economic recovery. At the same time, Lenin's regime snuffed out any hint of political freedom. Only the Communist Party could operate freely, and opponents of the regime were dealt with ruthlessly by the security services.

The rise of Stalin

Lenin died in 1924. The next few years saw a power struggle among Lenin's most prominent colleagues. It was not just a struggle between ambitious individuals, but also a clash of ideas about how Russia should progress to the stage of socialism. Communists believed that all resources should be used for the benefit of the population, not for the few individuals motivated by profit. But how was this to be achieved?

Stalin had not been one of the most prominent Communist leaders in 1917. He was not regarded as an equal by colleagues like Leon Trotsky. Trotsky had been Lenin's right-hand man during the Revolution and commanded the Red Army during the civil war. However, Stalin, as General Secretary of the Communist Party, controlled the Party machine and steadily built up a strong power base during the 1920s. He was able to outmanoeuvre and isolate rivals like Trotsky, who lacked the same level of support among the Party rank and file. By 1929, Stalin had emerged victorious in the power struggle. Initially he presented himself as a man of the centre, or a moderate. However, by 1928 he was proposing a hard-line approach to building socialism within Russia, which by now had become the Union of Soviet Socialist Republics (USSR). Stalin's road to socialism meant ending private ownership of the land and eliminating private enterprise from industry, so that the state would determine what should be produced, and how. The resulting economic shake-up, sometimes called Russia's 'second revolution', was every bit as significant as the political revolution of 1917. It set the framework for the Soviet political and economic system which was to outlast Stalin. Indeed, it was to form the basis of the Soviet Union right up to the early 1980s, only a few years before its sudden break-up in 1991.

Stalin's USSR: the 1930s

The 1930s were a traumatic time for the USSR. Stalin's regime carried out great economic and social changes at the same time as it locked up or killed millions of its citizens in the name of building socialism. The Party devoted most of its efforts to achieving five main objectives:

- **Achieving socialism:** for Stalin this meant completing the process of collectivisation of agriculture begun in the late 1920s. This had brought the countryside under the control of the Communists for the first time, as small farms were amalgamated into larger collective farms controlled by the Party.
- **Industrialisation of the USSR** through the mechanism of the Five-year Plans. These Plans provided the cornerstone of the Soviet 'command economy'.
- **Strengthening Soviet military capability**, principally to deter foreign enemies. This was seen as a priority in the later 1930s with the growing power of Hitler's Germany, which was an avowed enemy of Communism.
- **Mobilising the Soviet population** and ensuring loyalty through a mixture of propaganda and terror. This involved rooting out, punishing and eliminating real or potential opponents of the regime. For Stalin, such opponents included so-called slackers, 'saboteurs' and other 'enemies of progress'. Nobody could be allowed to undermine the achievements of the Soviet people.
- Ensuring that Stalin could **impose his will** on the Party and thereby the country at large. There was no room for criticism or doubt. Only the Communist Party, as the vanguard and conscience of the working class, could coordinate, inspire and manage the changes taking place. And who better than Stalin to be at the helm, as the visionary successor to Lenin?

▪ A closer look

Five-year Plans

The system of running the economy by Five-year Plans was adopted in 1928. All Soviet industry was run by this method. The State Planning Agency, Gosplan, decided what the regime's priorities were. Throughout this period they were mainly heavy industry and defence. The government then set targets for each industry and each factory, and allocated resources. Targets were set for a five-year period, then broken into shorter term targets for each enterprise. All was geared to producing what the state deemed as necessary, that is, the industrialisation and security of the USSR. What consumers might want was scarcely considered. Hence there was often a shortage of things to buy in the shops, for example shoes and basic household goods. The emphasis was on meeting targets, not the quality of the goods produced. The Plans did lead to big increases in production in some key heavy industries, and began the process of changing the USSR from a peasant-based economy into an industrial power. The first two Plans ran between 1928 and 1938. The Third Five-year Plan, begun in 1938, was interrupted by war in 1941.

The Five-year Plans, with some variations, remained the main mechanism for running the Soviet economy right up to the 1980s. The Plans initially showed great promise as a means of quickly dragging a 'backward' rural economy into the industrial age. However, the Plans relied on a heavy input of labour rather than modern machinery. Consequently, as the Soviet economy developed and its needs became more diverse, the Plans were to prove a much less effective method of increasing economic growth to the level of sophistication of the industrial economies of countries like the USA, Germany and Britain. In Britain and the USA in particular, business, because it was based on the profit motive, was much more responsive to the principle of supply and demand. In other words, businesses produced what people wanted to buy. In the USSR, in contrast, all decisions were made by authorities who decided what was good for the state, not the individual consumer. This need not in itself have been a permanent obstacle to growth, but the inflexibility of the Soviet system, its lack of concern with quality, its reliance on manual labour and over-bureaucratisation were all problems which were increasingly to plague the Soviet economy after 1945.

Fig. 1 *The USSR at the time of Stalin*

Stalin, and most other Communists, would not have seen any of these objectives as strange or contradictory, even though they caused immense dislocation to all aspects of Soviet society and the economy. Stalin was realising his vision of 'socialism in one country'. The disruption, the hard work, the elimination of opposition – all were justified as being necessary for the achievement of socialism. Beyond that lay the vision of Communism. This was a utopia in the distant future when the class divisions between workers, peasants and intellectuals, the three recognised classes in the USSR, would have been eliminated. Then everyone would work for the good of each other, and the need for organised government, let alone a Communist Party, would have disappeared. In Marx's words, the state would 'wither away'. Conflict would become a thing of the past. However, Stalin in the 1930s was building his version of socialism in a country surrounded by hostile capitalist states. These had already tried to destroy the new Soviet regime after the Revolution. Therefore, according to Stalin, far from 'withering away', the Soviet state, under his wise leadership, must actually be strengthened and be on its guard against internal and external enemies. Industrialisation fitted into the jigsaw well, since all Communists believed that a strong, socialist USSR depended on having a large industrial working class, known as the proletariat.

The USSR on the eve of war

Historians have often debated the extent to which Stalin had achieved his objectives by 1941. How far had the USSR become a powerful, industrialised, unified and stable state on the eve of the German invasion of the USSR? This was a major issue for the USSR. Stalin had been fearful of Germany since Hitler came to power in 1933. Hitler's Nazi regime was resolved to destroy Communism as an ideology, but was also committed to attacking the USSR in order to incorporate Russia into a new German empire. Yet Stalin had no powerful allies on which he could rely. Although Britain and France were fearful of German ambitions to dominate Europe, they were also suspicious of Communist Russia. For his part, Stalin feared that Britain and France wanted to embroil him in war with Germany. This suspicion of the Western powers was very real, since Communists remembered the period after 1917 when foreign governments had intervened in Russia to try to overthrow their new regime. Although there were negotiations between Britain, France and the USSR in 1939, following Hitler's takeover of Austria and Czechoslovakia and threats against Poland, these negotiations were half-hearted and came to nothing.

The strengths and weaknesses of the Soviet Union in June 1941

Historians have debated the strengths and weaknesses of the USSR on the eve of war in June 1941.

Economic strengths and weaknesses

There is no agreement on the precise impact of Stalin's Five-year Plans. There is an ongoing debate about the extent to which living standards rose or fell during the late 1930s. However, all historians agree that industrial production had increased considerably since 1928. It had probably increased by at least 200 per cent overall, and probably a lot more in some sectors of heavy industry. However, progress was often more evident in quantity than quality. The significant rise in economic production disguised considerable flaws in economic strategy:

- Resources were often used inefficiently and mistakes were made – for example factories were sometimes built on unsuitable sites.
- The emphasis on meeting numerical targets meant that quality was often sacrificed.
- There was low labour productivity, due to insufficient modern equipment and inefficient methods.

There was a shortage of skilled labour: many factories were heavily reliant on inexperienced workers, often women who were new to the labour market or peasants recently displaced from the countryside.

Planning was often very over-optimistic and sometimes bore no relation to reality.

Agricultural production was very slow to recover from the trauma of collectivisation – many peasants were unenthusiastic and unproductive members of collective farms.

The pressures created by the ceaseless effort to increase production, combined with a big increase in defence spending, pushed the economy towards a period of stagnation in the last years of peace, a period that coincided with the Third Five-year Plan.

Fig. 2 *Soviet poster showing the USSR standing firm against the Nazi threat*

Social strengths and weaknesses

Soviet society went through dramatic changes between 1928 and 1941. The process of turning the USSR into an industrial power resulted in winners and losers. Many people were ground down by Stalin's Terror. This was a period when thousands of Party members and other citizens had been arrested, imprisoned or executed as potential enemies of the regime. Many peasants were dispossessed, particularly the better-off ones who were forced off the land and were made to work in factories or became part of Stalin's convict empire. Many women were new to the workforce, but at the same time were expected to look after the home. Some groups suffered for different reasons: many religious believers were persecuted. Some were demoralised by the pressures of living in an authoritarian society, by the fear of persecution, and by the relentless propaganda. Some people just did not 'fit in'. Meanwhile, others gained: there was a great demand for skills, and there were opportunities for promotion and better education. However, not all citizens were equipped to take advantage of opportunities. Some more recent research suggests that the Terror had less of an everyday impact on people's lives than was commonly assumed. There were still many ordinary people prepared to complain about perceived injustices.

Political strengths and weaknesses

Assessing the political strength of the USSR in 1941 is a controversial area. Undoubtedly the power of both the Communist Party and the state bureaucracy increased throughout the 1930s. There was no way to oppose either the Party or state machine without extraordinary risks, and no channel through which to express any view which ran counter to the prevailing orthodoxy as defined by the Party. This is what made the USSR an authoritarian or totalitarian state. Historians attach different meanings to these terms. An authoritarian government is often described as one which rules firmly, but probably within the rule of law. A totalitarian system is usually defined as one in which the government or state tries to control not just people's behaviour but their thoughts as well, and adjusts laws as it sees fit, so there is no such thing as a 'rule of law' that guarantees real individual rights.

Although it made Stalin's personal position almost impregnable, since no one was likely to oppose his leadership, this was not necessarily a political strength. A state that exerts rigid control over everything also contains a weakness because it discourages initiative and enterprise. Even Party members found their influence declining during the 1930s as both the state and the Party machines became more centralised. Intellectuals, and indeed anybody with ideas and intelligence which might have helped society, were among those people most likely to be purged, because they were seen as dangerous and destabilising. There was therefore an absence of influences which might have breathed new life into the leadership. The disastrous effects of the fear of showing initiative were to be seen in the early stages of the war, when supposedly experienced officers were reluctant to act without clear orders from above in case they upset Stalin or their superiors. The Soviet army was to suffer large-scale casualties as a result. Historians also find it difficult to assess the health of the regime because in a society in which the use of force and propaganda underpin the regime, it is difficult to know exactly what most people were thinking. Did they support the regime because they wanted to or because they had to? There is no such thing as public opinion in an authoritarian society, only a lot of evidence from official propaganda of what the state wanted people to believe. Did this actually matter?

What historians tend to agree about is that the German invasion of the USSR in June 1941 put all Stalin's achievements at risk, as well as the very survival of the USSR.

■ Timeline

The colours represent different types of event as follows: Political, Economic, Social and International

1941	1942	1943	1944	1945
German invasion of USSR	Battle of Stalingrad begins	Battle of Kursk	Germans driven out of USSR	Yalta Conference
Siege of Leningrad begins		Teheran Conference		Potsdam Conference
Battle for Moscow				

1954	1955	1956	1957	1958
Khrushchev proposes Virgin Lands programme	Malenkov sacked as prime minister	Twentieth Party Congress and Khrushchev's 'secret speech'	Khrushchev defeated Anti-party Plot	Khrushchev appointed prime minister
	Warsaw Pact created	Beginning of de-Stalinisation	Launch of *Sputnik*	Pasternak forced to apologise for *Dr Zhivago*
		Suppression of Hungarian Rising		

1965	1966	1968	1969	1971	1972
Kosygin reforms begin	Sinyavsky and Daniel imprisoned	Invasion of Czechoslovakia by Warsaw Pact	Solzhenitsyn expelled from Union of Writers	Ninth Five-year Plan	Helsinki talks
	Brezhnev appointed general secretary	Brezhnev Doctrine announced			
	Politburo reintroduced				

1979	1980	1982	1984	1985	1986
Gorbachev elected to Politburo	Sakharov arrested and exiled	Death of Brezhnev	Death of Andropov	Death of Chernenko	Chernobyl nuclear disaster
Soviet troops invade Afghanistan	Moscow Olympics	Andropov elected general secretary	Chernenko elected general secretary	Gorbachev elected general secretary	Beginnings of Soviet withdrawal from Afghanistan
					Gorbachev calls for perestroika and glasnost

1946	1948	1949	1951	1953
Crackdown on 'cosmopolitan culture'	Berlin Blockade	Creation of Comecon	Fifth Five-year Plan	Doctors' Plot
Fourth Five-year Plan launched	Further Leningrad purge	First Soviet atom bomb		Death of Stalin
Leningrad purge				Collective leadership established and Beria executed
				USSR acquires hydrogen bomb
				Khrushchev elected first secretary

1959	1960	1961	1962	1964
Seven-year Plan	Intensification of Sino-Soviet split	Yuri Gagarin's space orbit	Liberman economic reform programme published	Khrushchev sacked
Khrushchev announces arrival of socialism		Seventh Five-year Plan	Cuban missile crisis	

1974	1975	1976	1977	1978
Solzhenitsyn expelled from USSR	Helsinki Accords signed	Helsinki monitoring groups set up	Brezhnev Constitution adopted	Trials of Orlov, Scharansky and Ginsburg
		Tenth Five-year Plan		

1987	1988	1989	1990	1991
Law on State Enterprises passed	Law on Cooperatives	Last Soviet troops leave Afghanistan	Party loses its leading role	Referendum on the Union
	Conflict in Nagorno-Karabakh	Elections to USSR Congress	Gorbachev elected Soviet president	Warsaw Pact dissolved
	Gorbachev elected head of state by USSR Supreme Soviet	Gorbachev elected chairman of Congress of People's Deputies	Russian Supreme Soviet declares its sovereignty	Coup against Gorbachev
	Estonia declares sovereignty	Fall of Berlin Wall	Yeltsin elected Russian president	CIS created
	Gorbachev announces arms reductions		Russia announces move towards a market economy	USSR broken up

The Great Patriotic War and its outcomes, 1941–53

The German invasion

In this chapter you will learn about:

- the progress and impact of the Russo-German war between 1941 and 1945

- how Stalin managed the Soviet war effort

- how the Soviet war economy was managed

- how the Soviet regime enlisted mass support for the war effort and dealt with opposition.

ПРИДЁМ К ИЗОБИЛИЮ!

Fig. 1 *Stalin in his marshal's uniform, with his facial pockmarks carefully airbrushed out*

'For the Motherland, for Stalin!'

1   *The battlecry of the Red Army during the Great Patriotic War*

The impact on the USSR of the German invasion and Nazi ideology from 1941

Military strengths and weaknesses in 1941

A strength of the Soviet military by 1941 was that the regime had devoted more money and energy to war preparations than other Great Powers, apart from possibly Germany. Along with the investment concentrated on heavy industry, this reduced the resources available to meet the everyday needs of ordinary citizens. The priority given to defence reflected the Soviet fear of foreign attack, although anti-Communists abroad were also likely to claim that it reflected a Soviet desire to spread Communism by force beyond its borders. There was a spurt of Soviet defence spending after 1937 in an attempt to update weaponry: Soviet defence spending trebled in this period. By 1941 there were over 5 million Soviet citizens in the armed forces, comprising about 6 per cent of the working population, while the defence industry was producing 230 tanks and 700 aircraft every month.

However, the USSR also displayed several military weaknesses, or at least aspects which in the eyes of foreign observers made the apparent strength of the large Soviet army and air force much less impressive in reality. The USSR did not plan for a specific type of war. Instead it built up its forces in an attempt to cope with any scenario, but also continually changed its military priorities. This was in contrast to Germany, which focused on **Blitzkrieg**, or 'lightning war', a method of warfare which helped the Germans achieve great successes in 1940 and 1941. Although German military policy concealed longer-term weaknesses, at least it showed evidence of coherent planning. The quality of Soviet military equipment and training methods was very variable. Furthermore, many of the Red Army's most experienced and skilful officers had been purged in 1937–38. They included some of the most innovative generals – those who, like their German counterparts, favoured mobile warfare. Their replacements were far less likely to show initiative, out of fear of failure or sharing the same fate as their predecessors. This was understandable given Stalin's unpredictability and tendency to look for scapegoats. However, some historians have tended to exaggerate the impact of the purges on the Red Army. Not all those who were purged were executed. A number of soldiers were rehabilitated after 1938, and the Red Army did address some of its deficiencies before 1941. Although the USSR produced some of the best tanks of the Second World War, Soviet generals tended not to adopt a flexible approach to strategy. Soviet military thinking by 1941 had reverted to the age-old strategy of trying to hold firm on the frontier and then planning a massive counter-offensive. This inflexible strategy was to cost the Soviets dearly in 1941 when facing fast-moving German tanks and aircraft. The USSR, like Germany, did not plan for a long war. When war came, therefore, there had to be a major rethink on how best to fight, at a time when the USSR was under severe strain and in danger of defeat. Insufficient thought generally had gone into war preparations. In particular, too many defence plants were situated in the south of the USSR and other areas close to vulnerable borders, with no plans for rapid evacuation. The Soviet population was also not prepared for the type of war which arrived in 1941. This was ironic, given the strident propaganda with which the regime had bombarded its population for years, on the theme of building up the

Key terms

Blitzkrieg: a method of warfare used by the Germans to great effect in the early years of the war. It depended on the daring use of mobile warfare, principally tanks supported by air power, to surprise the enemy, drive deeply into enemy territory, and disorientate and surround enemy forces. It proved very successful in the German campaigns in Western Europe in 1940 and in the initial stages of the invasion of Russia in 1941. It then proved less effective once German forces had become enveloped in the vast spaces of the Russian interior, with their supply lines stretched and facing an enemy which refused to give in.

Did you know?

Many military experts consider that the mass-produced Soviet T-34 tank was the most effective tank of the Second World War when used skilfully. It won the Battle of Kursk in 1943 against the much-vaunted German Panzers. The Soviets produced many more tanks than the Germans. The first T-34 tank to enter Berlin during the battle for the city in April 1945 is preserved at the Soviet war memorial near the Brandenburg Gate in Berlin.

USSR and being on guard against a ruthless enemy. Yet the Soviet people had also been told that if war came, it would never, as in the past, be fought on Russian soil. Rather, as soon as war broke out, the Red Army, under the banner of Lenin, would fight the war on enemy territory.

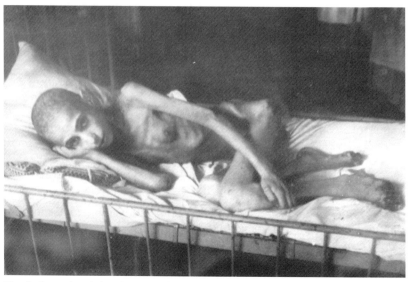

Fig. 2 *Starvation during the siege of Leningrad*

Nazi motives

The Germans launched their massive assault on the USSR on 22 June 1941. Hitler's assault on the USSR had three main motives:

Ideological

The attack was part of the Nazi drive to eliminate Communism and impose German domination over the Slav race. The Slavs were among those races designated by the Nazis as 'sub-human' and ripe for exploitation, enslavement and possibly extermination. The Nazis also regarded Communism (or 'Bolshevism') and the Jewish race as closely linked, and they estimated that several million Jews lived in the USSR.

Economic

Conquering the USSR would provide the Germans with much needed resources, such as oil and grain, as well as 'living-space' for German settlers once the war was won.

Strategic

The defeat of the USSR would leave Germany dominant on the continent, indeed virtually impregnable. The Germans had failed to defeat Britain in 1940 because they lacked the necessary air and sea power to make it safe for their victorious army to cross the English Channel. However, were the Germans to defeat Russia, the chances of a successful Allied invasion of Europe, even with American involvement, were slim. Had Russia been defeated, the German army would not have had millions of soldiers tied up on the Eastern Front, leaving just a handful of divisions in northern France, as was the case in 1944 when the Western Allies invaded Normandy.

Activity

Group exercise

In pairs, select five strengths and five weaknesses of the USSR on the eve of war in 1941. Prioritise these from the most to the least important and be prepared to justify your order as you compare your choices with those of others in your group.

Did you know?

Hitler was not alone in underestimating Soviet strength. British intelligence told the British government in 1941 that if Germany attacked the USSR, Germany would probably win within about six weeks. This attitude had been seen before in 1939, when the USSR attacked Finland, and some British politicians proposed declaring war on the USSR also, despite the fact that Britain was already at war with Germany. Few foresaw the resilience of the Soviet regime and its people.

German strategy

Hitler's strategy when attacking the USSR was based on two main assumptions:

- that the USSR was fundamentally weak and likely to collapse quickly after being attacked, in a matter of weeks or months, but certainly before winter arrived. This view was based partly on the supposed weakness of the Red Army folllowing Stalin's purges of the late 1930s
- that German Blitzkrieg tactics would enable the Germans quickly to surround and decimate a more cumbersome, demoralised and badly led Red Army.

The main stages of the war

Fig. 3 *The Great Patriotic War, 1941–42, showing the front line between German-occupied and non-occupied territory at different stages*

June–December 1941

German armies attacked on three broad fronts: in the north towards Leningrad, in the centre towards Moscow, and in the south towards the Caucasus and the oilfields. The Germans had major successes, overrunning the Baltic states (Latvia, Estonia and Lithuania), Russian-occupied Poland and large areas of Ukraine and Belorussia. In the process they captured or killed millions of Soviet troops, laid siege to Leningrad and, in the autumn, approached very near to Moscow. However, the Germans had not prepared for winter, and when it set in, the first successful Soviet counter-offensive took place. It was December 1941, by which time the German armies had become overstretched and weakened by a combination of the weather and ferocious Soviet resistance. Soviet forces drove the

Key chronology

The Great Patriotic War

1941

June	German invasion of the USSR
	Romania, Hungary and Finland declare war on the USSR
	Formation of GKO
July	Stalin's first wartime broadcast to the Soviet people
	Food rationing imposed in Moscow and Leningrad
September	German forces cut off Leningrad
	Germans begin offensive towards Moscow
October	State of siege declared in Moscow
December	End of German offensive against Moscow
	Soviet counter-offensive outside Moscow

1942

September	German offensive against Stalingrad
November	German army trapped in Stalingrad

1943

January	German surrender at Stalingrad
July	German offensive at Kursk fails

1944

January	Siege of Leningrad finally lifted
July	Soviet forces enter Poland

1945

January	Soviet forces invade Germany
April	Soviet offensive against Berlin
May	German surrender – victory in Europe

Germans back from the outskirts of Moscow and established a more stable front for the rest of the winter. Nevertheless, during the six months of fighting the USSR had lost a large amount of territory and resources. It had also lost over 3 million troops as prisoners, and probably close to 2 million soldiers had been killed, in addition to innumerable civilian casualties. These included those caught up in the fighting, and those murdered by the Germans, as the latter included over one million Russian Jews (who were mostly shot) and Communist Party members.

Spring 1942–February 1943

The Germans resumed their offensive in the spring of 1942. However, they now focused on a narrower front, heading towards the Caucasus and taking in the large industrial city of Stalingrad on the way. There were initial successes for the Germans, but in the autumn of 1942 a large German army became bogged down in Stalingrad, on the Volga. The Germans were cut off and surrounded by a Soviet counter-offensive. After one of the bitterest battles of the war, the Germans were ground into defeat and surrender by early 1943. The battle of Stalingrad is often regarded as the turning point of the war, certainly on the Eastern Front. It was the first major land defeat suffered by the Nazis, and thereafter their capacity to mount a sustained offensive petered out. However, some historians assert that the real Nazi failure was their inability to defeat Russia in 1941, since the whole German strategy and preparations had been geared to a quick knock-out blow.

Fig. 4 *Red Army machine-gunners during the war*

That failure gave the USSR a desperately needed breathing space. From then on the huge Soviet military and economic effort, much more geared towards **total war** than was the German effort before 1943, was gradually able to assert itself and grind down the Nazi war machine.

March 1943–June 1944

This period saw the Red Army build on its victory at Stalingrad. There was only one more major German offensive, at Kursk in July 1943. This was the largest tank battle in history. It resulted in a German defeat, a Soviet counter-offensive and a German retreat. Thereafter the Soviets always held the initiative. By the end of 1943 the Germans had been driven out of most of central Russia and Ukraine. In January 1944 the siege of Leningrad was finally lifted, followed by the destruction of German forces in Crimea and the liberation of Belorussia. By June 1944 Russia's allies had opened up the Second Front in Normandy, and the Red Army was poised to cross Soviet borders and drive the Germans back to Berlin.

Fig. 5 *The Great Patriotic War, 1942–44, showing the front line at different stages of the war*

July 1944 –May 1945

Although the war continued to be very costly for the USSR as well as the Germans, the Soviets now clearly held the initiative and it was just a matter of time before Germany was defeated. In July 1944 the Red Army crossed into Poland, and in the autumn it occupied Romania, Bulgaria, Latvia and Estonia. In January 1945, after a costly battle to capture Warsaw, the Red Army crossed the German border. It fought its way into Berlin. In the two weeks fighting for Berlin the Red Army suffered over 300,000 casualties – more than the total combined British and American military and civilian death toll for the whole war. Germany surrendered in early May. As a postscript, the USSR declared war on Japan, which was already reeling from the shock of the US atom bombs dropped on Hiroshima and Nagasaki, and the Soviets drove the Japanese out of Manchuria.

The effects of the war

Fig. 6 *Russian civilians executed by the German invaders*

Germany fought the war in Russia as a war of extermination. In response, the USSR fought ferociously, since it was a struggle for survival. The result was not just a war in a conventional sense, but a struggle to the death with appalling costs, both material and human, making it probably the most horrendous battlefront of the whole Second World War. The impact of the war on the USSR was not just immediate: it affected the USSR deeply for generations afterwards.

The costs of the war were immense.

The population as a whole

The USSR may well have lost up to one-fifth of its pre-war population. Soviet casualties were probably around half of the total loss of human life of all the countries involved in the Second World War combined. The figures for Soviet losses include both military and civilian casualties, but then the Germans doing the killing made little distinction between military and civilian personnel. Historians have long debated the precise figures and it is difficult to determine the exact truth. In his lifetime, Stalin did not want to give the impression that the USSR had been severely weakened, and therefore referred to 'only' 7 million Soviet deaths. Successive Soviet leaders then increased the estimates – they had to be estimates, since there were no Soviet censuses between 1939 and 1959. However, experts have calculated that at least 10 million more children might have been born in the USSR had there been no war.

Particular groups

Particular sectors suffered proportionately more than others. Broadly one in four of the Belorussian population, in the forefront of the German attack and occupation, died; Poland was the country next on the list of those countries that suffered proportionately the most casualties. During one period of the 900-day siege of Leningrad, in 1941–42 in particular, more of the city's population died (at a rate of over 4,000 a day) than the entire number of British casualties for the whole war. Eventually over one million Leningraders died, many of starvation.

Long-term factors

The human losses had a lasting psychological and material impact. Probably about three times as many Soviet men (totalling about 20 million deaths) died than women. This greatly exaggerated a trend evident before the war whereby there were already more women than men in the USSR. The result was that after 1945 millions of Soviet women had no chance of ever finding a husband. The gender imbalance has never been fully corrected to the present day. Other consequences flowed from this. For example, the shortage of males led to more inter-ethnic marriages in the USSR. This in turn increased the level of Russification, particularly through the infiltration of the Russian language throughout the various Republics.

The psychological impact

Psychologically the war was traumatic, not just because of the scale of the loss of life, but because of the nature of the deaths. Apart from the millions killed in battle or wounded – Soviet estimates were that about 18 million soldiers were wounded, frostbitten or suffered various sicknesses – many deaths resulted from torture or killings in cold blood. The Germans routinely killed hostages. Millions of Russian Jews were massacred. Whole villages were destroyed as reprisals for partisan action or simply out of sheer vindictiveness by German soldiers.

Fig. 7 *1945 Soviet poster showing the victory of the Red Army and Soviet people over the invader*

Fig. 8 *Soviet civilians discovering German atrocities against their family members*

Did you know?

Partisans played a valuable role in the war for the Soviets. They were men and women who fought behind enemy lines in German-occupied territory. They attacked German soldiers and destroyed German equipment. The aims were to tie up German troops who would otherwise have fought at the front and to disrupt the German war effort. It was a dangerous business. The Germans dealt brutally with captured partisans and their suspected supporters.

Prisoners

Over 3 million Soviet soldiers were captured by the Germans even before the end of 1941. By 1945 the total had risen to 6 million. Of these about 75 per cent were murdered, worked to death, or left to starve or freeze to death. The early experiments in gassing humans at Auschwitz death camp were carried out on Russian prisoners of war. The Nazis refused to treat Soviet prisoners according to the internationally recognised Geneva Convention. One of Stalin's own sons died in German captivity. Soviet treatment of German prisoners and later German civilians was often as brutal.

The political impact

The war also affected the Soviet political outlook. It fuelled existing Soviet suspicions of the outside world. The experience of the war goes a long way to explaining Stalin's hard-line approach to the Allies during and after the war, when he was involved in negotiations about the post-war settlement. Among other concerns, Stalin was determined to secure Soviet borders and Soviet influence in Central and Eastern Europe, in addition to extracting compensation for war damages.

The economic costs

The economic and financial costs of the war were extraordinary. Two-thirds of pre-war Soviet property was destroyed, as detailed in official Soviet records:

> The German-fascist invaders completely or partially destroyed and burnt 1,710 towns and settlements and more than 70,000 villages and hamlets; burnt and destroyed more than 6 million buildings and rendered homeless about 25 million people; destroyed 31,580 industrial enterprises … [They destroyed] 60 per cent of the steel, and mines yielding more than 60 per cent of the coal in the country; destroyed 65 thousand kilometres of railway lines and 4,100 stations, 36 thousand post and telegraph installations, telephone exchanges and other communications enterprises; destroyed and looted tens of thousands of collective and state farms, slaughtered, seized or drove back to Germany 7 million horses, 17 million cattle and oxen, 20 million pigs, 27 million sheep and goats. In addition they destroyed and looted 40 thousand hospitals and other medical establishments, 84 thousand schools, colleges, universities and research institutes, and 43 thousand public libraries.

2   *Extract from the official Soviet record*

Activity

Research task

Try to find out more about the Second World War experience of the USSR's allies, Britain and the USA, and compare the costs of the war for them with the Soviet experience.

The Soviet war experience as outlined above does not take account of other problems which followed on from the material damage. During the war there was inevitably a massive diversion of greatly needed financial and other resources from the civilian into the military sector. The loss of income, apart from other disruption caused by the war, has been estimated at the equivalent of about seven years' income from the pre-war period. All of this makes the Soviet recovery after 1945 the more remarkable.

Stalin's management of the war effort

Stalin's wartime leadership

Stalin's diplomacy before the war has been much criticised. He was rightly sceptical about British and French attempts to involve him in an alliance in 1938 and 1939. He recognised that these attempts were half-hearted, coming as they did from governments innately suspicious of Communism. Stalin felt that the West might simply be trying to involve the USSR in a war with Germany. Stalin himself was so desperate to avoid war with Hitler that he signed a Non-aggression Pact with Hitler in August 1939. The pact had secret clauses dividing Eastern Europe into German and Soviet spheres of influence and allowing for both powers to invade and carve up Poland. The USSR provided Germany with deliveries of valuable raw materials right up to June 1941.

In 1941, Stalin was still eager to avoid war and ignored the obvious build-up of German forces on the Soviet border, refusing to believe that Hitler would break the agreement and invade the USSR. He would not allow Soviet commanders to take sensible defence measures in case they 'provoked' Germany. Hence the USSR was virtually powerless when the Germans did attack. Stalin then blamed his commanders for the lack of effective defence. Several of them were arrested, brutally tortured into making confessions of treason and shot. In the first week of the war it is commonly assumed that Stalin had some kind of mental breakdown. He retired to his country retreat for ten days without issuing any orders. There were later claims, not very convincing, that some of his **Politburo** colleagues briefly discussed the possibility of arresting Stalin. The USSR, it may have appeared, lacked leadership at a critical time.

Key terms

Politburo (Political Bureau): the main decision-making body of the Party and the State, known as the Presidium between 1952 and 1966. It had a mixture of full and candidate members, usually no more than 20 in total, all leading figures in the Party. It functioned something like the British Cabinet, meeting regularly to discuss key policies, although Stalin often bypassed it, preferring to make decisions by himself or with individual colleagues.

Key profile

Vyacheslav Scriabin – known as 'Molotov' ('The Hammer')

One of Stalin's powerful colleagues, Molotov (1890–1986) was foreign minister from 1941 and a key figure in Soviet government and diplomacy. His power waned after Stalin's death. Popularly known as 'Iron Arse' for his ability to drink his colleagues under the table and his hard-line negotiating tactics, Molotov was descibed by Churchill as a 'robot' with 'a smile of Siberian winter'. Molotov's wife, Polina, was imprisoned in 1949, accused of being part of a Jewish conspiracy against Stalin. She was not released until after Stalin's death, but Molotov continued to serve Stalin loyally.

The reality was less dramatic. While it is true that Molotov, not Stalin, made the radio announcement that the USSR had been invaded, more recent evidence proves that during this whole period Stalin was very active. He received a constant stream of visitors and drafted orders, apart from two days when he may have been in a state of temporary depression. On the other hand, some historians believe that Stalin was silent during this brief period to test his colleagues' loyalty, to see how they would react – which, given Stalin's paranoid tendencies, is entirely credible. Stalin was then persuaded to set up GKO (see below). A sure sign of real recovery was his radio speech to the Soviet people on 3 July 1941, in which he called for fierce resistance to the invader.

Fig. 9 *Stalin, Voroshilov and Molotov discussing strategy*

The centralisation of power

Having recovered his nerve, it was not in Stalin's nature to give up any personal control. However, fortunately for the USSR, Stalin and other Politburo members realised that effective decision-making was crucial. Decisions could not get bogged down in the usual Soviet bureaucracy.

Speed and decisiveness were vital. The result was the creation of GKO (the State Defence Committee). This was suggested to Stalin by Molotov, and was set up at the end of June with full control over wartime decision-making and 'the entire plenitude of power in the country'. Its decisions had the force of law: Stalin described GKO as having 'all the power and authority of the State' behind it. It met frequently and whenever was thought necessary.

GKO acted almost as an inner Politburo. The original members of GKO were Stalin, Molotov, Georgy Malenkov, Lavrenti Beria and Kliment Voroshilov. It was simply superimposed on existing systems but crucially, it had the power to bypass complex bureaucracy and ensure that quick and flexible decisions could be made. Each member of GKO took responsibility for a particular sector, such as armaments production. Sometimes GKO left business to committees once decisions were taken. If necessary, when meetings were held, a particular expert might be co-opted into the discussions. Despite Stalin's presence at meetings, and people's fear of crossing him, accounts from members attending GKO insist that there was genuine discussion and debate. The discussions could range from economic policy to military strategy, from ideology to foreign policy. GKO took direct responsibility for the defence of Moscow in 1941.

■ Cross-reference

For more about Malenkov's struggle for the succession after Stalin's death, see Chapter 3.

■ Key terms

NKVD: the Soviet security services, commonly referred to as the secret police. It was run by Beria. It was the forerunner of what later became the KGB, and was responsible for internal state security. It had great power, and was effectively answerable to Stalin.

Key profiles

Georgy Malenkov

During the war, Malenkov (1902–88) was in charge of military equipment. After Stalin's death he was a leading figure in the struggle for the succession. Although involved in brutal enforcement of the regime under Stalin, after 1953 he advocated a more moderate form of Stalinism which paid more attention to the needs of ordinary Soviet citizens. However, Malenkov was defeated by Khrushchev in the power struggle following Stalin's death.

Lavrenti Beria

Possibly the most feared man in the USSR, as Stalin's brutal head of the **NKVD**, Beria (1899–1953), was possibly also one of the most intelligent of Stalin's colleagues. Beria was given extraordinary powers by Stalin during the war, to ensure that key tasks were carried out. Beria was utterly ruthless in his treatment of colleagues, and was reputed to have taken part in the torture of those interrogated by his security forces. Because he was so feared, colleagues quickly had him arrested and then shot after Stalin's death.

Kliment Voroshilov

An early comrade of Stalin, Voroshilov (1881–1969) was a member of Stalin's 'inner cabinet' early in the war, although later described by a Soviet general as 'incapable of understanding modern warfare', since his early military experience had been as a cavalry commander in the Civil War. Stalin eventually recognised Voroshilov's incompetence and he fell out of favour, although he remained important in the Party and was buried in Red Square with full military honours.

Before the war Stalin's personal power had grown, and frequently he did not summon the Politburo but dealt instead with individuals. This trend continued during the war, and indeed strengthened. The Politburo and other Party organisations met infrequently.

The centralisation of control in the war did not prevent some conflicts between different bodies and individuals, and did not mean that all issues were quickly resolved. War causes disruption, and sometimes the notorious 'fog of war' prevents the central administrative and command structure from knowing exactly what is happening and where. In the USSR, it could not always ensure that orders from Moscow were carried out as intended, particularly when communications were disrupted. This problem was made worse by the fact that during the war there was a rapid turnover of local officials. Often relatively inexperienced officials had to show initiative in the absence of direction from above. For example, local Party organisations sometimes took over the management of enterprises such as factories. It was simply not possible in wartime to refer all decisions to Moscow.

Military leadership

The centralisation of the state administration, with its flaws as well as its advantages, was reflected in the direction of military operations. At the start of the war there was no centralised military command which could coordinate a response to the German invasion. Very quickly, two days after the German invasion, Stavka (the Soviet High Command) was created. From August it was led by Stalin as supreme commander. Stavka also included Molotov and the heads of the armed services, and its meetings were attended by GKO representatives. Stavka directed strategic and military operations. When decisions had been made, the details were then worked out by the General Staff.

Stalin's chosen method of running the war had important implications. Many historians believe that the Soviet system was much more efficient than Hitler's equivalent structure. Hitler operated very much as an individual, frequently playing one general off against another. He often acted on his 'intuition' or personal hunches to direct events, rather than rely on an organised command and administrative structure. Hitler often flew into rages when contradicted and was increasingly surrounded by yes-men. He lost touch with reality and made sometimes disastrous decisions. Stalin was also capable of making major errors, such as his refusal to allow Soviet forces to retreat at Kharkov in 1943, resulting in their encirclement and destruction in Germany's last real victory inside Russia. However, Stalin, while also sometimes playing off individuals against each other, did learn during the war to take advice – he certainly learned better than Hitler did. There was a clear principle from the start of the war that the Soviet armed forces were under political control. This principle was reinforced by the reintroduction from July 1941 of the old Leninist system of having political commissars attached to army officers at all levels. This was to ensure political reliability and obedience to political directives. However, there was an important change in October 1942. As the war situation improved and military commanders grew in confidence and influence, the political commissar system was abolished. Stalin began to listen more to senior and successful officers like Marshal Zhukov. These generals were able to make a genuine contribution to military debate in a way which Hitler rarely allowed. Stalin was still clearly in charge. He would decide who was to command which operations. He also had the confidence of knowing that he was backed up by Beria and the NKVD, which was active in ensuring the continued enthusiasm of the Soviet people for the war effort.

An evaluation of Stalin as war leader

Since Stalin dominated both military and civilian command structures, he clearly took responsibility for all Soviet actions during the war and probably exerted more power than any other war leader. He brutally punished failure, for example having generals who allowed their forces to be defeated early in the war executed. Yet he too made 'mistakes', such as refusing to allow strategic retreats which might have saved thousands of lives. Most historians have blamed Stalin for major disasters, such as allowing the encirclements of Kiev and Leningrad in 1941. He was also guilty of obsessions with pet preferences, such as a love for cavalry. This dated back to his experience of the Civil War after the Revolution, even though cavalry had limited value in the Second World War and suffered disasters in some campaigns as in Crimea.

However, there were also some positive aspects to Stalin's war leadership:

■ Stalin was prepared to sack incompetent generals, including his old comrade Voroshilov. In this he showed more wisdom than Hitler, who was prone to tolerate incompetent generals provided they were yes-men.

■ He proved to be a very effective symbol of resistance for the Soviet people to cling to.

■ He had the sense to make concessions which strengthened the regime, for example reopening churches in order to get the support of the faithful, whom he had previously persecuted.

■ Stalin did develop a good grasp of strategy. He was able to some extent to build on his considerable experience of the Civil War of 1918–21.

■ Stalin allowed considerable authority to able subordinates, particularly Molotov (Deputy Chairman of GKO and Commissar for Foreign Affairs, and therefore responsible for diplomacy); Voznesenski (responsible for economic planning and Gosplan); Malenkov (responsible for Party organisation); and Beria (responsible for security, including the NKVD).

Stalin employed experts to check on the work of colleagues. He also increasingly showed a willingness to welcome a clash of ideas in order to resolve a problem. A notable example was in 1945 when he told two leading and rival commanders, Marshals Konev and Zhukov, to produce plans for the final assault on Berlin. Stalin also used 'plenipotentiaries', people with a personal mandate from Stalin to resolve a problem, using whatever ruthless measures were necessary. This helped to resolve some crises: for example, Kaganovich sorted out the major crisis caused by evacuation in the face of the German advance.

Stalin was clearly a powerful force. In the words of one historical work, Stalin's 'accumulation of major responsibilities, together with the enormous prestige which the Red Army's victories in time brought him, made his predominance even greater during the war than before it' (Barber, J. and Harrison, M., *The Soviet Home Front, 1941–1945*, 1991).

■ Did you know?

Some Soviet historians became critical of Stalin's leadership after his death. They unearthed some evidence, still controversial, that in October 1941, when the Soviet position was desperate, Stalin put out peace feelers to Hitler. He was supposed to have tried to persuade Hitler to halt the invasion by offering to cede Germany huge amounts of land in the Baltic Republics, Ukraine and Belorussia. A confident Hitler, already occupying most of these territories, is supposed to have rejected the proposals. If these claims are true, Stalin's offer may not have been genuine, but a delaying tactic to persuade Hitler to pause his attack.

The nature of the wartime economy

The effectiveness of the Soviet war economy

The heroism and sacrifices of the Red Army and Soviet people as a whole helped to grind down the German war machine. However, it was the strength of the Soviet war economy which built on these foundations to pave the way for eventual victory. In essence, the USSR greatly outproduced Germany in all key areas. Investment by the Soviets in steel, machine tools, chemicals and power enabled the production of modern weapons and munitions. Provision for rapid increases in war production had been made during the 1930s. For example, factories had been given the extra capacity to produce more weapons and munitions if required. However, the degree to which the Soviet economy was well prepared for war is a matter for controversy.

Some evidence suggests that the Soviet economy was not well geared to war needs. The regime did not give sufficient attention to ensuring that war industry was located away from the vulnerable western and southern regions, both of which were to be occupied by the Nazis. By November 1941 the Germans occupied an area containing two-thirds of the Soviet population and one-third of its labour force, in addition to well over half of its big industries and industrial capacity, including heavy industry and weapons production. This area also contained two-fifths of Soviet pre-war grain production. The USSR destroyed much of this capacity in order to forestall a German takeover, and the Germans did the rest once they arrived.

The USSR evacuated some industrial equipment from the path of the German advance from June 1941 onwards. This is often presented as a great achievement, which made it possible for the USSR ultimately to win the war. However, a more balanced assessment would be that although helpful to the Soviet war effort, the contribution has been exaggerated. There was no predetermined, coordinated relocation plan, partly because Soviet assumptions had been that any war would be fought on foreign, not Soviet, territory. Although some industry was successfully relocated to the east, much was left too late, or else it was relocated to areas which were not far enough away to be safe. There were also transport difficulties. There was simply not enough transport available, although historian Holland Hunter has claimed that the railways 'weathered a massive invasion … and, through flexible adaptations and energetic responses, carried the troops and material responsible for the Soviet ejection and defeat of the Nazis' (Hunter, Holland, 'Successful spatial management', in Linz, S. (ed.), *The Impact of World War II on the Soviet Union*, 1985)

By 1942 production of key resources like coal, steel and oil was down. Productivity in areas where industry was relocated was relatively low due to the strain on communications and basic services. There was a serious economic crisis in 1942. At the end of 1942 Soviet productive capacity was only 68 per cent of pre-war capacity (it was still 12 per cent lower in 1945). Agriculture also suffered badly, as Soviet historians accepted, although they disagreed on the impact on production. Harvest losses during the war are usually estimated at about a third, with 1943 being a particularly bad year. Much of the land selected for resowing was unproductive.

During the war 3,500 large new factories were built. However, they did not operate at the same capacity as those factories built in peacetime. Most of the new enterprises were built in the Urals and western Siberian regions, previously neglected. When territory was liberated from German

Fig. 10 *A civilian munitions worker*

Fig. 11 *1942 propaganda poster: 'Soldier of the Red Army, come to the rescue'*

■ Exploring the detail

The role of Soviet women

Soviet difficulties were added to by the loss of available labour in occupied areas. To make up the shortfall, the Soviets had to make more use of previously 'unemployed' female labour, schoolchildren and students. Workers and soldiers were also recruited from the countryside, but the denuding of rural areas added to the problems already experienced by Soviet agriculture. The make-up of the Soviet workforce had changed dramatically by 1943. Sixty per cent of the industrial workforce was now female. Over 25 per cent of the workforce was aged under 19 or over 50. Men had virtually disappeared from the countryside. Workers had to be speedily trained for vital war work, on a massive scale. The importance of women should have come as no surprise, since already in the 1930s they had played a major role in enabling Stalin's industrialisation programme to succeed by working in the new factories.

occupation from 1943 onwards, it took a long time to get efficient full-scale production going again.

Another major problem was a shortage of labour. This had been an issue before the war, because the Soviet economy was very labour intensive, with no spare capacity even before 1941. By 1942 the USSR had mobilised virtually all possible labour resources, to the extent that if more labour was required for one enterprise or sector, it could only be found by transferring it from another sector which was also regarded as essential. There was a real possibility that it would become impossible to replace equipment needed by the armed forces. By the end of the first fortnight of the war there were already 10 million Soviet citizens in the armed forces (there were 5 million in the standing army at the start of war, and 5 million more were mobilised in the first week of war). There were simply too few people to go around. The economy was therefore strained almost to breaking point, simply papering over the cracks. Soviet workers, who included children and old people, worked long hours in difficult conditions. Many post-war accounts made glib assertions about Russia's supposedly 'inexhaustible' supplies of labour, soldiers and equipment as a major factor in the Soviet victory. The reality was very different, and in some ways made the Soviet effort even more remarkable, but it was a difficult struggle which took its toll on everyone.

There is, however, some evidence suggesting that the Soviet economy was not so badly geared to war requirements (see Table 1). About one-eighth of Soviet industrial assets were relocated, and this *might* have tipped the balance towards survival in the winter of 1941. Marshal Zhukov later wrote: 'The heroic feat of evacuation and restoration of industrial capacities during the war meant as much for the country's destiny as the greatest battles of the war' (Zhukov, G., *The Memoirs of Marshal Zhukov*, 1971).

Soviet historians refuted the claims that Soviet preparations for war were insufficient. They claimed that it was the socialist nature of the Soviet economy that was decisive, fulfilling Lenin's assertion that a country in which peasants had been given land and workers controlled factories would have a much higher defence capability than a capitalist country in which ordinary people were exploited. One Soviet historian claimed that moving industry eastwards was 'the most massive and most effective evacuation ever undertaken in history … a whole industrial country was moved thousands of kilometres to the East' (Rzheshevsky, O., *World War II: Myths and the Realities*, 1984). This view was echoed, for example, by a British historian, Chris Ward, who claimed that the evacuation of industry was 'one of the most stupendous and successful of such operations ever witnessed' (*Stalin's Russia*, 1999).

Table 1 *Evidence about the effectiveness of the Soviet wartime economy*

Positives	Negatives
The USSR had a large industrial capacity	Much Soviet industry was in vulnerable areas
The USSR was able to quickly mobilise large numbers of people and other resources	There was a shortage of skilled and experienced labour
The USSR was able to relocate some industry	Evacuation and relocation were fraught with difficulties
The USSR massively outproduced Germany	Labour productivity fell under the pressures of war

The Soviet workforce

Because, as the evidence above details, the USSR was already fully mobilised for war by 1942, and indeed almost at breaking point, it is possible to talk of the USSR experiencing 'total war' in a meaningful sense. There was certainly no respite. For example, when in 1941 and 1942 particular areas were under threat of German attack, workers volunteered or were forced to march out of their factories and join Soviet soldiers in the fighting. Often untrained and poorly equipped, these workers suffered great losses, and then there was the added problem of how they were to be replaced, even if the German attack were repulsed. Elsewhere millions of people of all ages were occupied in desperately building defences on the outskirts of cities, often using the simplest equipment.

To coordinate the problems of mobilising the workforce as described above, a Labour Committee was set up at the beginning of the war. Management of the workforce became more systematic later in 1941 and 1942. This was necessary to prevent anomalies that arose earlier in the war, for example when workers essential to war production found themselves conscripted into the armed forces. However, it was not until November 1942 that the Labour Committee acquired sufficient authority to prevent various agencies 'poaching' labour for their own needs from elsewhere. Only then was the wartime economy, and in particular the management and allocation of labour, effectively coordinated. Before then, as two historians have written, 'there were too many soldiers and too many munitions workers compared to the few left in the supporting civilian infrastructure' (Barber, J. and Harrison, M., *The Soviet Home Front, 1941–1945*, 1991).

Partly as a result of full employment, labour productivity in the USSR had been notoriously low since the early 1930s, despite intensive propaganda urging people to work hard for the glory of socialism. This could not be allowed to continue in wartime. As early as 26 June 1941 the government abolished holidays and introduced compulsory overtime of up to three hours per day. There were harsh penalties for the traditional vices of absenteeism or slacking. Tens of thousands of Soviet workers were fined or sent to the notorious labour camps. However, despite official pressure, many workers continued to leave their jobs illegally or simply swapped jobs. Not surprisingly, given all the pressures, labour productivity remained a problem. Typical was the coal industry, where unskilled workers, inexperience and poor working and living conditions led to a big fall in productivity.

Productivity

The results of all the various incentives and pressures on the working population and the economy as a whole were varied. In the munitions factories, which were favoured in the allocation of resources, output doubled during the war. However, in other sectors such as transport, construction, agriculture and trade, output fell back. The propaganda issued about Soviet war production was therefore slightly misleading, because, although the efforts might have been heroic, Soviet wartime productivity was not exceptional, even when measured against other countries. Nevertheless, in terms of sheer quantity, there were some impressive figures: during the war 100,000 tanks, 130,000 aircraft and half a billion shells were produced. All were necessary to feed the Soviet war machine and replace the great losses caused by the intensive fighting, wasteful tactics and the inexperience of many soldiers. The output of defence materials peaked in 1944.

 Activity

Challenge your thinking

Is economic strength as important as military power in modern warfare?

 Exploring the detail

Prison camps

Prison labour was part of the Soviet war effort. The Gulag, or system of Soviet labour camps, had been greatly extended during the 1930s as part of Stalin's campaign of Terror. The camps were used for political as well as 'ordinary' prisoners, and were notoriously harsh, especially those in Siberia and the Arctic Circle. Prisoners had helped to build some of the achievements of the Five-Year Plans such as the White Sea Canal. Thousands died in the camps, through a combination of hunger, disease, hard work and general brutality. The camps continued their role during the war, when the number of prisoners doing forced labour fell, but still amounted to over 600,000 by the beginning of 1944. The effectiveness of prison labour in contributing to the Soviet economy has always been a controversial topic. Whatever its exact value, it is unlikely to have been a major factor either positively or negatively in the context of the whole Soviet war effort.

Lend-lease

Allied help to the USSR was also significant, particularly the provision of American trucks and jeeps after 1942 under the **Lend-lease** scheme. There have been strong debates about how significant this aid actually was. It may have accounted for one-fifth of Soviet resources from 1943, but Soviet estimates were much lower. Some Western historians have claimed that without Allied aid, it would have taken the Soviets several more years to defeat Germany. However, there have been dissenting voices: for example, in his study *Barbarossa* (1965), Alan Clark claimed that the Soviets could have fought Germany to a standstill without foreign aid. Soviet historians have also tended to emphasise the importance of the 1941–42 period in deciding the outcome of the war, before Lend-lease had even taken effect.

Interpretations of the economic impact of the war

Although the economic costs of the war were an enormous burden, some historians have emphasised that participation in the war also brought gains, notably the acquisition of new territory and new technology. Also significant, although less easy to evaluate in its impact, may have been the social unity that developed among the Soviet people, which came from sharing the burden of such a massive war effort. This has to be balanced against what became a burden as a result of the war, namely the costs of occupation in Eastern Europe, maintaining the military power to underpin the USSR's new world power status, and having to try to keep pace with the USSR's chief rival, the United States.

A closer look

Soviet–US rivalry

The USSR and the USA were allies in the war against Germany, and the USA provided valuable resources under Lend-lease to support the Soviet war effort. This was also in the American interest, since the Soviets were doing the bulk of the fighting against Germany, at least on the ground. However, the ideological differences between on the one hand the USA, a society based on private capitalism and free-market enterprise, and on the other the authoritarian, state-dominated USSR were always just beneath the surface. President Roosevelt had a rosier view of Stalin than many of his fellow Americans, but relations between the two great powers remained reasonably smooth as long as Germany was the common enemy.

After the war, the latent tensions between East and West soon surfaced. Mutual distrust led to the Cold War, a state of armed tension punctuated by crises such as the control of Berlin and the Korean War. The USA often appeared to have the upper hand, because its economy was much stronger. Both sides directed enormous resources at building up their defence forces. The Soviet economy ran into difficulties from the 1970s, partly due to Soviet attempts to keep pace with America. Indeed, some commentators believe that competition between the two superpowers was deliberately promoted by the USA in an attempt to bankrupt the more vulnerable Soviet economy in its efforts to keep up and maintain a world role.

Soviet historians looking back on the war tended to very positive about the Soviet war effort on the home front, particularly praising the efforts in 1941. They claimed that the expansion of arms production at the expense of contracting basic industries simply proved the great flexibility of the Soviet planned economy. The reality was that the divergence between these sectors was not planned. More successful was the regime's ability to adapt under pressure in 1941. Although costly, the regime's efforts bought time and space for the Soviets to regroup. Survival was only the first stage:

> The emergency regime of 1941 averted Soviet defeat, but it could not supply the means of Soviet victory. In the summer and autumn of 1941 resource mobilisation was pursued without regard to economic balance, and by the winter the imbalances in the economy had reached an extreme pitch of crisis.

3   Harrison, M., *Soviet Planning in Peace and War 1938–1945*, 1985

There was a new development as the war entered 1943:

> The arms mobilisation continued, but the emergency shifted to the condition of the basic industries. The third period, 1943, saw arms mobilisation reach a peak, while economic expansion resumed. The fourth period began during 1944 when expansion penetrated even the most devastated regions and sectors.

4   Harrison, M., *Soviet Planning in Peace and War 1938–1945*, 1985

Activity

Revision exercise

Based on your reading so far, explain how well the Soviet economy was able to respond to the needs of war.

The actions of the Communist regime to enlist mass patriotism for the war effort

Fig. 12 *Red Army and American troops meet at the River Elbe in Germany, 25 April 1945*

Propaganda and the popular response

Propaganda had always been an integral part of the regime's strategy for enforcing its hold over the Soviet population. In June 1941 this initially worked against the regime. For years the Soviet regime had assured the people that it would not permit a foreign power to invade its territory.

Therefore when the initial attack came in 1941, people either refused to believe it and carried on as normal, or else they panicked. Some even dared to criticise the regime. However, when the truth of the German invasion finally emerged, the people rallied to Stalin and the motherland. Large numbers immediately volunteered for war service or extra work, even before the government called up reservists and passed an emergency decree compelling all able-bodied men between 18 and 45 and women between 18 and 40 to work on defence construction or in war industries, if they were not already employed. For once, by the end of June, the regime told the truth about the situation. The Central Committee condemned complacency and called for a 'scorched earth' policy, which meant the destruction of anything in the path of the invader which might prove useful to him. The Central Committee also called for partisan warfare behind enemy lines and the mobilisation of all resources. The tone was repeated by Stalin in his first meaningful speech of the war, on 3 July:

> A great danger hangs over our country … It is essential that our people should appreciate the full immensity of the danger … The issue is one of life and death for the Soviet state, for the peoples of the USSR. The issue is whether the peoples of the Soviet Union shall remain free or fall into slavery. All our work must be immediately reconstructed on a war footing, everything must be subordinated to the interests of the front and the task of organising the demolition of the enemy.

5   *Pravda, 3 July 1941*

The public response was very impressive. One million Leningraders alone worked on constructing tank traps, ditches, barricades and other defences outside their city. Similar efforts were made in other cities, even when their exhausted inhabitants were already under attack. Martial law was enforced, because the authorities were terrified of a collapse of discipline and order. This was a real danger, and actually happened for a few days in October 1941 when there was looting and panic in Moscow as party officials and their families were seen leaving the city because an imminent German attack was expected.

Mostly the regime relied on traditional methods of control. For example, it withheld bad news which might damage morale. It also made exaggerated claims of German losses. The Battle of Stalingrad was scarcely reported at all until the Soviets knew that they were winning it. The regime also introduced new, tougher measures: there was even stricter censorship; all radios had to be handed in; and refugees were kept out of large cities in case they spread panic. The regime was also afraid of a 'Fifth Column' of traitors who might try to destabilise Russia from within. Therefore the NKVD rounded up anyone who already had a record of opposition. Drastic action was taken against 'defeatists' and 'rumour-mongers'. Thousands of 'suspects' were shot by the NKVD. Soldiers who retreated on the battlefield were also arrested or shot.

Did you know?

One major operation undertaken at this time was the evacuation of Lenin's embalmed corpse from its Red Square mausoleum lest it fall into German hands in the event of them occupying Moscow. Lenin's body was taken to a safer destination, accompanied by scientists responsible for ensuring the preservation of the body. Nevertheless, although the body was later returned and is still on display in Red Square, rumours always persisted that it was damaged during the evacuation, and that the resulting corpse is not in the state that it was before 1941.

Fig. 13 *1941 propaganda poster invoking the spirit of past Russian heroes such as General Suvorov*

The efforts to maintain morale had mixed results. Inevitably, bad news did leak out, and accounts of people who experienced the war suggest that this caused some scepticism regarding official propaganda. On the other hand, there were few occasions when public order and morale did not hold firm. What is difficult to know is whether this was due to the regime's morale-boosting measures, whether it was due to people's hatred and fear of a barbarous enemy, or whether it was later the result of pride in Soviet successes. The regime should probably be credited for recognising the need to adapt some of its propaganda to the different conditions of war, notably:

- a focus on national pride and patriotism, and the defence of the motherland, rather than urging people to fight for the traditional Communist themes such as Marxism-Leninism or the international proletariat. Stalin acknowledged privately that Russians were fighting not for 'us' (that is, the Party), but for Russia

- widespread adoption of the title 'The Great Patriotic War'

- applauding the deeds of pre-Communist Russian heroes such as Alexander Nevsky, conqueror of the Teutonic Knights in the Middle Ages, and also Russian generals who had fought in earlier wars against Napoleon

- the whipping-up of hatred against the Germans generally, not just the Nazi regime

- above all, Stalin's name was constantly held up as a patriotic symbol. He was presented as the leader of the country rather than leader of the Party.

Cross-reference

For Stalin's cult of personality, see also Chapter 2.

This new version of Stalin's cult of personality was prominent from early 1943, once the Soviets were confident of winning the war and it was safe to talk up Stalin's role as commander-in-chief. This could not be done when the Soviets were losing battles. There are many accounts of the great impact which this Stalin cult had on ordinary people: Stalin had always been feared and respected, but now he was even loved.

Strangely, given the fact that the Soviet war effort involved the whole Soviet Union, the emphasis of Soviet wartime propaganda was mostly 'Russian'. Much less publicity was given to the role of other Soviet nationalities.

People's Militias

Other methods were used by the regime to enlist popular support. One was the creation of local 'People's Militias', made up of volunteers, to back up the overstretched Red Army. Because some of these militias were formed spontaneously, and the regime always distrusted 'unofficial' gestures, they were treated suspiciously at first. However, the value of extra personnel could not be overlooked, and the militias were used in many different capacities, including combat. Many of the militia members were killed, since they were often sent into battle with inadequate training or weapons. In reality, their early combat efforts were probably very wasteful, because they would have been better employed in the workplace.

Fig. 14 *Red Army soldiers greeted as heroes on their return from war in 1945*

Religious concessions – the Russian Orthodox Church

Another very successful propaganda exercise by the regime was to restore the Russian Orthodox Church to favour. The Church had never been formally banned in the USSR, but ever since 1917 it had suffered harassment and loss of influence and resources. Many churches had been closed and priests killed. However, Stalin, who as a result of his early priestly education had always remained very interested in religion, met the Head of the Orthodox Church. In return he was given the Church's blessing for the war effort. This may have counted for something in enlisting support from Russia's persecuted Christians. The Church had already been involved early in the war, before Stalin's official attempt at a reconciliation. Without waiting for permission, it had begun to put out propaganda leaflets against the Germans and was making collections to raise money for the war effort, even though such an unofficial action was illegal. The Church even funded a tank brigade.

Later the Church pleased Stalin by campaigning for the Allies to open up a **Second Front**. Under the Church's new alliance with the State, the number of bishops was increased, and by the end of 1943 there were over 15,000 functioning Orthodox churches. The Church was able to preserve its traditional structure, although its function had to remain essentially spiritual. It was not allowed to have a social role in local communities. In the long run Stalin got the best of the bargain: he secured Christian backing during the war. And when, after the war, the need for the Church's support was gone, the regime reverted to a mixture of persecution and discouragement of religious activity.

Soviet historians found it difficult to acknowledge the value of the religious concessions, insisting that the essential principle of the separation of Church and State continued to be upheld during the war, and that no religious body was allowed to participate in state affairs. Indeed, one Soviet historian wrote that:

> The influence of the Orthodox Christian and other religions on the population was a far cry from what bourgeois historians claim it was and could not serve as a source of inspiration in the struggle against the enemy.

6   *Rzheshevsky, O., World War II: Myths and the Realities, 1984*

Interpretations of the Soviet victory in the Second World War

Western interpretations

There have been several interpretations of why the USSR won the Second World War, all of which have elements of accuracy but do not tell the whole story. There has in the past been a tendency in the West to emphasise the importance of Soviet heroism in standing up to the German invasion, but to downplay some of the other positive factors. Sometimes there has been a focus on Stalin's errors and indecisive leadership, especially early in the war. Sometimes there has been an emphasis on German 'errors', for example their lack of preparation for a long war and their reliance on Blitzkrieg tactics; Hitler's interference in strategy; strategic errors such as delaying the campaign against

Key terms

Second Front: a term commonly used after 1941 when the bulk of land fighting was taking place on the Russo-German Front. The idea was that the British and Americans would open up a 'second front' by invading Western Europe, so relieving some of the pressure on the USSR, which was doing the bulk of the Allies' fighting. Stalin felt that the Allies were dragging their feet. The Normandy invasion eventually took place in June 1944. By then it was technically the third front, since Allied forces had already invaded Italy in 1943.

Moscow until too late in 1941, and allowing their forces to be diverted uneccessarily towards Stalingrad in 1942; and not cultivating the anti-Communist sentiment among some of the Soviet nationalities and turning it against Stalin's regime.

The German failure has sometimes been attributed to their inability to cope with the severe Russian winter in 1941. This was a factor, but the assumption is sometimes made that severe weather conditions only affected one side – the Germans – and not the other. Marshal Zhukov emphasised this in his memoirs: 'It was not the rain and snow that stopped the Nazi troops at Moscow. The more than a million-strong elite Nazi force was crushed by the iron will, courage and heroism of the Soviet troops who were there to defend their people, their capital, their country' (Zhukov, G. K., *Reminiscences and Reflections*, 1985).

More positive or balanced interpretations, while accepting some of the points above as contributory factors to success or failure, nevertheless have highlighted some more positive features of the Soviet experience, such as:

- Stalin's growing qualities as a war leader
- the skills of Russian generals such as Zhukov
- the activities of partisans, tying up German forces behind enemy lines
- the heroism of ordinary people, both civilian and military
- the strength of the Soviet economy.

The truth is a combination of all these factors. A typical balanced account is the following by Richard Overy:

> The war effort was not the product of one man, nor could it be made to bend entirely to his [Stalin's] will. The role of the party in sustaining popular mobilisation, of the apparatus of terror under the grotesque Beria or of the Red Army itself ... is as much a part of the history of the war as Stalin's personal dictatorship.'

 7

Overy, R., Russia's War, 1997

Soviet interpretations

Soviet historians often resented the way in which the war on the Eastern Front was analysed in the West. They challenged particular claims. For example, they refuted the idea that it was the Germans' own fault for losing the war because the popular struggle against the Nazis was only triggered by their 'error' in not making use of the anti-Stalinist feeling prevalent in many parts of the USSR. Soviet writers emphasise that there was determined resistance by the people from the very start of the war. Soviet historians refuted some Western interpretations that the Communist Party's role in the Soviet victory was not significant, and the claim that Soviet resistance was due more to national patriotism than support for the regime. A variation on this was the idea that the Soviet people were driven by fear of the regime rather than patriotism. Soviet historians talked up the role of the Party by emphasising that 70 per cent of those who were awarded the highest military title of 'Hero of the Soviet Union' were full or candidate members of the Communist Party. Soviet historians also claimed that the West greatly exaggerated the impact of Western support, particularly the provision of military equipment, as a significant factor in the Soviet victory. Soviet historians refuted the claim sometimes made that the Red Army was wasteful and careless with human life, and relied on successes against the Germans essentially by relying on brute force. They attacked the idea that Soviet victories were achieved only at enormous cost against a German enemy that in essence was more skilful but was overcome by the sheer weight of Soviet numbers. They also claimed that Western historians overestimated the role of other Allied operations in contributing to Germany's defeat, rather than recognising the prime importance of the Red Army in defeating Germany.

The Communist Party during the war

Between 1937 and 1941 the Communist Party had recruited increasingly from the white collar sector, particularly when filling gaps left by Stalin's purges. The Party was therefore becoming less 'working class'. This trend continued when the 1939 Party Congress relaxed the recruitment criteria to make it easier for people from other groups besides workers to join the Party.

The war brought further significant changes. Up to 75 per cent of the Party membership joined the armed forces during the war. Despite heavy losses, Party membership rose, partly because it now seemed more of a patriotic duty to join. By 1945 two-thirds of all Party members had been recruited since 1941. Like the workers, the proportion of peasants in the Party also fell. The proportion of women in the Party rose, although only to a figure of 18.3 per cent. As well as being younger, the Party membership was also better educated. A high proportion of military commanders joined the Party, although full-time Party members lost the power officially to interfere in military decisions, as the army became more confident and professional and Stalin trusted it more. Party members gradually changed their function during the war, becoming less involved in military and political activity and more involved instead in economic organisation and carrying out administrative functions.

Activity

Thinking point

Why did the USSR win the war against Germany? Taking account of the interpretations in this section, put forward the case for two main reasons for the Soviet victory. Then read your reasons to others in the group and see if they share the same ideas.

■ A closer look

The impact of the war on the city of Leningrad

Leningrad was a prime example of how drastic and long-lasting the impact of the war on the USSR was. Leningrad, which was the name given (after Lenin's death) to the old Russian capital of St Petersburg or Petrograd, was the USSR's second city after Moscow. It was a great political, economic and cultural centre. Because of its historic connections with Lenin and the Russian Revolution, Leningrad had a particular fascination for Hitler, and he was determined to wipe out the city completely. By the autumn of 1941 German forces had surrounded and cut off the city. Starvation and disease began to take their toll. By 1943 the population of Leningrad had fallen from a pre-war figure of 3.2 million to 639,000 inhabitants. The siege took a terrible toll on human lives and much else besides. The siege and enemy action destroyed 25 per cent of its capital stock and 16 per cent of its housing stock. Many of the city's architectural and other treasures were destroyed. However, there were also other longer-term consequences, although the population had recovered to its pre-war level by the late 1950s. Leningrad lost a high proportion of its skilled workforce and therefore also lost its pre-eminent position among other Soviet industrial centres. Its once powerful political elite lost its standing during the war. Its previous prominent position was taken over by Moscow after the war, and Leningrad clearly emerged from the war demoted to the USSR's second city. In several respects, therefore, Leningrad never really recovered from the war.

Fig. 15 *One of the iconic Soviet posters of the war, from 1943: 'For the Motherland!'*

The extent of wartime opposition within the USSR and the regime's treatment of it

Stalin's regime had always relied upon a mixture of propaganda and coercion, or the threat of force, to maintain itself in power. However, for many Soviet citizens, it appeared that the terrible experience of war formed a new bond with their leader, who became the personification of victory. The regime acquired more legitimacy than before because the survivors felt that all of them, including the Party faithful, had been through the ordeal of total war together. Everyone had contributed. Stalin's own status as a successful war leader had been boosted enormously. He was now genuinely popular.

The nationalities

Most of the nationalities of the USSR were fully involved in the Soviet war effort, even those whose territory was not directly threatened. The Soviet regime, despite utilising the resources of the various republics, saw the multinational nature of the USSR as a weakness, and indeed a threat. The regime did have grounds for concern. In some areas, for example in Ukraine, the invading Germans were regarded as liberators or allies in a struggle for independence from Moscow. The Nazis signally failed to capitalise on this because of their slavish adherence to a racial theory which could not recognise the worth of the Soviet nationalities. In spite of the Nazi neglect of popular dissatisfaction, possibly a million or more people from various national groups did become collaborationists and fought on the German side. The most famous group was Vlasov's 'Russian Liberation Army'. Vlasov was a Red Army commander captured by the Germans in 1942. He then fought alongside the Germans. He was captured by the Americans in 1945. They returned Vlasov to the Soviets, who hanged him. Some Soviet citizens also joined Hitler's SS, and some **Cossacks** collaborated, believing that the Germans might help them build an independent state.

Collaboration was not widespread. Yet Stalin's regime branded several nationalities as traitors, real or potential, or 'guilty by association'. Some national groups were deported. The Crimean Tatars were deported in 1943–44 to Kazakhstan and Central Asia. The Volga Germans, who had been settled in the USSR for generations, were deported in 1941 to Siberia and Central Asia. Many Soviet citizens were also exiled from the Baltic states, Ukraine and Georgia. Stalin was obsessed with a supposed threat to national unity. Along with the deportations there was a revival during wartime of Russian nationalism, which was a change from the pre-war emphasis on furthering the concept of 'Soviet man' and 'Soviet woman'.

Proportionately Soviet Jews suffered the most of all the Soviet nationalities. They lived mostly in western Russia, Ukraine and

Activity

Research task

Investigate the fate of some of the other Soviet national groups during the war.

Belorussia. All these areas were occupied by the Germans in 1941 and 1942, and by 1945 half of the approximately 5 million Jews who had lived in the USSR in 1941 had disappeared. Many were killed outright by the Germans, sometimes with the help of local nationalists.

It is difficult to be precise about the numbers involved in deportations. Early in the war over one million people were deported from western Belorussia and the western Ukraine. In June 1941 134,000 people were deported from the Baltic states and sent to convict camps. Overall, between 1941 and 1948, a period which therefore included the post-war years, probably about 3.3 million Soviet citizens were deported.

A closer look

The fate of Soviet prisoners of war

A high proportion of Soviet prisoners of war never survived German captivity because of the brutal treatment they received. However, even for those who survived both imprisonment and Stalin's retribution for allowing themselves to be captured, life remained hard. Until the break-up of the USSR in 1991 and even beyond, many of these survivors were virtually shunned and treated as second-class citizens. They were regarded even in the popular mind as cowards or weaklings who had let their comrades down. They often found it difficult to get work, their names were left off war memorials, and they did not receive a proper pension until many years after the war. The memory of the war remained extremely strong in the USSR for generations after 1945, and it was very common, for example, for veterans to go into schools to talk to young children about their war experiences. But ex-prisoners were never invited. As late as the 1980s, someone filling in an application form for most things in the USSR had to respond to a question which asked whether they were closely related to anyone who had been a prisoner of war or had been imprisoned during the war. One of the most famous victims was the future Russian writer Alexander Solzhenitsyn, a Red Army officer. Upon his release at the end of the war, he was treated with suspicion by the Soviet authorities, along with other prisoners, and sentenced to a prison camp. It was as a result of these experiences that he began his writings about the Stalinist prison camp system, writings that eventually achieved fame throughout the world.

Internal security

During the war the security services continued to exert the massive authority under Beria which they had enjoyed before 1941. While there was no mass purging as in the 1930s, the NKVD continued with undiminished zeal in the task of ensuring compliance from the population. It punished incompetence and failure, at the highest military level as well as among the civilian population. The NVKD arrested those suspected of disloyalty. It had a particular role in dealing with 'suspect' national groups, as described above. It monitored those Soviet citizens who had lived under German occupation, and these people were investigated for loyalty. The NKVD was also involved in using convict labour for the war economy. Beria was a member of GKO and used by Stalin as a troubleshooter in several capacities, to sort out problems in his usual ruthless manner. All this made Beria one of the most powerful and feared Communists in the USSR.

The relationship between the Soviet people and Stalin's regime by 1945

Many Soviet citizens were hopeful in 1945 that they would experience better living and working conditions as a reward for the great sacrifices endured during the Great Patriotic War and the 1930s. They probably also hoped for greater personal freedom after the years of Stalin's Terror. Soviet citizens were understandably proud of the massive contribution they had made to the Allied victory over Germany. The USSR was now one of the world's two superpowers, to be feared as well as respected. Although there was no such thing as free public opinion in the USSR, since all media was controlled by the state, it is likely that many Soviet citizens felt not just relief and pride at the end of the war, but also a hope that the regime would treat its subjects with more humanity. The years of sacrifice must mean more than simply the glorification of Stalin and his regime's ideology.

Any such optimism was misplaced. This was not really surprising. During the war the regime had shown the same zeal for persecuting its own citizens as it had during the 1930s

Fig. 16 *Soviet war propaganda: Soviet forces fighting under the banner of Lenin*

purges. The message was always the same. There must be an unceasing struggle against the enemies of the world's first socialist state. There must be continual sacrifices in the cause of consolidating this state and moving forward to the eventual triumph of Communism. Stalin declared that as the USSR grew stronger, so its enemies would become more desperate in their efforts to destroy Soviet achievements. Eternal vigilance and struggle were the watchwords.

This message was clear even before the final defeat of Germany. The Party had never relaxed its grip on the Soviet population, while Stalin's own grip on the Party had been intensified. His prestige and power were greater than ever. His determination to root out 'enemies' – what some historians have called his paranoia – continued unabated. After 1945 many millions of Russians and other Soviet citizens would be imprisoned, tortured or killed during the remaining eight years of Stalin's life.

Summary questions

1 To what extent was the strength of the Soviet economy responsible for the Soviet victory in the Second World War?

2 How important was Stalin to the Soviet victory?

High Stalinism, 1945–53

Fig. 1 *Stalin and Zhukov at the 1945 Moscow victory parade*

In this chapter you will learn about:

- how the USSR was governed under Stalin between 1945 and 1953

- the extent to which the Soviet economy recovered from the impact of the 1941–45 war

- how the USSR was affected by Cold War politics.

A column of Soviet citizens, all a hundred years old or more, was marching through Red Square on the May Day celebration. The citizens came from Lithuania, Armenia, Uzbekistan, Georgia and other Soviet Republics. They carried a placard which read: 'Thank you, dear Comrade Stalin, for our happy childhoods.'

Stalin is confused. He stops the column and says: 'But I wasn't around then.'

'That's exactly why our childhoods were happy.'

1 *A post-1945 Soviet joke*

Stalin's dictatorship, 1945–53

Ideological developments

Andrei Zhdanov was a leading figure in the Soviet regime after 1945, as a member of both the Secretariat and the Politburo. It is possible that Stalin, in his own mind, had marked out Zhdanov as his eventual successor. Zhdanov certainly promoted Stalinist themes, by emphasising strict conformity to the Party line. There was no place for genuine discussion about any 'alternative' policies to those agreed by the regime. Any Soviet citizen, however prominent or insignificant, who did not follow the Party line, risked not just exile to the political wilderness but imprisonment or worse – although far fewer leading Communists were liquidated in the 1945–53 period than had been the case during the **Great Terror** of the 1930s.

Key profile

Andrei Zhdanov

Zhdanov (1896–1948) rose to prominence in 1934 as one of Stalin's favourites. According to Molotov, Stalin 'valued Zhdanov above everyone else'. The two men loved discussing Russian history and culture, and Zhdanov provided the piano accompaniment to Stalin's singing when the leader was relaxing. When Sergei Kirov, head of the Leningrad Party organisation and one of the rising stars of the Party, was assassinated in 1934, it marked the start of Stalin's Great Terror. Zhdanov took over Kirov's post and led the purge in Leningrad. By 1939 he was a member of the Politburo, and his son married Stalin's daughter Svetlana. Zhdanov's reputation was as a hard-liner and someone who strongly opposed any 'Western' influences being allowed to enter the USSR. For example, he denounced jazz. It was Zhdanov who laid down what could be published in the USSR and seen on stage and in film. It was his influence which determined that Stalinist culture was largely sterile and totally subservient to the task of glorifying Stalin and the benefits of socialism. Although Zhdanov suffered from ill-health before his death, Stalin believed that he had been murdered, and this led to several arrests. However, there is also speculation that Zhdanov, who had his own enemies such as the police chief Beria, was losing influence and would himself have been purged had he not died first.

Zhdanov, undoubtedly reflecting Stalin's own views, ensured that all intellectuals – whether writers, artists, scientists, musicians or economists – followed the Party line. It was dangerous not to follow to the letter directives from on high. Sometimes these intellectuals, who might have been helping to formulate opinion in more liberal or democratic societies, had to try to second-guess what was the orthodox line that the Party wanted. This carried its own risks, so independent thought was stifled. Religion, at least in the form of the Russian Orthodox Church, had been harnessed by Stalin to boost support for the regime during the war. However, after 1945 religious practice was tolerated only in so far as it conformed and presented no threat to the State's control of 'public opinion'. In reality, much religious sentiment was channelled into a glorification of the Stalin cult.

Key chronology
Stalin's dictatorship, 1945–53

1945	
May	End of the Great Patriotic War
July	Potsdam Conference
1946	Fourth Five-year Plan announced Purge in Leningrad
1947	Declaration of US Truman Doctrine and Marshall Plan – denounced by Zhdanov
1948	Dispute with Western powers over Berlin Death of Zhdanov and further purge in Leningrad
1949	Campaign against 'Western' influences in USSR Testing of first Soviet A-bomb Stalin's seventieth birthday
1950	Outbreak of Korean War
1951	Fifth Five-year Plan
1952	Politburo renamed Central Committee Praesidium Possibility of 'Peaceful Co-existence' raised
1953	'Doctors' Plot' announced
March	Death of Stalin

Exploring the detail

Anti-Semitism

Anti-Jewish prejudice had long been a feature of Russian history. Before 1917, most of Russia's several million Jews had been confined to certain areas of Russia, and had been subject to vicious racist attacks. Many educated Jews joined political groups such as the Communists. Yet although many leading Communists, including Trotsky, Kamenev and Zinoviev, were Jewish, prejudice against Jews persisted, and was exploited by Stalin after the war. A Jewish Anti-Fascist Committee had been set up during the war. Members of this committee were now arrested. Its leader, the actor Solomon Mikhoels, was killed in a motor 'accident' arranged by the police.

A new Terror

Despite the unity in Party and government that apparently prevailed after 1945, there were rivalries beneath the surface. Stalin was old and increasingly frail, although this was not acknowledged publicly. Some historians believe that he had become an alcoholic. It was therefore inevitable that other leading Communists would manoeuvre for influence for the time when Stalin died, although this was a dangerous game. The manoeuvring became more evident following Zhdanov's sudden death in 1948. Beria, the feared head of the security services, conspired with Zhdanov's rival Malenkov to launch a major purge in Leningrad. This must have been agreed by Stalin. Over 200 leading Leningrad Party officials were arrested and in some cases shot. Leningrad had achieved a heroic, almost mythical status for holding out against the Germans during the 900-day siege between 1941 and 1944. During that period over one million Leningraders had died of enemy action, disease or starvation. This apparently meant little to Stalin. He remembered instead 1934, when the assassination of Leningrad's Party chief (and Stalin's potential rival for the leadership) Kirov marked the beginning of the Great Terror. For Stalin, the loyalty of the Leningrad Party was in doubt. He also saw Leningrad, traditionally Russia's 'window on the West', as a place where foreign influences might enter the USSR, given its reputation as a great intellectual and cultural centre as well as being the birthplace of the Revolution. Stalin preferred to promote Moscow as a more 'traditional' Russian capital.

There is no convincing evidence of any plot against Stalin. The Leningrad purge victims were posthumously rehabilitated in the Gorbachev era in the 1980s. The purge in Leningrad was simply the prelude to an extension of the Terror across the USSR. In 1948 there was a new outburst of anti-Semitism. A small number of prominent Russian Jews were tortured into confessing treasonable activities and were shot. Thousands of other Jews were arrested, sacked from their jobs or harassed in other ways. Even Molotov's Jewish wife was arrested.

The purge then spread into the Party itself. Several security officials and administrators in Georgia were arrested. Stalin despised his fellow Georgian, Beria, although he had relied upon him as his security chief for many years. The Georgian purge was therefore seen as an attack on Beria, although he was allowed to survive for the time being. In 1953 the Terror was further extended with the bizarre 'Doctors' Plot'. Leading Kremlin doctors, many of whom happened to be Jewish, were accused of poisoning Zhdanov and plotting the deaths of Stalin and some of his colleagues. The fact that Stalin was ill at this time could only have added to his paranoia. In 1952 Stalin had already begun to criticise leading subordinates such as Molotov and Mikoyan. It is likely that Stalin was on the verge of a massive new purge. If so, only his own sudden death in March 1953 stopped it in its tracks, and possibly saved some of his successors such as Khrushchev from liquidation. Stalin's death left his subordinates in a state of both relief and uncertainty: relief because they had survived, but uncertainty because there was no clear line of succession to Stalin and each saw the others as potential rivals.

The government of the USSR under High Stalinism

Stalin was clearly the very hub of government. Some of his colleagues claimed after his death that he had become conceited after the victory against Germany and came to see himself as infallible. He appeared to take fewer decisions, leaving much to his subordinates, but at the same time encouraging an atmosphere of secrecy and even mystery, playing off

Fig. 2 *Stalin represented at the peak of his power* – Anthem of People's Love *by Igor Reznik*

his colleagues against each other. These colleagues often had to second-guess what Stalin really wanted, as although he gave fewer orders he insisted on being consulted about everything. At the same time the Party leaders were terrified of getting it 'wrong', since Stalin was unpredictable and his temper might suddenly explode. Colleagues like Molotov and Khrushchev reported that when Stalin did give an order, it was obeyed without question. According to Molotov, 'government ceased to function', with Stalin dealing directly with individual officials rather than leading Party colleagues as a group. He seemed to be constantly suspicious or jealous of those around him. He spent much of his later years watching films and forcing subordinates like Beria into all-night drinking sessions. Some like Zhdanov became alcoholics as a consequence.

Interpretations of Stalin's rule

Some historians, for example Peter Kenez (in *A History of the Soviet Union from the Beginning to the End*, 1999), have emphasised the deliberate nature of Stalin's method of ruling, arguing that he always retained full power, even when growing old and somewhat weary. Although some of Stalin's subordinates became associated with particular policies – for example Zhdanov and his 'anti-cosmopolitanism' – this was only so that, if the policies were later deemed unsuccessful, Stalin could demote the person held responsible. He could thereby avoid any implication that he himself had been responsible for the policy in the first place. Some historians also argue that in essence the USSR was a strongly totalitarian state in which the Party reigned supreme. They suggest that where there were limitations on Stalin's power, it was not due to lack of will but simply inefficiency, because decisions were sometimes made haphazardly, or because Stalin became personally more isolated. Other historians, for example W. Hahn (in *Postwar Soviet Politics: the Fall of Zhdanov and the Defeat of Moderation 1946–53*, 1982), have taken the view that Stalin's power was less supreme than is popularly imagined. For example, in the immediate post-war years Stalin found himself having to compete for popularity with famous Red Army commanders. Stalin's daughter later maintained that he did not control his personal staff, and Chris Ward (*Stalin's Russia*, 1999) described Stalin as 'no self-confident tyrant in charge of a smoothly functioning totalitarian machine, but a sickly old man – unpredictable, dangerous, lied to by terrified subordinates, presiding over a ramshackle bureaucracy and raging, like Lear, against failure and mortality'.

Thinking point

How much power do you think Stalin had after 1945?

Exploring the detail

Satellite states in Eastern Europe

Stalin was obsessed with the security of Soviet borders, which had been crossed by invaders several times in recent history. At the end of the war, Stalin used his strong bargaining position to ensure Soviet domination of several countries in Central and Eastern Europe, principally Poland, Czechoslovakia, Hungary, Romania and Bulgaria, as well as the Russian zone of Germany. The Red Army already occupied these areas. Between 1945 and 1948, the USSR used its influence to ensure that Communist Parties came to power in these states, either by election or force. They then followed Moscow's line.

A feature of the USSR between 1945 and 1953 was the apparent ease with which the regime continued to manage the vast territory of the USSR and its new satellite states in Eastern Europe. The regime had never lost its hold over its own population, even during the most difficult war years of 1941–43. This was due to Stalin's personal prestige and the grip of the Party on the country, which had been very strong ever since Stalin's rise to power a generation before. Nevertheless, it was a great achievement to maintain stability after 1945 given the appalling costs of the war and the need to mobilise the population to bring about recovery, while simultaneously ensuring that the USSR played a leading part in the new world order after 1945. The strength of the regime did not just rest on fear, although this was certainly a significant element.

In one important sense Stalin was all-powerful, shifting his colleagues from post to post, creating fear and uncertainty, and acting unpredictably or arbitrarily on many occasions. This was seen, for example, when demoting the war hero Marshal Zhukov. However, the Party also had a life of its own. At a local level, Party organisations had their own ways of doing things, involving patronage, nepotism and internal rivalries. The leadership probably did not care, provided there was no actual opposition to directives from Moscow. Certainly, when abuses of power at the local level were identified by inspectors from Moscow, drastic action rarely followed. Stalin himself rarely left Moscow except when on vacation in the south. He never visited his 'subjects' and relied on information from those around him. Probably, in his final years, the information he was given was very selective. It is not certain exactly how much Stalin really knew about the USSR in his final years.

Key profile

Marshal Georgi Zhukov

The Red Army's greatest commander, Zhukov (1896–1974) had fought in the Red cavalry in the Civil War after the Russian Revolution. He became a professional soldier, seeing action during the Spanish Civil War and against the Japanese during the 1930s. In January 1941 he was appointed chief of the general staff. During the first year of the war, he was at various times in charge of the reserve army, of Leningrad and of Moscow. He was promoted to marshal in January 1943. Zhukov led the assault on Berlin and received the German surrender in 1945. After the war Stalin saw Zhukov as a rival in the popularity stakes, and posted him to a remote area. He resurfaced briefly to serve as minister of defence under Khrushchev.

Most historians accept that Stalin's personal position as leader was secure, and that the Party held sway over all aspects of Soviet life. However, because of of Stalin's increasing isolation, they sometimes argue that his position within the totalitarian state was perhaps more complex than was once believed. This is because an increasing number of power bases were developing, particularly at the lower levels, as his rule entered its final years.

The various interpretations of Stalin's last years can probably be narrowed down to two main schools of thought. One interpretation of Stalin's rule in this period is that as he aged, he became less in control and more isolated from reality, possibly even believing his own propaganda.

Khrushchev's memoirs painted the picture of a man who was often ill, afraid of assassination and avoiding large political meetings. Instead Stalin would socialise with colleagues, especially the ones he promoted after the war, usually inviting them to late night evening sessions where they watched films, danced, sang, and most important of all, drank heavily. During these sessions Stalin might discuss policy with advisers, but he was equally liable to turn on colleagues and embarrass, humiliate or threaten them. Government suffered because Stalin took increasingly longer holidays in the south rather than staying at the helm in Moscow.

Another interpretation might be that Stalin remained very much in control of events. If he gave the impression of being less active, it was because he preferred to let his colleagues pursue particular policies. If these policies failed, Stalin could avoid association with the policy but instead demote the colleague whose name was attached to it. Stalin deliberately provoked colleagues into distrust of each other, so they felt isolated, and thereby reinforced his dominance. He did not rely on formal bodies such as the Politburo, which very rarely met after 1945. Instead he relied more on 'unofficial' sources of information, such as the security agencies.

Activity

Group discussion

Divide the class into two groups. Each group should take one of the two interpretations above and produce at least five points to support its argument.

Government and Party structures

The basic structures of government and society under Stalin had not changed significantly from pre-war days. The 1936 Constitution was still in place. This promised various civil liberties which did not exist in reality. However, it also laid down the principles of government. The USSR had a parallel Party and government structure.

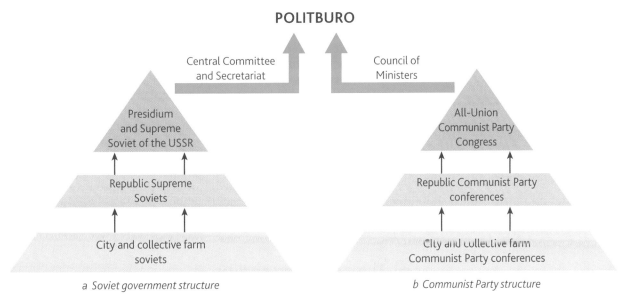

Fig. 3 *The Government and Party Structures*

The structure of the elected soviets (a Russian word meaning 'council') involved a system which reached upwards from local, district, farm and city soviets, eventually to Republican soviets and finally to the Supreme Soviet of the USSR. The Supreme Soviet met only once or twice a year. Although in theory the soviets elected the Central Committee and ultimately the Politburo, in reality the Supreme Soviet meekly approved laws drafted by the Communist Party. Elections to the soviets were open to all sane and free citizens over 18. However, candidates were usually Party members, drawn from a list put forward by the unelected Party organisation.

Although there were sometimes heated debates at Soviet election meetings, the actual elections were presented as the opportunity to show support for the Party and regime rather than allow citizens to influence policy or put forward alternative views. All citizens were urged to vote, and election turnouts were usually put at about 99 per cent.

The Communist Party under Stalin after 1945

The Communist Party structure paralleled the Soviet structure, although its members were not elected. The number of Party members varied, but was usually around 10 per cent of the population. People joined the Party for various reasons. However, the two most obvious motives were ideological commitment to what the Party stood for, or career advancement, since it was difficult to progress far in any sphere of Soviet life without being a Party member. Being a full Party member, which was only possible after a probationary period, did carry responsibilities. For example, at a low level, it could mean organising Party meetings in the workplace to explain Party policy to workmates. Party members at the higher levels, who were full-time Party operators, got certain privileges. These included access to special shops which provided a range of consumer goods completely unavailable to the rest of the population. However, being a Party member also carried risks as well as privileges. Party members were more likely to be the victims of Stalinist purges than non-Party members. Except in the extraordinary periods of Terror, when Party members were among the many Soviet citizens who were arbitrarily arrested, imprisoned and sometimes killed, 'purging' usually meant being expelled from the Party for unsatisfactory behaviour. This might mean insufficient enthusiasm or an anti-social offence such as alcoholism.

The Party clearly controlled all aspects of Soviet life, and holders of State positions were also Party members. Party delegates attended regular conferences at local and Republican levels. The more infrequent All-Union Congresses listened to speeches from the hierarchy, but under Stalin the meetings were little more than staged events to applaud the leadership. At the highest levels, the Politburo was self-selecting, usually drawing its members from the Central Committee, although even the Politburo, originally the chief policy-making body, rarely met under Stalin in its original form. His ministers did meet without Stalin being present, and some historians have suggested this as evidence that Stalin's grip on power was being slowly loosened. However, Russian sources tend to contradict this interpretation, since they show that Stalin nearly always insisted on ratifying any proposals made in his absence before they could be put into practice.

■ The cult of personality

Even before the 1941–45 war, Stalin had been portrayed as almost a god-like figure. His cult-like status was reinforced by the Soviet victory in 1945, and the uncertainty and possibly failure of nerve shown by Stalin at the time of the German invasion of June 1941 was never mentioned. In private Stalin voiced disapproval of the excesses of the Stalin cult, expressed in many ways such as vast parades, posters, and Stalin's name appearing throughout the media. However, in practice he showed little sign of wanting to curb these excesses.

It is not clear exactly what Stalin thought about the adulation heaped upon him. Some have argued that, as he was renowned for being a pragmatist, he was not taken in by his own propaganda, but simply recognised the political advantages of allowing his subordinates to promote the image of the all-seeing, all-knowing supremo. He was presented as the leader who at the same time cared for his people and was ruthless in protecting their interests as defined by Stalin and the Party. When meeting with colleagues after the war to discuss a new edition of one of the official biographies of him, Stalin objected to the emphasis put on him as being the fount of all wisdom and the leading interpreter of Marxism. He declared that 'We already have the teaching of Marx and Lenin. No additional teachings are required. Nowhere is it said clearly that I am Lenin's pupil ….. I considered and still consider myself the pupil of Lenin.' Stalin frequently made irritable outbursts when he detected excessive flattery. And yet he allowed the publication to go ahead. The next edition in 1947 exaggerated his role in the Second World War, playing down the contribution of other individuals to the Soviet victory.

Propaganda both subtly and blatantly promoted Stalin's positive image: for example, in the frequent propagandist portraits of Lenin and Stalin together, Stalin began to appear as slightly taller than Lenin, which had not been the case in real life. Official portraits or photographs of Stalin were airbrushed to disguise flaws such as his pock-marked skin (see page 10). The reality was that although Stalin on the surface might have been somewhat cynical about how his image was promoted, either he was flattered at least to some extent, or he was too lazy to prevent it from happening. He surely recognised the political advantages such adulation had in reinforcing his position. Probably it was a combination of all these factors.

Stalin had already amassed honours before 1945. At the end of the war he had been awarded more titles, among others that of generalissimo, although he resisted suggestions of renaming Moscow 'Stalinodar'. However, the cult of Stalin was at its height at the celebrations held for his seventieth birthday in December 1949. Celebrations, festivals and processions were held throughout the USSR, culminating in a vast balloon floated in the sky above the Kremlin, with Stalin's face projected on it. None of his colleagues took seriously Stalin's statement before these events that he did not want excessive celebrations.

Economic recovery after 1945

One of the main reasons for the Soviet victory in the Second World War was Stalin's success in industrialising the USSR during the 1930s. However crude and fraught with problems this process had been, it had enabled the Soviets to build up a strong base of heavy industry and an armaments programme which meant that the USSR was able to massively outproduce the Germans. However, much of this economic base had been damaged, destroyed or exhausted by the war itself. It was therefore scarcely surprising that one of Stalin's first priorities in 1945 was rapidly to rebuild the Soviet economy, so that the country could recover and also to provide a sound foundation for the USSR's new superpower status. This would involve maintaining a massive military establishment. Stalin was convinced in 1945 that another war was likely, this time with his former allies in the struggle against Hitler. As in the years before 1941, industry was seen as the key factor in economic recovery and progress.

Economic organisation

Although the fundamentals of the Stalinist economic structure remained unchanged, there were some modifications in its management. Reflecting the growing complexity of the Soviet economy, there were now more economic ministries, with less direct Party interference in their everyday

Activity

Thinking point

Why do you think a cult of personality was created around Stalin?

running. However, this was not the case with agriculture, which was more closely controlled than ever before. At the end of 1947, Gosplan, the State Planning Commission, had its responsibilities limited to planning the economy, and its previous responsibility for arranging the supplies necessary for carrying out the plans was transferred elsewhere.

The Fourth Five-year Plan, 1946–50

The Soviet approach to industrial recovery was traditional, based as it was on the mechanism of the Five-year Plans. These were first introduced in 1928. The Fourth Plan, just like its predecessors (the Third Five-year Plan, begun in 1938, was effectively brought to a premature end by the German invasion of 1941), worked by the State setting priorities and targets for the next five years, determining what should be produced and where. The Fourth Plan had the same advantages as its predecessors: it was a relatively effective method of producing large amounts of basic raw materials or capital goods (sometimes referred to as 'producers' goods') such as coal and steel. Almost 90 per cent of industrial investment between 1945 and 1950 went into capital goods industries. The Plan also had the same defects as before. Although it was broken down into shorter-term targets for individual enterprises to meet, the system was inflexible:

- Most emphasis went on meeting quantitative, not qualitative, targets. An enterprise manager was expected to meet the targets, not worry about whether the product was produced efficiently or whether it was any good at all.

- The Plan was based on government priorities, taking no account of what consumers, that is ordinary people, actually wanted. Therefore products such as clothing, food and household goods were given a low priority and were often in short supply.

- Soviet industry was very inefficient and heavily labour intensive – that is, it depended on masses of workers, often with not very high productivity, working with inefficient and even obsolete machinery. The problem was worsened by heavy Soviet losses of man- and womanpower during the war.

- The USSR had lost the economic help provided during the war by its then allies, the Americans and the British.

Nevertheless, the gains made were impressive, as the table here indicates:

Table 1 *The Fourth Five-year Plan (rounded to nearest whole number)*

	1945	Planned 1950 target	Actual 1950 results
Coal (million tons)	149	250	261
Oil (million tons)	19	35	40
Steel (million tons)	12	25	27
Cement (million tons)	2	10	10
Electricity (billion Kwhs)	43	82	91
Tractors (thousands)	15	112	242
Number of workers (millions)	27	33	39
Index of producers' goods (1940 = 100)	112	-	205

Adapted from Soviet sources
Note: Due to statistical manipulation by the Soviet authorities, it is not possible to vouch for the complete accuracy of the statistics, although the general trends are likely to be realistic.

Industrial production in 1950 was almost 75 per cent up on 1940. There were big increases in the production of capital goods such as coal and steel. Some of the pre-Second World War propaganda showpieces which had been destroyed, such as the great Dnepropatrovsk hydro-electric power station, were rebuilt. The reconstruction of the Soviet railway system was a notable achievement. Defence, as always in the USSR, received the most favoured treatment in the allocation of resources, including skilled labour, although understandably there was a drop in armaments production in the first year of peace. Much of the early investment after the war went into regions which had been occupied by the Germans and had therefore suffered the most, for example the Donets mining region. Soviet industry also gained from the policy of stripping assets from countries which it occupied at the end of the war, especially eastern Germany, although some historians like Alex Nove (*An Economic History of the USSR*, 1988) doubt whether this factor was significant in comparison to the Soviet people's own efforts. Areas of industry such as the Urals, which had escaped destruction by Germany and had contributed greatly to the Soviet war effort, continued to boost industrial output figures in the years of peace.

The successes that were achieved were due above all to the hard work of men and, increasingly, women, who had to compensate for the loss of manpower during the war. There may have been some of the enthusiasm akin to that shown in the early 1930s by committed young people who believed that they were building socialism. However, much of the effort after 1945 was made by workers who were tired and sometimes hungry. They were trying to avoid the penalties of lower wages or arrest if they were thought to be slacking, yet they had little prospect of better living and working conditions in their lifetime. The slogans encouraging endless sacrifice for the future, part of the staple propaganda of the 1930s, were wearing thin in the grim aftermath of the war. Although it is difficult to gauge the popular mood, it cannot have been helped by the State taking what appeared to be some arbitrary decisions which affected everyday life. One such was the 1947 currency reform, which drastically reduced the amount of money in circulation. Everyday products such as clothes and shoes were even scarcer than they had been before the war. In order to acquire basic necessities, people often had to pay much higher 'unofficial' prices on the Black Market.

But in a society in which the State rigidly controlled the media, it was difficult or dangerous for citizens to voice any discontent. Stalin remained apparently convinced that the economic strategies he first introduced in the late 1920s remained the way forward over 20 years later. In his last book, *The Economic Problems of Socialism in the USSR* (1952), he insisted that the priority must be to continue developing heavy industry, with consumer goods being very much a secondary concern. Meanwhile, he insisted, developing competition between **capitalist** countries would eventually result in a new world war, so the USSR must remain strong and on its guard.

However, economic policy drifted in Stalin's final years. The Fifth Five-year Plan, which should have begun in 1951, was not drafted and approved until October 1952. It planned significant further increases in industrial and agricultural production, but it was difficult to see how this could have been achieved in agriculture since nothing was done to increase investment in rural areas. In any case, the Plan was overtaken by events, as Stalin's death in 1953 created the possibility of significant changes of direction.

Did you know?

The idea of State planning in the form of the Five-year Plans arose from observations by Communist leaders like Lenin and Stalin of how the Western Allies had organised their economies during the First World War. The Communists chose a period of five years since it seemed to fit the period of time needed to complete major works such as hydro-electric power stations – although in practice, constant revisions meant that the actual length of each Plan varied.

Key terms

Capitalist: countries like the USA and Britain where, despite some government regulation, the economy was based on the free movement of private capital or wealth. People could own private property and dispose of their income as they wished, which meant that business responded by producing goods that people wanted to buy, and thereby also made profits for businessmen and their shareholders.

Interpretations of industrial progress

Most historians recognise the achievements of the industrial recovery. For example, Alex Nove commented that 'The USSR could face the arms race, which in 1950 was again beginning, with a stronger industrial structure than before the war' (*An Economic History of the USSR*, 1988). Peter Kenez agreed: 'Even if we take into consideration the exaggerations built into Soviet statistics, it is still indisputable that the Stalinist methods worked, and that the speed of reconstruction was impressive' (*A History of the Soviet Union From the Beginning to the End*, 1999).

Agriculture

Agriculture in 1945 was in an even worse condition than industry. For many years before the war it had been the poor relation of industry. Soviet agriculture had been collectivised in the late 1920s and early 1930s.

The trauma of collectivisation had disrupted agricultural production, which by the late 1930s had scarcely returned to pre-First World War levels. Under Stalin, farming was treated as a source of revenue gained from exporting grain, even if Soviet citizens went hungry. The revenue gained by the State from exporting agricultural produce helped to pay for imports of industry and technology, while displaced peasants were an additional source of labour for the expanding industrial economy. The prime duty of the collective farm was always to supply the State. After 1945 the State took between 60 and 70 per cent of harvested grain. Stalin continued to distrust the peasantry, regarding peasants as too individualistic to make good socialists. On top of this, much of the better agricultural land in the western regions had been laid waste during the war, and parts of the Soviet countryside had been depopulated, at least of men. In 1946–47 there was famine, brought on by drought in Moldova and the middle Volga region. Meanwhile the regime extended collectivisation to the Baltic states, which the USSR had annexed in 1940.

Despite drastic efforts by top officials, the targets for collecting farm produce were rarely met. Even so, after grain collections the collective farmers in many areas were left with nothing other than the food they managed to grow on the small private plots of land which they were allowed to maintain for their own use. Peasants were even denied food rations from October 1946.

Table 2 *Agricultural output under the Fourth Five-year Plan (rounded to nearest whole number)*

	1945	Planned 1950 target	Actual 1950 results
Agricultural production (1940 index = 100)	60	127	99
Grain harvest (million tons)	47	-	81

Adapted from Soviet sources

Most workers on the collective farms in this period were women. The shortage of labour was such that the regime tried to persuade more Party members to join the rural labour force, but this was unpopular. Although life was also hard in the towns, most people thought that conditions in the countryside were even worse. Despite these problems, or because of them, State regulations and demands became even tougher from 1947 onwards. There were increased delivery quotas and taxes and restrictions on peasants selling produce from their own plots on the open market. Most farmers earned less than half what they had in the 1920s.

Investment in farming was still low. The government forced many farms to amalgamate, not so much in a bid to make them more productive but rather to make it easier for the state to control them. Between 1950 and 1952 the number of collective farms more than halved. There were other attempts to solve the agricultural 'problem', such as organising farms into small groups and paying farmers by results, while in 1950 groups of up to 100 peasants were organised into brigades. Bureaucracy in rural areas was reduced. Millions of trees were planted in the southern steppes to reverse soil erosion. However, nothing worked, and the regime continued to export grain at the same time that Khrushchev was reporting cannibalism among starving peasants in **Ukraine.** Despite what Soviet propaganda claimed to the contrary, the 1946 grain harvest was one-third of the 1940 one, and the 1940 figure was not even reached in 1952. The 1954 grain harvest was still below the 1913 figure. Stalin's rural economy grossly underperformed and was a fundamental weakness in the Soviet system, as it was to remain throughout the Soviet period. In the words of Alex Nove (*An Economic History of the USSR*, 1988), Soviet agriculture in Stalin's final years was characterised by 'ill-judged interventions of authority, excessive centralisation of decisions, extremely low prices, insufficient investment and lack of adequate incentives.'

The impact of Cold War politics on the USSR

The international context

The USSR suffered staggering losses during the Second World War. Nevertheless victory did not just bring great prestige to Stalin but also resulted in an enormous expansion of Soviet influence both in Europe and the wider world. The USSR recaptured the Baltic states plus territory in the east previously lost to Japan, and also now dominated several Eastern European countries – Poland, Hungary, Czechoslovakia, Bulgaria and Romania – in addition to having partial control or influence in Germany, Austria, China, Albania and Yugoslavia. This sudden change in international status was bound to have an impact within the USSR itself, as well as affecting its status abroad.

Some of this spread of Soviet influence was the result of agreements with wartime allies, the USA and Britain, resolved principally at the Yalta and Potsdam Conferences. However, these agreements were often grudging, and the outcomes added to already existing Western fears about Communist expansionism. Equally, there were strong Soviet concerns about hostile Western attitudes towards the USSR, demonstrated as recently as 1918 when foreign powers had invaded Russia in support of Russians opposed to the new Soviet state. Stalin was particularly fearful because the USA and Britain had refused to share with him their knowledge of the atom bomb, which had been first used against Japan in 1945. The USSR did not succeed in producing its own bomb until 1949.

Soviet interference in Eastern European elections, disagreements over reparations and joint control of Germany, and Soviet suspicions of American involvement in Europe, demonstrated in initiatives such as the Marshall Plan and the Truman Doctrine,

Fig. 4 *The first Soviet atomic test, 29 August 1949*

Exploring the detail

The Yalta and Potsdam Conferences

These conferences were held between the Allied powers in 1945, principally to decide the fate of post-war Europe. The conferences were largely dominated by Stalin, whose Red Army already dominated Eastern Europe. The conferences decided on spheres of influence and made key decisions concerning issues such as the division of Germany and Berlin. Stalin dealt with Allied leaders such as Churchill, Attlee, Roosevelt and Truman.

Cross-reference

For more on the Doctors' Plot, see page 38.

all built on existing suspicions between East and West. These suspicions had only been papered over during the Second World War in the interests of defeating Hitler. The combination of mistrust and fear for the future, on both sides, led to the rapid development of the Cold War. This can be defined as a state of tension between the superpowers that stopped short of outright military conflict but which poisoned the relations between the world's leading powers.

Soviet nationalism

Stalin's USSR had already shown great distrust of the capitalist West long before 1945. Stalin was an orthodox Marxist-Leninist in the sense that he believed it was very difficult if not impossible for socialist and capitalist powers to live alongside each other without eventually fighting for ultimate supremacy. The Cold War simply intensified Soviet paranoia about the West's intentions, which some historians argue was understandable, since there were hostile politicians in the West who wanted to put pressure on the USSR's very existence. This was demonstrated in two particular, but linked, ways.

First, there was a campaign against 'cosmopolitanism'. This was associated particularly with Zhdanov, but also reflected Stalin's own paranoia. Partly, 'cosmopolitanism' was associated with increased anti-Semitism, evident in increased discrimination and violence against Jews. Many Soviet Jews lost their posts in the Party or the bureaucracy. The 'Doctors' Plot' was just one aspect of this wider suspicion of supposed evil Jewish influence. But cosmopolitanism was also reflected in a campaign to eliminate virtually any contact with the outside world. Only high-ranking Party officials were allowed to travel abroad. Marriage with foreigners was forbidden. Foreign films, books and art were denounced. Saxophones were banned because of associations with Western jazz. There was rigorous official policing of what Soviet artists and intellectuals were allowed to produce.

Second, there was a related upsurge in Russian nationalism. This took the form of praising all things Russian, but was often difficult to distinguish from an ideological commitment to spreading Communist ideology. It was evident to many Russians who had had contact with the West during the war years that Soviet propaganda had painted a false picture of the West. To these people, the West clearly demonstrated examples of much better living conditions and technological and scientific advances than the USSR could demonstrate. But the official Soviet line, which reached its peak in 1948 and 1949, was that anything Russian was greatly superior to anything in the West. Prominent Russians from the past such as Tsar Peter the Great, once dismissed as tyrannical representatives of an old pre-revolutionary regime, were now praised for leading Russia to victory over foreign aggressors. All major scientific achievements of previous generations, such as the invention of the radio, were now attributed to Russians. Even Karl Marx, the German founder of Communist ideology, was held up as an 'honorary' Russian. This excessive nationalism resulted in part from feelings of backwardness and insecurity, reflected in Russia's experience of being invaded by powers with superior technology, but it also reflected Stalin's personal fear of his regime being undermined by the West.

Ultimately, it was the USSR which suffered most from this self-imposed isolationism. Banning most foreign contacts had negative consequences, particularly for Soviet science, which had to operate in a vacuum, unable to share experiences and expertise with the West.

Activity

Research task

Research briefly the process by which the USSR gained control over Eastern Europe between 1945 and 1948. Consider the decisions made at Yalta and Potsdam and then take one Eastern European country. Examine how Soviet influence was used to ensure that Communists took power in that country.

Fig. 5 *The dead Stalin lying in state before his funeral*

Stalin's legacy

One of the curiosities of this period is that historians have paid far less attention to Soviet domestic history during Stalin's final years as leader, 1945–53, than to the earlier period of his leadership. Particular interest has been shown in the 1930s when Stalin consolidated his power and carried out massive social and economic changes. There has also been great interest in the war years when Stalin led the Soviet people to victory in what the Germans intended as a war of virtual extermination.

The comparative neglect of the final years has been partly due to the relative lack of evidence, much of which remained locked away in secret archives for decades after 1953. It also reflects the lack of systematic procedures in Stalin's methods of rule, which has made analysis difficult. There has therefore been historical debate about the exact nature of that rule. Some commentators now believe that post-1945 Soviet society was much more rigid than in the 1930s. In the 1930s dynamic changes were taking place, politically, economically and socially, for good or ill. Christopher Read has written that the post-war years suggest a society:

> much more rigid and cowed – through exhaustion and shortages as well as political repression – pursuing a grim, grey existence picking through endless bureaucratic obstacles to obtain limited resources of food, housing and other basics ... Political oppression appeared to be at a peak in these years ... These years, rather than the thirties, probably fit the totalitarian model more closely. The grimness of the time – a consequence of purges, wartime regimentation, outside hostility in the form of the Cold War and shortages resulting from wartime destruction – was all the more disappointing for a society expecting some reward for its wartime sacrifices and victory.

2 *Read, C., The Stalin Years, 2003*

And yet, despite this grim analysis, when Stalin's death was announced in March 1953 Russians wept in the streets. They could scarcely remember a time before Stalin; they were used to him as leader, and saw him as a symbol of stability and victory. As his mummified body was laid in the Lenin mausoleum in Moscow, grieving Muscovites were crushed to death among the mass of mourners. There are even reports of many prisoners in Stalin's prison camps crying when they heard the news of his death. The dead tyrant was mourned by millions who were living in difficult times but now feared an even more uncertain future.

Learning outcomes

Through your study of this section you should have a good understanding of how the USSR became involved in the Second World War and how the USSR not only survived the German attack but went on to win the war. You have learned about Stalin's leadership and the contribution of key aspects, such as the harnessing of the Soviet economy, which helped bring about Russian victory. You should also have a good understanding of the nature of Soviet politics, economy and society during the period of High Stalinism, 1945–53. You will be aware of how the USSR was affected by its experience of the Second World War and how reconstruction took place, while the Stalinist regime at home was consolidated and the USSR adjusted to a new world order following the defeat of Nazi Germany and its allies.

AQA Examination-style question

To what extent did the development of the Cold War after 1945 influence Stalin's policies inside the USSR?

(45 marks)

This question covers a variety of factors: certainly political, but also economic and social. You will probably introduce your answer by putting the Cold War into context, explaining how old suspicions between Stalin and his Western allies were resurrected and were heightened by events following Germany's defeat in 1945. However, you are not expected to know Stalin's foreign policies in detail. You should focus on developments **inside** the USSR. You should certainly analyse economic policy and the extent to which it was designed to strengthen the USSR in a hostile world. You should try to relate Stalin's leadership style and political developments to the impact of the Cold War. You should also analyse the impact of policies designed to isolate the USSR and prevent 'harmful' foreign influences from entering the USSR. You might also want to discuss the extent to which these policies were due directly to Stalin or to other people such as Zhdanov. As in any essay answer, you should aim to reach some sort of judgement and support it with plenty of evidence, in order to achieve a high mark.

3 The emergence of Khrushchev

Fig. 1 *Stalin and Khrushchev conferring during the war*

In this chapter you will learn about:

- how Khrushchev emerged as Soviet leader after Stalin

- the significance of Khrushchev's 'secret speech' at the 1956 Party Congress.

At the Twentieth Party Congress, Khrushchev was giving details of all Stalin's crimes when a voice came from the back of the hall: 'And where were you then?'

'Would the person who asked that question stand up,' said Khrushchev.

The frightened questioner did not stand.

'That's where we were, too!' retorted Khrushchev.

1   *A story circulating in Moscow after the 1956 speech*

Key chronology

The emergence of Khrushchev

1953

January   Death of Stalin

Collective leadership established

Malenkov gives up leadership of the Party

July   Beria arrested

September   Khrushchev elected first secretary of the Communist Party

1955

February   Bulganin succeeds Malenkov as prime minister

1956

February   Twentieth Party Congress

Khrushchev's 'secret speech'

The emergence of leaders after Stalin

An uncertain succession

On Stalin's death in March 1953, all the leading Communists agreed on one thing: the excesses of Stalin's personal rule were no longer appropriate to the USSR's needs, if they ever had been. Stalin had achieved great things. He had turned the USSR from a backward rural nation into an industrial power; he had led the country to victory in a brutal war; and he had presided over a remarkable recovery since 1945, while giving the USSR a prominent place on the international political stage. These processes had been marked by economic and social changes and accompanying hardships and state brutality, on an unprecedented scale. Many of Stalin's colleagues had been leading figures in that process and believed that many of the sacrifices had been necessary and justified. However, it was time for the country to move on. People needed a respite from the years of repression and the constant calls for hard work and vigilance. New generations had different expectations and the Party needed to give more consideration to the needs of ordinary people when policies were being decided.

None of Stalin's colleagues had the will or possibly the imagination to want drastically to change the 'system' that had allowed them to rise to powerful positions and secured some remarkable achievements for the USSR. They fervently believed in the leading role of the Party and the fundamentals of Stalinism such as economic planning, which was supposed to ensure that both the needs of the people and the ideological demands of socialism were satisfied. The Party leaders were looking for modifications of Stalinism, not its destruction. At the same time, as ambitious politicians, they wanted to secure their own positions in the system. The real issue was whether Stalinism could be modified in such a way that what were believed to be its benefits were kept, while the excesses were removed. Were the next generation of leaders committed or skilful enough to make it happen, or want it to happen?

There was already considerable rivalry between the leading contenders for power before Stalin's death. This was inevitable because, as so often in the USSR, no clear line of succession had been established to replace the previous leader. Also, in Stalin's case, it would have been extremely dangerous for any individual to have pushed himself too strongly into the limelight while Stalin was still alive, since Stalin was notoriously sensitive to perceived threats to his own pre-eminence as leader.

The contenders for power

Nikita Khrushchev

Khrushchev (1894–1971) emerged from a working class background in Ukraine. His father was a coal miner. When his family moved to the Donets basin, Khrushchev became a pipe fitter and joined the Communist Party. He fought for the Reds in the Russian Civil War after the Revolution, and then received a secondary education in a school for workers. He eventually became a full-time Party worker, making his way up the Moscow Party organisation before being promoted to run the Ukraine Party in 1938, and joining the Politburo in 1939. During the war years he was trusted with important tasks such as incorporating Polish territory occupied by the Red Army in 1939 into the USSR, and transferring Ukrainian heavy industry to eastern regions of the USSR to avoid its capture or destruction by the invading Germans. In the role of political adviser, he was active in the crucial battles of Stalingrad and Kursk.

In 1944 Khrushchev was given the task of rebuilding Ukraine, shattered by German occupation. He was temporarily demoted in 1946, but came back as Ukrainian Party leader in 1948. His really big break came in 1949, when Stalin brought him to Moscow to head the Moscow Party organisation and become a secretary of the Central Committee. Through a mixture of luck and keeping a relatively low profile, Khrushchev survived the difficult final years of Stalin's rule and was therefore well placed to be a contender for power in 1953.

Fig. 2 *Nikita Khrushchev*

Advantages in the struggle to succeed Stalin:

- seen as down-to-earth, prepared to take on challenges and showing native cunning – described by a colleague as having 'native wit and resourcefulness, peasant cunning and gumption, with the ability to take the initiative and win over people of all sorts'
- very good at political in-fighting
- built up a power base by appointing followers (local Party bosses) to the Central Committee
- as Party leader, gained from the fact that the Party had a more important role after the death of the dictator Stalin
- colleagues like Molotov reported that Khrushchev listened to what people said and was respectful of them
- good at putting ordinary people at their ease and was prepared to get out of Moscow and meet them in the outlying provinces
- had a record of success in several key positions
- was lucky – he survived difficult situations which could have led to his downfall during Stalin's rule.

Disadvantages:

- sometimes seen as crude, impulsive and too embarrassingly unsophisticated by colleagues
- prone to overreach himself and regard himself as an expert on everything
- sometimes failed, for example when, despite his reputation as an agricultural expert, his proposals for agricultural reform were defeated in the early 1950s
- closely associated like many colleagues with the old Stalinist regime, for example being implicated in the purges
- although effective at carrying out orders, as he had shown under Stalin, he was not so good at thinking strategically and seeing the 'big picture'.

Georgi Malenkov

Malenkov (1902–88), who was descended from a long line of high-ranking tsarist civil servants, served as a young political officer in the Red Army during the Civil War. He was a prominent Party official in the 1920s and 1930s, and his dominant wife helped to get him promotion. An educated, close family man, he was heavily involved in the Great Terror of the late 1930s. He prospered because he was friendly with both Beria and Stalin. He was to become a regular member of Stalin's inner circle, and was careful to keep relatively quiet and dutifully follow Stalin's instructions. Malenkov joined the Central Committee in 1941 and was a member of Stalin's State Defence Committee during the war. Mainly because of his talent for administration and his political skills, he was made deputy prime minister in 1946 and a member of the Politburo, where he remained until 1957. He had a reputation for ruthlessness, seen in his part in organising the Leningrad purge; and he was a strong enemy of Khrushchev and Zhdanov. When Stalin died in 1953, with Beria's support Malenkov became both head of the party and prime minister. When it was decided he could not hold both posts, he gave up the role of head of the Party, which was probably a mistake because it opened the way for Khrushchev. Malenkov claimed, probably falsely, that it was he rather than Khrushchev who organised the coup against Beria. After his attempt to challenge Khrushchev in 1957 failed, Malenkov was exiled to the management of a power station a long way from Moscow, and disappeared from the political stage.

Malenkov has been described as 'small, flabby and moon-faced' with 'broad, female hips, a pear shape and a high voice' (Simon Sebag Montefiore, *Stalin: The Court of the Red Tsar*, 2004). Zhdanov nicknamed him 'Melanie' Malenkov, and he was known to take walks along Moscow's famous Gorky Street with the equally fat Khrushchev, surrounded by secret policemen.

Advantages in the struggle to succeed Stalin:

- was steadier and less concerned with hogging the limelight than the more impetuous Khrushchev
- had been an ally of the powerful Beria
- appealed to the more intellectual wing of the Party
- was prepared to court popularity by promising reforms to raise the standard of living and improve agriculture.

Disadvantages:

- was hated by several important colleagues such as Molotov and Kaganovich
- was regarded as somewhat colourless
- made some crucial errors of judgement: for example, paying more attention to the state bureaucracy than the Party; giving up the post of head of the Party and opening the way for Khrushchev.

Nicolai Bulganin

Before the Revolution, Bulganin (1895–1975) had fought in the Tsar's army. However, in 1918 he joined the Cheka, Lenin's secret police. Later he was regarded as an economic expert. In the 1930s Bulganin was active in the Moscow Soviet, working with Khrushchev, and rose to become deputy prime minister in 1938. Bulganin helped to organise the defence of Moscow during the Second World War. By now a marshal of the Soviet Union, he was minister of defence, 1947–49 and 1952–55. As one of Stalin's inner circle, the endless late night carousing almost turned him into an alcoholic. Bulganin joined the Politburo and later became head of state. He worked closely with Khrushchev, often accompanying him on foreign visits. However, having become one of the Anti-Party group opposing Khrushchev, he was expelled from the Presidium in 1958.

Advantages in the struggle to succeed Stalin:

- his only real advantage was that he was prominent in the Party, with an impressive record of service in key positions, especially in Moscow.

Disadvantages:

- had powerful enemies such as Malenkov
- lacked the political skill or drive to outflank rivals
- compared to his rivals, was too naive and indecisive, and lacked leadership qualities.

Lavrenti Beria

Beria (1899–1953), a Georgian like Stalin, wormed his way into Stalin's favour and became his agent in the Caucasus in the 1930s. He achieved great power when Stalin appointed him head of the NKVD, or secret police. Between 1941 and 1953 Beria was in charge of Soviet security, and after Stalin's death was briefly minister of internal affairs until he lost out in the power struggle to succeed Stalin and was executed. Beria's influence was extensive: he even controlled Moscow Dynamo, Russia's most famous football team. Everybody feared Beria because of his powerful position, his deviousness and his brutality. He personally took part in torture sessions of purge victims and was an alcoholic. He cruised around Moscow picking up women, drugging them, taking them home and raping them. He also propositioned the wives of prominent colleagues.

Advantages in the struggle to succeed Stalin:

- had a very strong power base through his position in the security services, and knew everything about everyone else in the Party hierarchy
- was utterly ruthless and cunning.

Disadvantages:

- his very power and ruthlessness made him feared and hated: because he created fear and insecurity, colleagues took the opportunity to unite against him and liquidate him after Stalin's death
- was prone to underestimate his colleagues and also to humiliate them publicly.

Khrushchev's victory in the power struggle

Collective leadership

Because there was no clear line of succession, a collective leadership took over the running of the USSR after Stalin's death. Before the dying Stalin had breathed his last, leading colleagues met to determine the next stages. Khrushchev, because of his Party role, chaired the meeting. Colleagues were proposed for various posts, and after strong debate, Malenkov was appointed prime minister. He and Beria were effectively the two key players. Beria was a deputy prime minister, but more importantly, head of the powerful merged Ministry of Internal Affairs (MVD) and Ministry of State Security (MGB). Molotov became minister of foreign affairs and Bulganin minister of defence. Voroshilov became head of state. A small Politburo was appointed (less than half the size of the previous one). Malenkov was initially in charge of both government and Party. Khrushchev was a Central Committee secretary and had no government post. But he was to use his Party role to seize the initiative.

The fall of Beria

Khrushchev and the other leaders moved swiftly against Beria, enlisting Marshal Zhukov's help. Beria proposed significant reforms, aimed at removing Party influence from the government, believing that the interlinking of the two made government inefficient. He wanted the Party to confine itself more to ideology and propaganda. This was heresy to most Communists. However, the proposals were typical of Beria's practical approach, as was his insistence that about

Fig. 3 *Beria, feared head of the Soviet security services, 1938–54*

Activity

Group discussion

Consider the strengths and weaknesses of the contenders for power after Stalin and rank them in order of their qualities. Students could be in groups, and each group could make its case for a particular leader, responding to questions from other groups.

1 million of the 2.5 million prisoners in the Gulag prison system be released. This was not done out of humanity but because he saw the current practice as inefficient and not helping the economy.

Beria was cleverer than many of his colleagues, but undoubtedly underestimated them. Whatever he now proposed was unlikely to save him, particularly since he had no power base within the Party. Even former allies like Malenkov were terrified of Beria's power and reputation for ruthlessness. He was also deeply implicated in Stalin's Terror. The collective leadership accepted the conclusion of an inquiry set up by Beria, which found that the Doctors' Plot had been a fraud. However, Beria was accused of trying to stir up trouble between the Republics and informing on his colleagues (he certainly had enough information on them to have done so). Senior officials in some Republics were replaced.

Beria's colleagues took their opportunity while he was away in East Berlin. Khrushchev led colleagues in a plot, and Beria was arrested on 26 June 1953, soon after his return. Zhukov ensured that the military stayed loyal to the conspirators. It is not clear what precisely happened at the Presidium meeting. Malenkov supposedly lost his nerve, and Khrushchev had to tell Beria that he was under arrest. One version is that Beria was immediately taken down and shot in a Kremlin basement. The other version is that he was given a secret trial and was not executed until December 1953. Whatever the truth, the way was now clear for Khrushchev and Malenkov to fight it out for supremacy in a more civilised manner.

The struggle between Khrushchev and Malenkov

The two main contenders for influence in the post-Stalin reorganisation, Malenkov and Khrushchev, had different policies and strengths. Malenkov, being more powerful in the state administrative sector, favoured power being concentrated in the government and the government effectively controlling Presidium decisions. Khrushchev, as first secretary of the Party, was more concerned to use his Party base to ensure that the Party dominated the government – more in keeping with the old Stalinist approach.

Both men favoured economic reform. However, the emphasis was different. Malenkov believed that more effort should now be put into light industry and consumer goods. Khrushchev countered this by allying himself with the heavy industry and defence sectors, arguing that if the USSR was to catch up with the West, there must be a continued emphasis on these sectors. Both men also advocated agricultural reform. Malenkov carried out some reforms, reducing taxes on peasants' private plots and paying more for deliveries of produce to the State.

In the months following Stalin's death, Khrushchev showed himself better equipped for the in-fighting, which had long been one of his strengths. He showed himself to be more ambitious than Malenkov, who also misread the situation, wrongly assuming that the State institutions would prevail. Meanwhile Khrushchev mobilised support within the Party and undermined Malenkov's position. In February 1955 Malenkov admitted to some mistakes in policy and resigned, although remaining in the Presidium. His replacement as head of government, Bulganin, was no match for Khrushchev, who was quickly establishing his dominance.

■ **Exploring the detail**

First secretary of the Party

The post of first secretary was created in 1919 but was renamed general secretary in 1922 when Stalin was given the position. In 1934 the title became simply secretary and did not revert to general secretary until 1966. Leaders from Brezhnev down to Gorbachev continued to use the latter title. Whatever the official title, it was the key position in the USSR, because as leader of the Party, the office holder dominated decision-making. It was the means by which Stalin had increased his power in the 1920s, since as Party leader he controlled key appointments and had access to personal information on other Party members.

The 1956 Twentieth Party Congress and Khrushchev's 'secret speech'

Fig. 4 *Khrushchev making his famous speech in 1956 denouncing Stalin's crimes*

Background to the speech

The reshuffles in the leadership had put Khrushchev in a strong position, but he was not yet an unchallengeable leader. He was well aware of the desire for change in the USSR. He too wanted to move on from the Stalinist era, but this was fraught with difficulties. Khrushchev like all his colleagues still accepted the fundamentals of Stalinism, in particular the domination of the Party. He was as much a part of that system as anyone else. While anxious to shift the blame for past 'errors' onto Stalin, he had to avoid criticism of the Party's role in events, since such criticism could as much be directed at himself as anyone else – for example for his ruthlessness in implementing the Stalinist purges.

Khrushchev knew that reform was necessary, particularly in the economy. He also wanted to encourage initiative, which had been stifled under Stalin out of people's fear of the consequences of failure or making 'mistakes'. But any tinkering was fraught with difficulty. Governments, especially dictatorships, are often at their most vulnerable when beginning to reform, a process sometimes taken as a sign of weakness rather than strength. Khrushchev wanted to avoid opposition and not give his rivals the opportunity to strike against him. Yet at the same time, as a politician used to in-fighting, he was looking for opportunities to discredit his oponenents.

The repressive hold which Stalin's ghost still had over the country had to be broken. But would the reputation of the Party suffer a terminal collapse if Stalin's crimes and mistakes were uncovered? Would they emerge anyway, and therefore was it better to bite the bullet now? Could Khrushchev make a break with the past and convince the Soviet people that they no longer had to fear arbitrary terror, while preserving the basic structure and ideology of the socialist state?

Khrushchev was not a liberal, and he was often intolerant of opposing arguments. But as well as being a staunch Communist, he was a realist and believer in reform within limits. He was also an ambitious politician who wanted to strengthen his political position. Khrushchev had to reconcile all these positions, and this was the background to his speech at the Twentieth Party Congress on 24 February 1956.

The speech

The delegates to the Congress had already completed official business before 24 February. The Congress had been a satisfactory affair, with optimistic reports on the economy. Delegates were preparing

Exploring the detail

The 1924 Testament

Just before his death in 1924, Lenin had condemned Stalin as too coarse and untrustworthy to be his successor as leader. Lenin recommended that other colleagues should demote Stalin. However, the Party leaders decided after Lenin's death not to act on the Testament in the interests of Party unity. Had the Testament been published soon after Lenin's death, it is unlikely that Stalin would have emerged as leader.

to return home when they were suddenly recalled for a special 'closed' session from which foreign guests and delegates were excluded. Khrushchev faced the bemused delegates and launched straight into a four-hour speech, focusing on Stalin's excesses. There was direct criticism for the first time of Stalin's activities. Lenin's criticism of Stalin in his 1924 Testament was mentioned. Stalin's behaviour in the 1934 Kirov assassination was described. His arbitrary policies during the Great Terror were condemned, because thousands of innocent Soviet citizens had suffered. Stalin's reputation as an infallible war leader was destroyed, with criticism of his behaviour and some of his decisions. Stalin's cult of personality was condemned. Khrushchev declared that Stalin's behaviour went against the essence of Marxism-Leninism:

> It is foreign to the spirit of Marxism-Leninism to elevate one person, to transform him into a superman possessing supernatural characteristics akin to those of a god ... The negative characteristics of Stalin ... transformed themselves in the last years into a grave abuse of power ... which caused untold harm to our party ... Stalin practised brutal violence, not only towards everything which opposed him ... but also toward that which seemed contrary to his beliefs ... Stalin originated the concept 'enemy of the people' ... This term made possible the use of the most cruel repression ... leading to glaring violations of revolutionary legality ... After the war began, the nervousness and hysteria which Stalin demonstrated, interfering with actual military operations, caused our army serious damage ... We must restore completely the Leninist principles of Soviet Socialist democracy ... We are absolutely certain that our Party ... will lead the Soviet people along the Leninist path to new successes, to new victories.

2

*Adapted from Daniels, R., **A Documentary History of Communism, Volume 1**, 1987*

Delegates strongly applauded parts of the speech, although they were shocked at the content. Nothing like it had been heard before in Soviet history. However, as an analysis of the truth the speech had major limitations:

- the speech mentioned very little about Stalin's wrongdoings before 1934, for example ignoring the brutal treatment of the peasantry during collectivisation
- the focus of the speech was on Stalin, presenting the Party as a victim like everyone else in the USSR – it appeared to absolve other leading Communists such as Khrushchev himself from any blame for previous excesses
- there was no suggestion that there were any serious flaws in the Communist system itself – by appealing to 'Leninist principles', for example, Khrushchev ignored Lenin's own ruthless contribution to the creation of arbitrary State power and preparing the way for Stalin's later excesses
- the speech accepted the correctness of some of Stalin's major policies such as industrialisation and forced collectivisation
- although the speech called for the rehabilitation of some of Stalin's victims in the Terror, some of the most prominent victims such as Bukharin and Trotsky were not rehabilitated for several decades
- while the speech broke new ground in trying to explain some aspects of the past, it offered no blueprint of how the future might be improved, other than a few exhortations.

Fig. 5 *Khrushchev (on the right) with Romanian Communist leader Gheorghe Gheorghiu-Dej*

Activity

Challenge your thinking

Was Khrushchev's speech more to do with his personal ambition, or was it rather a genuine attempt to change the course of Soviet rule?

Reactions to Khrushchev's speech

Khrushchev did not allow a full written reproduction of the speech. An edited version was sent out to local Party committees to be discussed by Party members. Although not published officially in the USSR, it was read to several million Soviet citizens in their workplaces and high schools. It was also quickly leaked and published around the world. Inside the USSR there were strong reactions. Some of the relatives of purge victims, such as Trotsky's widow, asked in vain for the rehabilitation of their loved ones. Some welcomed the denunciation of Stalin, but felt that the blame should have been spread more widely. Others were angry at the denunciation of Stalin and by implication much of Soviet policy during the previous generation. The speech was also an implied attack on those like Malenkov and Molotov who had been in Stalin's inner circle.

The speech created waves within the leadership: although nobody was dropped from the Politburo, Khrushchev succeeded in getting some new supporters added to it, including the future leader Brezhnev. By 1956 half of the Central Committee members of 1952 had been replaced. Some of the strongest opponents of the criticism of Stalin were veterans of the war and others who felt that Stalin had provided stability and had strengthened the USSR. Intellectuals and those wanting more freedom in the arts were more inclined to support Khrushchev's interpretation. However, the USSR was still a closed society and it is impossible to evaluate exactly how much of the popular response to the speech, such as it was, was positive or negative. It is also difficult to evaluate the longer-term impact of the speech within the USSR. Although Khrushchev did not set out to damage the reputation of the Party, his revelations about Stalin probably had that impact. However, the stability of the regime survived intact. The essential features of Stalinism, such as the planned economy, the one-party state and limitations on personal freedom, continued. The use of arbitrary terror did virtually disappear, and citizens who conformed could feel reasonably safe – but any opposition or overt criticism of the regime was still suppressed.

■ Activity

Thinking point

What was the significance of the 1956 speech inside the USSR? Write a reply to the speech in a way that might have come from a Stalin loyalist.

John Keep has emphasised both the innovative qualities and the flaws in the speech:

> [The speech] substituted new myths for old ones as a way of legitimising the Party's continuing monopoly on power and information. It was far from clear how the 'cult of the individual' … could really be overcome. Even so, for all its faults the 'secret' speech was an act of considerable political courage. Khrushchev had grasped the nettle. He also exhibited a characteristic recklessness. The road ahead would be rockier than he expected, for he overestimated ordinary people's gullibility. In a sense the whole of later Soviet history may be seen as a reaction to his revelations.

3   *Keep, J.,* **Last of the Empires***, 1996*

What was of more immediate significance was the impact of the speech on the satellite states of Eastern Europe and other Communist regimes.

Fig. 6 *Stalin's funeral procession. In the foreground from left to right are Beria, Voroshilov and Khrushchev*

■ Summary questions

1 Why was Khrushchev able to overcome his rivals for the leadership of the USSR?

2 What was Khrushchev's purpose in making the 1956 'secret speech'?

Khrushchev's leadership and the impact of de-Stalinisation

Fig. 1 *How the regime liked to show the peasantry: contented peasants bringing in an abundant harvest*

In this chapter you will learn about:

- why Khrushchev wanted to reform Soviet agriculture and industry
- how effective Khrushchev's reforms were
- what impact Khrushchev had on other aspects of the USSR
- the impact of de-Stalinisation
- how Khrushchev was removed from power in 1964 and why this occurred.

In 1956, two Russians were discussing the future of the USSR.

One asked, 'What do you think the future will be like in three or four years?'

His friend replied, 'Don't ask me. I don't even know what our past will be like in three or four years.'

Q: What is the difference between a Soviet pessimist and a Soviet optimist?

A: The pessimist says, 'Russia has become hell. Everything is so bad it couldn't become any worse.'

The optimist says, 'It will, it really will.'

1

Soviet jokes

■ Khrushchev's motives for industrial and agrarian reform

Once in power Khrushchev embarked on a policy sometimes called 'Reform Communism'. He had both political and economic motives. The economic motive was based on the fact that although there had been some growth in the Soviet economy since the early 1950s, there were still major weaknesses. Ordinary consumer goods such as refrigerators and radios were now in more plentiful supply, but the quality of goods was poor and they were often expensive. More luxurious goods such as cars were beyond the reach of anyone except for the most privileged. Military spending at the level needed for a superpower was a drain on an economy which was much weaker than that of its main rival, the USA. The USSR lagged behind the more sophisticated capitalist economies which were less labour-intensive and more productive. All this was galling for Khrushchev, who publicly stated that he wanted the USSR to catch up with and overtake the capitalist West.

The political motive was linked to the economic one. The new regime did not want to rest on the fear that had characterised much of the Stalinist era. It wanted to rely on popular consent. But for this to happen, the regime had to offer more than calls for sacrifice and hard work. People needed to see the fruits of their labour in terms of more goods in the shops and the prospect of better housing, particularly for those who lived in the poorly built, overcrowded communal apartments in cities like Moscow. Communist ideology must mean something more than wishful thinking about a better future. Socialism must deliver. The dilemma for reformers like Khrushchev was how to achieve this within the planned economy created by Stalin. Communists saw this Stalinist system as essential if the country was to progress to the promised land of Communism – a promised land that would destroy the inequalities of wealth that characterised Western capitalism.

■ A closer look

Communist ideology and socialism

These phrases had very specific meanings in the USSR. Socialism was the preliminary stage after the Revolution when the state took over the means of production and ran the economy supposedly in the interests of the proletariat or working class instead of for the benefit of capitalists. Capitalists (or the 'bourgeoisie') made profits from the labour of ordinary people. Communism would be the eventual future when all the remains of private exploitation had disappeared. Then the state would 'wither away', with all people working for the good of each other – in Marxist terms, 'From each according to his ability, to each according to his needs.' There would be no need for all the organs of repression which the state had to employ to protect the working class from capitalist exploitation.

The terms socialism and Communism are often, and confusingly, used interchangeably. Stalin claimed to be creating a socialist state. Khrushchev talked about 'approaching Communism'. But the Soviet regime never talked about having actually arrived at a Communist society – that was a distant utopia. However, Westerners often talk about 'Communist **countries**' because they were run by Communist **parties**.

In 1959 the Party Congress declared that the USSR had achieved full socialism and that the construction of Communism had begun, with a move towards a classless society and the elimination of differences between urban and rural society – although Soviet citizens would probably not have noticed any differences. Moreover, the state certainly did not begin to 'wither away'.

The problem in agriculture was even worse than in industry. Although there had been some recovery in production since the war, agriculture was still performing poorly. It lacked sufficient investment and innovation and was probably the weakest sector of the economy. Khrushchev admitted that productivity was too low, with too much inefficiency and few incentives for peasants. He regarded himself as an agricultural expert. Both agricultural and industrial reforms were high on Khrushchev's agenda, even before he was securely in power.

Industrial reform

Khrushchev's strategy for improving industry included the reorganisation of its structure and management. This was to address the inflexibility and lack of initiative that increasingly hindered the planned economy, as the USSR tried to get to grips with changed circumstances from the early 1930s. Then the priority had been to industrialise the country quickly from a low base. Now, in the 1950s, the economy was more complex, and simply throwing resources at industry without sufficient concern for efficiency or quality was not the answer.

Khrushchev initially tried decentralisation. Existing economic ministries in Moscow were abolished and replaced by 105 regional ministries corresponding to existing administrative regions. The Party ensured its influence in these ministries. The principle of central planning remained, although the Five-year Plan begun in 1956 was put forward for revision in 1957, rejected, and eventually abandoned in 1959 in favour of a Seven-year Plan (1959–65). This was designed to take advantage of newly discovered mineral resources and fit in with the recent reorganisation of industry described above. Table 1 outlines the Plan and its achievements.

Table 1 *The Seven-year Plan (figures rounded to nearest whole number)*

	1958	1965 Plan	1965 Actual
Gross output (index):			
Producers' capital goods	100	185–188	196
Consumer goods	100	162–165	160
Steel (million tons)	40	65–70	66
Coal (million tons)	493	600–612	578
Oil (million tons)	113	230–240	243
Electricity (billion Kwhs)	235	500–520	507
Machine tools (thousands)	138	190–200	185

Adapted from figures in Nove, A., **An Economic History of the USSR**, *1988*

■ Activity

Thinking point

Consider Table 1. What does this table tell you about the priorities of the Seven-year Plan? What does the table reveal about the success of the Plan? How useful are these statistics to a historian?

Forty per cent of the investment was to be put into the relatively neglected eastern regions of the USSR. There were some impressive gains, but not all the Plan's targets were met. The Seven-year Plan suffered from many of the same faults as its predecessors: resources got diverted to the wrong places or ended up stranded in railway sidings; managers were afraid to innovate with new production methods for fear of disrupting production and falling behind their factory targets; there was still sometimes confusion about whether Party or government organs were giving the orders. The main difference from Stalinist days was that more attention was now given to the everyday needs of consumers. However, this did not prevent continued shortages and the production of poor-quality consumer goods.

Fig. 2 *A 1960s satirical cartoon about the quality of consumer goods available in Soviet shops*

The Seven-year Plan was itself replaced by the Seventh Five-year Plan in 1961.

Khrushchev's administrative reforms did not really help the economy. Each region jealously guarded its own resources. **Gosplan**'s functions were divided. In 1963 some of the regional ministries were merged and there were new planning regions. The Party was split into industrial and agricultural wings, but the industrial sectors of the Party did not match the geographic divisions of the ministries. New investment priorities were suddenly added to the equation, for example to boost the chemical industry. This created shortages in other key areas such as steel, while the much needed housing programme was cut back. At the same time a rise in military spending (up by 30 per cent in 1963), together with massive investment in the space and missile programmes, were further complications. There was no clearly coordinated, coherent structure, and the economic growth rate in 1963 and 1964 fell to its lowest peacetime level since 1933. Khrushchev's declaration that the USSR would catch up with and outstrip the USA within a few years was an empty boast that was to come back to haunt him.

■ **Did you know?**

Soviet consumer goods were not only of poor quality but very unreliable. One alarming feature of television sets in this period was a tendency suddenly to explode.

■ Key terms

Gosplan: the State Planning Agency originally created in the 1920s. It was the main agency for deciding the Five- and Seven-year Plans and allocating the resources. The plans were then broken down into shorter-term plans, and each enterprise was given targets to be met in particular months and years. Targets were sometimes revised while the plans were in progress.

Agricultural reform

The Virgin Lands

Khrushchev had already begun the process of agricultural reform before he was in charge of the USSR, with a scheme he got approved by the Central Committee in 1954 to increase food production. This was the Virgin Lands scheme, designed to open up previously neglected areas, mostly in Siberia and Kazakhstan. Initially, thousands of volunteer Party and **Komsomol** members travelled to these outlying areas to work on large state farms (*sovkhozes*).

Initially the scheme was successful, with grain production, particularly maize, increasing by at least 50 per cent by 1958. This was despite the fact that, contrary to Khrushchev's belief, land beyond the Urals was simply not as fertile as the plains of the USA or Canada. However, from 1958 the Virgin Lands scheme proved a failure, partly because the designated land had unsuitable soil and suffered from wind and dust erosion. There were also serious faults in the planning and administration of the scheme:

- the initial planning was done hastily and had many flaws
- the management was inexperienced and ineffective, without effective coordination
- insufficient fertilisers were provided to replenish the soil
- insufficient thought was given to the living and working conditions of volunteers who went out to the Virgin Lands; many workers became disillusioned and returned home.

Table 2 *Agricultural production 1953–58 (million tons)*

	1953	1956	1958
Total grain harvest	82.5	125	134.7
Virgin Lands	26.9	63.3	58.4
Meat	5.8	6.6	7.7
Cows	24.3	27.7	31.4
Pigs	28.5	34	44.3
Sheep	94.3	103.3	120.2
Gross agricultural production (1953 = 100)	100	132	151
State procurement			
Grain harvest	31.1		56.9
Virgin Lands	10.8		32.8
Meat	3.6		5.7

*From Soviet sources, adapted from Nove, A., **An Economic History of the USSR**, 1988*

Other agricultural reforms

While the Virgin Lands scheme was under way, Khrushchev made other changes in agriculture:

- The State paid more for deliveries from the collectives, and some quotas were reduced.
- Overall taxes on produce from private plots were reduced.

Key terms

Komsomol: the All-Union Leninist Union of Youth, formed out of various youth groups in 1926. It was for aspiring Party members between the ages of 14 and 28. Children under 14 could join the Young Pioneers.

Exploring the detail

'Membership of the Komsomol'

By 1982 there were over 40 million members of the Komsomol. Members learned to be good Communists and were required to volunteer for unpaid work, such as cultivating the Virgin Lands. By the 1980s the organisation was tainted with corruption and it was dissolved in 1991.

Fig. 3 *Khrushchev helping to bring in the harvest*

Activity

Thinking point

What does Table 2 tell us about the success of Soviet agriculture in the period 1953–58?

Exploring the detail

Machine Tractor Stations

These had been established throughout the USSR in 1930 as part of collectivisation. Each MTS hired out machinery to several collective farms and was paid in kind. The stations provided some basic mechanisation and helped to control the collectives. Khrushchev decreed that it was time for collective farms to own their own machinery, but the farms were obliged to buy from the MTS not just tractors but old machinery they did not want. Mechanisation was never effective: there was a shortage of mechanics and machinery was often old and unreliable.

Exploring the detail

Comecon

The Council for Mutual Economic Assistance was founded in 1949 and included the USSR and most of the Eastern European Communist states. It was designed to promote trade and industrial development among the Communist states, although trade terms were often designed to be favourable to the USSR.

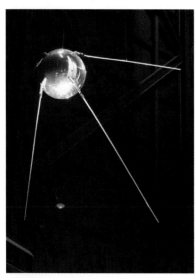

Fig. 4 *Sputnik 1*

Many collectives farms were merged into larger State farms. These ensured that the government had more direct control, while giving the State farms themselves more freedom of action. For example, they were allowed to buy their own machinery instead of hiring it from the Machine Tractor Stations, which were abolished in 1958. The acreage of land in State farms increased by almost 500 per cent between 1953 and 1965 and the number of workers on State farms trebled to over 8 million.

Workers on State farms received a fixed wage and also social benefits not available to peasants on collective farms. Peasant incomes rose at a faster rate than other sectors of the population.

Peasants no longer had to make compulsory deliveries of produce to the State from their private plots.

In 1958 the government decreed that city dwellers who owned plots of land could no longer keep cattle on them. This hit many citizens badly: they now had to buy meat and dairy products from State shops that often did not have enough supplies.

The impact of Khrushchev's economic reforms

Khrushchev's economic reforms had a variable impact. Foreign trade, two-thirds of which was with Comecon countries in Eastern Europe, considerably increased. There was an improvement in living standards for ordinary citizens. This may not have been solely due to Khrushchev's reforms, but also the result of peace and recovery after 1945. By Western standards, living conditions were still backward: for example by the time of Khrushchev's fall in 1964 only 5 in 1,000 citizens owned a car, only 82 in 1,000 owned a television and only 40 in 1,000 owned a refrigerator. In 1963 the USSR had to import grain from the capitalist West to compensate for shortages. Also there was still a major housing shortage in towns and cities, despite the construction of over 15 million new prefabricated flats, often of poor quality. In 1956 a minimum wage was decreed (slightly higher in towns than rural areas) in an attempt to reduce growing wage differentials between different jobs and professions. Working conditions improved with a shorter working day, more holidays, longer maternity leave, lower penalties for absenteeism from work, better pensions and other social benefits. It became easier for workers to change jobs, although not easier to get permission to move to large cities.

The Khrushchev era saw other social reforms:

educational reforms in the poorer Republics and in 1956 a decree promising secondary education for all in towns, and eventually also in rural areas: student numbers increased considerably

improved medical care: infant mortality lessened dramatically between 1950 and 1965

in 1957 women were banned from manual labour in mines.

Soviet propaganda often focused on prestige projects, which were well resourced. Scientific and technical education was made a priority. Sputnik I, the world's first artificial satellite, was launched into space in 1957. Sputnik II took a dog into space and between 1959 and 1962 there were unmanned missions to the Moon, Venus and Mars. In April 1961 Yuri Gagarin became an international celebrity as the first man to travel into space and circle the world. In June 1963 Valentina Tereshkova became the first female cosmonaut. In 1964 the Soviets launched the first multi-manned space mission, and a cosmonaut completed the first space 'walk' in 1965. It appeared that Soviet space technology was superior to that of the West, although there were several fatal disasters in the Soviet space programme that were not reported at the time. These were very much prestige projects, trumpeted as examples of the superiority of socialism, but Khrushchev was also a realist. He made a point of admitting the need to improve the lives of ordinary people in a series of striking statements such as 'It is useless if everyone has the right ideology if they have to walk around without any trousers.'

Interpretations of Khrushchev's economic reforms

John Keep (in *Last of the Empires*, 1996) was positive in recognising that Khrushchev 'had kept peasant affairs at the centre of attention for an entire decade. No other Russian ruler had ever done this, or would do so.' However, he also pointed out that agriculture received half the investment of industry and 'was insufficient to meet rural Russia's needs … By subsidising socialised agriculture the State was ensuring that it remained inefficient.' In industry, while economists were now more prepared to recognise openly that there was a need for more flexibility and realism in planning, there were still strict limits to what could be debated: 'It was heresy, to say, for example, that there was a "contradiction" between the interests of the State and those of producers or consumers.' Peter Kenez (*A History of the Soviet Union from the Beginning to the End*, 1999) identified some sound logic in some of the agricultural reforms, while recognising that agriculture remained a major problem. Kenez emphasised the impressive industrial growth, which took place 'despite appalling inefficiencies and irrationalities'. He also emphasised that the problems in industry were not caused by Khrushchev but 'were the consequence of the very nature of the highly centralised Soviet planned economy, based at least partially on Marxist ideology', although Khrushchev 'sometimes made it worse by creating confusion'. Donald Filtzer (*The Khrushchev Era*, Macmillan, 1993) acknowledged the increases in agricultural output, although they were not enough. He stated that Khrushchev's reforms were based on the assumption that agriculture would receive many more resources than he was able to obtain, because other sectors of the economy prevented diversion of resources from themselves. However, Khrushchev also failed because 'he pushed through his policies bureaucratically and often with little foresight or planning' and 'he could not solve the essential problems: improving peasant morale and incentives, and giving them better equipment and investment resources with which to work'. Filtzer blamed poor preparation and bureaucratic obstructionism among the reasons for the difficulty in making the industrial reforms effective.

Most interpretations of Khrushchev take the line that he was intelligent enough to recognise the need for reform and brave enough to attempt it. However, some of the failures are attributed to Khrushchev personally, especially the lack of effective planning of the reforms and the confusion which sometimes arose. Other problems were inherent in the Stalinist structure, especially in industry; and there was the lack of enthusiasm for change by many Party members, bureaucrats and managers. Ultimately, Khrushchev was attempting to reform a structure without destroying its basic rationale. This may have been an impossible task, especially so soon after Stalin's death. Until Gorbachev's emergence a generation later, no other Soviet leader had the will or courage to introduce even the limited reform that Khrushchev attempted and which helped to bring about his downfall.

Activity

Group activity

In groups, decide on answers to the following questions:

1 How successful were Khrushchev's economic reforms?

2 Was the Soviet economy fundamentally different under Khrushchev compared with the economy under Stalin?

Fig. 5 *A Soviet hero: Yuri Gagarin*

Key chronology

Khrushchev's leadership, 1959–64

1959		
	January	Seven-year Plan formally adopted
		Congress announces the achievement of socialism
	July	Khrushchev promises to 'teach America a lesson' and 'bury you all' or 'outlast you all'
	September	Russian rocket Lunik II lands on the Moon
1960		
	January	Armed forces halved in size
1961		
	April	Gagarin orbits the world in Vostok
	October	Seven-year Plan replaced by Seventh Five-year Plan
1963		
	June	Tereshkova becomes the first woman in space
	August	Bad harvest forces USSR to import grain
1964		
	October	Khrushchev forcibly retired

The reasons for the ousting of Khrushchev

The Anti-Party conspiracy

Although Khrushchev had outmanoeuvred his rivals in the period after Stalin's death, and appeared to have asserted his primacy by the mid-1950s, he was never totally secure as Stalin had been as leader. There was opposition to some of Khrushchev's reforms, particularly following his attempts to reorganise economic planning and administration and his alteration to the Party structure. In particular, his attempts to decentralise control by creating ministries in the provinces aroused much resentment from government officials. They were horrified at the prospect of being moved from the relative comfort of Moscow to the provinces. For officials at a lower level, opposition could only be expressed by a lack of enthusiasm in implementing changes, combined with using bureaucratic procedures to slow down initiatives. Colleagues at a higher level could be more direct. They were particularly alarmed at the decline in their own influence and what they saw as Khrushchev's rash promises of reform, presented as a campaign to overtake the West. Consequently in May 1957 a majority group of Presidium members, including Malenkov, Molotov, Bulganin and Kaganovich, plotted to demote Khrushchev to the post of minister of agriculture. The plotters became known as the 'Anti-Party group', because they were opposing the influence of the Party, represented by Khrushchev, over the government.

In a Presidium meeting in June, from which Khrushchev was absent, the members agreed to act: the first time in Soviet history that the top political body made a formal attempt to remove the leader. However, the plotters had failed to convince the war hero, Marshal Zhukov, a candidate member of the Presidium, to join them. Zhukov appeared at the critical meeting with some members of the Central Committee and threatened the Presidium with a military takeover unless it agreed to a Central Committee meeting to decide Khrushchev's fate. The plotters gave in, Zhukov ensured that sufficient Khrushchev supporters were flown into Moscow and the tables were turned. It was at the resulting meeting that Khrushchev's chief rivals, including Malenkov (described by Khrushchev as the 'ideological leader' of the plot), Molotov and Kaganovich, were removed from the Presidium.

▪ A closer look

The June 1957 Central Committee plenum

The June 1957 Central Committee plenum at which Khrushchev trounced his rivals was a fascinating insight into the workings of the Soviet political system and the rivalries among its leading participants. Only Molotov stood up to the accusations thrown at the plotters and refused to vote for his own demotion. Accusations and counter-accusations were flung about, particularly about the responsibility of various individuals for their part in the Stalinist purges. At one point Khrushchev shouted at Malenkov, 'Your hands are covered with blood, Malenkov; your conscience isn't clean; you're a vile person.' He described Bulganin as ending up 'on a pile of manure' and declared that Molotov was the only one of the plotters he respected. During the arguments, Khrushchev told his rivals, 'Why do you all keep on about Stalin this, Stalin that? All of us taken together aren't worth Stalin's s …'.

Despite the denunciations and bitterness of the arguments flung about during the plenum, the results set a new humane trend compared with past Soviet standards. Khrushchev himself was part of the system and realised that if the Party and even Stalin's reputation were completely discredited, so also would he be personally. Although the plotters were demoted, they were not formally charged with any crimes and they were allowed to remain in the Party. This would have been very improbable at the height of Stalin's power. The new leniency in approach was demonstrated starkly two days after the plenum. Kaganovich, implicated in the purges, was in fear of his life and telephoned Khrushchev, saying, 'I beg you not to allow them to deal with me as they dealt with people under Stalin.' Although Kaganovich had authorised the execution of thousands of purge victims, Khrushchev told him, 'Comrade Kaganovich, your words confirm again what methods you wanted to use to attain your vile ends … You wanted to kill people. You measure others by your own yardstick. But you are mistaken. We apply Leninist principles with vigour and will continue to apply them. You will be given a job. You will be able to work and live in peace if you work honestly like all Soviet people.' True to Khrushchev's word, Kaganovich survived: he was sent to manage a cement factory in the Urals and lived in retirement into the Gorbachev era. In his old age he could be found sitting on a Moscow park bench continuing to defend Stalin vigorously.

Changes in the Party

Khrushchev learned quickly from his narrow escape. In October 1957 he sacked Zhukov, who along with Khrushchev's support from the KGB and ordinary Party members had helped him defeat the Anti-Party plot. Despite Zhukov's help, Khrushchev could not tolerate the implied threat of military force against the government. By now Khrushchev also had his own supporters in crucial positions. In March 1958 further sackings were made, including Bulganin, and Khrushchev assumed the position of commander-in-chief of all Soviet forces. He now held the same posts as Stalin had done. There were, however, at least two differences from Stalin's day: first, Khrushchev never exerted the unchallenged authority of Stalin, and secondly, Khrushchev set a new, more humane trend by not imprisoning or liquidating his defeated rivals. Instead he simple demoted them to minor positions away from the centre of power. Molotov ended up as Soviet ambassador in Mongolia.

Khrushchev then embarked on further changes to the Party. He wanted to get away from the practice of 'jobs for life', which created a culture of privilege and complacency and in turn created resistance to reform. In the 1961 22nd Party Congress, Khrushchev got a rule passed whereby, depending on the level of organisation, there had to be a substantial proportion of new people elected (for example at CC and Presidium level, at least one-quarter of members had to be new; in elections at the lowest levels of organisation, one-half had to be new; at Republican level, one-third had to be new). This reform was combined with the division of the Party into industrial and agricultural wings.

■ **Cross-reference**

For more on the industrial and agricultural splits in the Communist Party, see page 64.

Ousting Khrushchev

It was obvious that several of Khrushchev's reforms had not succeeded. There had been attempts to frustrate them, particularly by bureaucrats and Party members who disliked them on ideological grounds or because they threatened the privileges and job security of many citizens, particularly in the Party. Several of Khrushchev's colleagues also had long-held and strong reservations about his populist, brusque style. Traditionalists in the Party felt this was unbecoming in a leader who was prominent on the world stage. These factors alone would probably not have accounted for Khrushchev's downfall in 1964. However, a series of foreign policy adventures and difficulties in Communist Eastern Europe added to the disquiet and provided the final straw for many colleagues.

The Cuban missile crisis may have been the first occasion when the Presidium seriously considered Khrushchev's dismissal. However, there were claims later that colleagues such as the future leader Brezhnev had several times suggested that Khrushchev be killed in an arranged 'accident'.

■ **Cross-reference**

For the significance of the Cuban missile crisis, see page 77.

Khrushchev was called to a Presidium meeting while on holiday by the Black Sea, in October 1964. On his return to Moscow, he had to listen to a list of his shortcomings, with no opportunity to reply to his accusers or the public at large. With nobody speaking up for him, he was forced to resign. The official reasons given were his old age and ill health, although when *Pravda* (the official Party newspaper) released the news, it went much further in condemning his 'hare-brained schemes, hasty conclusions, rash decisions and actions based on wishful thinking'.

There were many reasons for Khrushchev's fall, some to do with his personality and style, some to do with his domestic policies, and some to do with his ventures into foreign affairs.

Criticisms of Khrushchev's personality and style

Khrushchev was disliked by many colleagues for his brash style. He ignored advice, appeared to make off-the-cuff decisions, and insulted colleagues publicly and very crudely. He was accused of developing a personality cult, something for which he had condemned Stalin in 1956. While there was no propaganda campaign to boost his image as in Stalin's day, undoubtedly Khrushchev enjoyed the limelight, especially when representing the USSR abroad. This approach affronted colleagues who preferred their leader to operate largely behind closed doors, except when celebrating the big State and Party celebrations.

Criticisms of Khrushchev's policies inside the USSR

Many Party members disliked Khrushchev's attempts to reform the Party, especially in the 1961 programme. They objected to policies to decentralise the Party, to remove privileges and job security, and weakening Party control of the economy. They objected to any reform which appeared to threaten their privileged position in Soviet society. Colleagues objected to his rash statements to the effect that the USSR was catching up with the USA and that the USSR was well on the way to achieving Communism.

His economic policies failed to meet several of their objectives:

- Economic growth declined from more than 10 per cent per annum between 1950 and 1956 to about 5 per cent between 1959 and 1963, although Khrushchev claimed that the latter years were the most successful.
- He failed to solve the shortfalls in agricultural production which forced the USSR to import grain, while living standards in the countryside did not improve significantly.
- Heavy industry continued to grow at a much quicker rate than consumer goods, despite Khrushchev claiming the contrary; ironically, some colleagues criticised Khrushchev for, in their eyes, failing to give due attention to heavy industry.
- Reorganising the planning and administration of industry did not significantly improve industrial progress.
- Reducing expenditure on conventional armed forces in order to give more priority to nuclear weapons upset the military hierarchy, which wanted a large, powerful army.

While living standards improved, there were also failures – particularly in the quality and range of housing construction. Khrushchev had raised expectations which he could not meet. Colleagues also objected to his educational reforms, particularly the requirement that their children in higher education were expected to learn a trade in a factory or on a farm for one day a week.

Criticisms of Khrushchev's foreign policies

Khrushchev faced the general charge of 'adventurism': that is, behaving rashly in foreign affairs and bringing the danger of war. There were specific cases:

- In 1956, threatening the West during the Suez crisis almost brought war.
- Khrushchev behaved provocatively towards the West over Berlin, threatening war if its status was not resolved.
- The large amount of economic aid given to Third World countries such as Iraq, Syria, India and Indonesia did not produce many beneficial results and did not even ensure governments being friendly towards the USSR, for example that of Iraq.
- Above all the Cuban crisis almost led to war with the USA but then led to accusations of backing down in the face of a strong American response.
- Khrushchev's de-Stalinisation led to a dangerous situation in Hungary and the Eastern European bloc.
- De-Stalinisation also upset China, the USSR's Communist ally.

Activity

Group or individual exercise

Having read this chapter, make a list of what you think were the five main reasons for Khrushchev's fall from power. Rank your choices in order of importance, explaining your reasons. Then compare your choices with other individuals or groups.

Did you know?

After his dismissal, Khrushchev was allowed to live with his family in near obscurity in a dacha (a house in the country) on the outskirts of Moscow, apart from a summons in 1971 to explain to the authorities how his dictated memoirs had come to be published in the West. Khrushchev denied any role in this. He died of a heart attack in September 1971, almost as a 'non-person', with no official announcement and only a private funeral.

Cross-reference

For more on Khrushchev's attack on Stalin, see pages 57–60.

Khrushchev's general conduct of foreign affairs provoked criticism from colleagues. During his many long journeys abroad, often accompanied by his family, he was prone to major gaffes: for example telling the German ambassador in Moscow that the Soviets would 'wipe all you Germans off the face of the earth'.

When Khrushchev returned home after resigning, he said, 'Well, that's it, I'm retired now. Perhaps the most important thing I did was just this: that they were able to get rid of me by simply voting, whereas Stalin would have had them all arrested.'

The impact of de-Stalinisation within the USSR

The death of Stalin had opened the way to a new era in Soviet development. Khrushchev issued a new Party programme in 1961, full of optimism:

> In the current decade, 1961–70, the Soviet Union, in creating the material and technical basis of communism, will surpass the strongest and richest capitalist country, the USA, in production per head of population, the people's standard of living and their cultural and technical standards.
>
> The material and technical basis of communism will be built up by the end of the second decade, 1971–80, ensuring an abundance of material and cultural values for the whole population. Soviet society will come close to a stage where it can introduce the principle of distribution according to needs … A communist society will in the main be built in the USSR.
>
> The majestic edifice of communism is being erected by the persevering efforts of the Soviet people – the working class, the peasantry and the intelligentsia … There will be a further strengthening of the role and importance of the Communist Party as the leading and guiding force of Soviet society.
>
> THE PARTY SOLEMNLY PROCLAIMS: THE PRESENT GENERATION OF SOVIET PEOPLE SHALL LIVE IN COMMUNISM.

2   *Sakwa, R., **The Rise and Fall of the Soviet Union 1917–1991**, 1999*

What was de-Stalinisation?

'De-Stalinisation' can be a confusing term. It was not a phrase used in Khrushchev's time. Sometimes historians use the term specifically to refer to Khrushchev's attack on Stalin's reputation in the 1956 'secret speech'. Sometimes the term is used for Khrushchev's policies generally within the USSR, particularly the moderate concessions to cultural and intellectual freedom. Sometimes the term embraces all Khrushchev's reforms; and sometimes it is used just in connection with the events which took place in Eastern Europe, including the 1956 Hungarian rising, which followed directly from Khrushchev's actions within the USSR.

Whichever definition is adopted, the concept of de-Stalinisation should be used with caution, for two main reasons:

- Nearly all the fundamental features of 'Stalinism' remained in place, throughout and beyond Khrushchev's rule, including the command economy, the one-party State and the State's monopoly of information.

Khrushchev himself was not trying to destroy the 'system' of which he himself was very much a part. He believed in the essentials of Stalinism. All he was trying to do was to humanise it to the extent that the regime no longer relied for legitimacy on the use of arbitrary terror, implemented by all-powerful security services. He also wanted to make the economy more efficient. Khrushchev was blaming Stalin rather than the system itself for past mistakes and excesses.

Cultural reform

Khrushchev's policy of 'Reform Communism', as suggested in earlier chapters, was designed to give the regime some basis of popular consent rather than relying on blind obedience to the State or Party. This was to be achieved partly by improving living standards but also by allowing more personal freedom to Soviet citizens. The Soviet people had become used to having their actions and even their thoughts manipulated by the Party, which decided what people could see, hear and do. Reform Communism was an attempt to get away from the rigid conformity which had characterised the Zhdanov era less than a decade before.

Sometimes known as the 'Thaw', a more accurate term than de-Stalinisation, the reforms had some positive effects for Soviet citizens. For the first time since the early days of the Soviet regime citizens could get access to a wider range of foreign literature and films, although they still had to be passed as 'safe' by Soviet censors. For the first time people could listen to some foreign radio stations. Some famous artists such as the composer Shostakovich, who had been heavily criticised in Stalin's day for writing classical music which was 'inaccessible to ordinary people', suddenly found their reputations and artistic freedom restored. The regime actively encouraged Soviet intellectuals to publish franker accounts of Soviet history, particularly when they reinforced Khrushchev's campaign against the excesses of Stalinism. Thus, for example, Solzhenitsyn was allowed to publish *One Day in the Life of Ivan Denisovich*, a graphic account of one prisoner's day in a Stalinist labour camp.

The USSR was opened up to the outside world to the extent that foreign visitors were encouraged to visit the USSR, while a limited number of carefully vetted Soviet citizens was allowed to travel abroad. There were increased cultural and sporting contacts with non-Communist countries, so that famous organisations like the Bolshoi Ballet and the Red Army Choir toured abroad. The fact that Stalin's excesses were now officially condemned was confirmed by the release of many thousands of 'political prisoners' from the prison and labour camps. Stalin was relegated to the status almost of a non-person. Towns were renamed: for example, Stalingrad

Key chronology
Cultural reform
1954 Publication of Ilya Ehrenburg's novel *Thaw*, which gives its name to the period of post-Stalin reform
1955 Warsaw Pact signed
1956 Hungarian rising and violence in Poland
1958 Pasternak affair
1960 Sino-Soviet split worsened
1961 Soviet legal reforms
1962 Cuban missile crisis
Solzhenitsyn's *One Day in the Life of Ivan Denisovich* published

Cross-reference
For Zhdanov's policies see page 37.

Fig. 6 *The composer Shostakovich (right)*

became Volgograd. Streets were also renamed and statues of Stalin removed from many a city square, except in his native Georgia. Here there was public hostility to the campaign against the respected dead leader. The ultimate sign of Stalin's loss of favour was the removal of his body from its place alongside Lenin in the Red Square Mausoleum and its nearby burial in a much less obtrusive grave.

Legal reform

Citizens were given more security by a new criminal code issued in December 1958. Civilians could no longer be tried by emergency or military courts, or be convicted for vague 'crimes' that included being 'an enemy of the people', being related to someone already convicted, or belonging to a particular social group. Defendants could not be convicted purely by their own confession – a major concession since torture had been used in Stalin's day. The death penalty was restricted to the crime of treason. The length of imprisonment for many offences was significantly reduced. Minor offences could now be tried by 'comrade courts', set up by local soviets (councils), trade unions or housing committees. These courts could not imprison people but could fine them, sentence them to corrective labour, sack them from their jobs or downgrade their place in the housing queue.

Some of these initiatives were flawed. For example, the comrade courts encouraged blackmail, bribery and other abuses at the local level. The reforms were modified. The death penalty was reimposed for large-scale 'economic crime' in 1961, because of concerns about widespread corruption and the Black Market. In 1961 it was also decreed that 'parasites', meaning people 'who do not work honestly according to their abilities' or 'gain unearned income', could be exiled for up to five years. The KGB was still active in monitoring the population, although it no longer arbitrarily arrested 'suspects' as in Stalin's day.

Limits to de-Stalinisation

Khrushchev's regime had no intention of turning the USSR into a liberal democracy. The 'Thaw' was never announced as a coherent policy, and in practice there were limitations which were often determined simply by the whims of those in authority:

- Solzhenitsyn's novel served a purpose for the regime: to highlight Stalinist excesses. But Boris Pasternak's internationally renowned novel *Doctor Zhivago* was banned. Pasternak was condemned by *Pravda* as 'a weed on Soviet soil' and was prevented from travelling abroad to collect the Nobel Prize for Literature.

- Writers classified as dissidents, because they were too outspoken against the regime, were harassed and imprisoned – despite Khrushchev often asserting that there were no political prisoners in the USSR.

- The Party spoke out strongly against what it saw as the import into the USSR of degenerate Western behaviour, particularly a youth culture that was enthusiastic about capitalist fashions such as jeans and pop music. The Party was very concerned about an increase in youth 'hooliganism', blamed on these Western influences.

- Khrushchev himself was conservative in his views and very critical of what he saw as worthless artistic experimentation in fields like abstract art. He closed the USSR's first exhibition of abstract art, declaring that the pictures looked as if they had been painted 'with the tail of a donkey'.

Fig. 7 *A Soviet cartoon satirising Western culture, called 'Miss Muddleheaded'*

Activity

Discussion point

What message is Figure 7 putting across?

The regime showed an almost Stalinist zeal in its persecution of particular groups. Russian Jews were barred from emigrating to Israel. Khrushchev resurrected the anti-religious campaign of the 1920s and 1930s, which Stalin had called off during the Second World War. Between 1960 and 1964, seminaries for the training of priests were closed down; the number of churches was more than halved, with many being converted into museums or other uses; and many priests were imprisoned or even killed. Some children were removed from Christian parents. Islam was also persecuted. Although the USSR was not officially an atheist state, atheism was taught in schools. Church-going, while not banned, was discouraged. Those attending church were often harassed, and church-going was certainly a bar to progress in a career.

Many of the 'liberal' reforms attempted in the first flush of de-Stalinisation were already being modified even before Khrushchev's fall. The next regime reverted to encouraging and sometimes enforcing conformity. Although Stalin's Terror was not repeated, the Party continued to be a dead weight on cultural and social life and still tried to determine what were acceptable outlets for popular expression. It also meant that there was still political interference in the legal and judicial processes, albeit on a smaller scale than in Stalin's day. Khrushchev defined the limitations quite clearly in a speech to Moscow metal workers in 1963:

Fig. 8 *Inside the Gulag: a drawing of one of the camps by an ex-prisoner. Many prisoners were released by Khrushchev*

Some creative intellectuals have drawn the wrong conclusions from the Party's efforts to overcome the injurious consequences of the Stalin cult. They failed to understand that struggle against the cult does not mean weakening authority. Some have even begun to assert that the time has come when everyone can determine his own conduct without considering the interests of society and the State. This is nothing but an anarchist idea, hostile to Marxism-Leninism.

3   *From a speech by Khrushchev*

In other words, the Party would still decide what was good for the Soviet people.

The popular response

There is little evidence that most Soviet citizens resented the treatment of those such as dissident writers who criticised the regime. If anything they were seen as unpatriotic or simply foolish. Soviet citizens who conformed, at least outwardly, were safe from persecution, although they might grumble about everyday annoyances such as shortages in the shops. If Khrushchev's aim had been to modify Stalinism and persuade Soviet citizens that they had a stake in preserving the regime, he probably succeeded.

The impact of de-Stalinisation on Soviet relations with the satellite states

Khrushchev and the Communist world

After the Second World War, Stalin ensured that Communist parties had secured control of the satellite states of Eastern Europe. These were bound to the USSR by political and economic ties. The Communist parties of East Germany, Poland, Hungary, Czechoslovakia, Bulgaria and Romania relied ultimately on Soviet military support and basically took their orders from Stalin. In 1955 these states were militarily bound to the USSR by the Warsaw Pact, set up to counter the Western NATO alliance (North Atlantic Treaty Organisation).

Khrushchev also tried to improve Soviet relations with Yugoslavia and Albania, both Communist states but free of direct Soviet influence. He failed. His efforts to strengthen Soviet influence in the poorer Third World countries in Africa and Asia also did not bear much fruit. Khrushchev upset the Chinese Communist regime with his policy of de-Stalinisation, and his attempts to forge close links with Cuba and counterbalance American strength by placing missiles in Cuba brought the world to the brink of nuclear war. This was ironic given that Khrushchev had been vocal in advocating 'peaceful co-existence'. This was the idea that the USSR could compete peacefully with the capitalist world and not risk the war which previous generations of Soviet leaders had always thought to be inevitable. Khrushchev's failures and conduct of foreign policy were to be major factors in his fall from power. The Thaw in the USSR which was associated with the campaign against Stalin's memory had a major and potentially devastating effect on Khrushchev's standing and Soviet relations with the Eastern European satellite states.

A closer look

The Cuban missile crisis

The USSR was conscious of its inferiority to the USA in sophisticated nuclear weapons, particularly missiles, and Khrushchev saw the opportunity to address this in 1962. He had already tried to bully the new and inexperienced US president Kennedy, and was encouraged by the American failure to overthrow Castro's regime in Cuba. The USSR signed an agreement with Castro and stationed Soviet missiles in Cuba, close to the American mainland. The USA responded in 1962 by asserting that an attack from Cuba would be treated as an attack from the USSR, and placed a naval blockade on Cuba to prevent the delivery of more Soviet missiles. With threats and counter-threats, there seemed a real possibility of nuclear war. In the end, both sides backed down, with the removal of Soviet missiles from Cuba and a promise by the USA not to invade Cuba. Khrushchev was seen within the USSR as weak for backing down. However, the USSR did not yet have the naval power to match the USA, and Khrushchev had also won American agreement to remove its missiles from Turkey, close to the Soviet border. This crisis was one of the major flashpoints of the Cold War.

Exploring the detail

The Warsaw Pact

The Warsaw Pact was signed in 1955 following West Germany's admission to NATO the year before. The signatories recognised the equal sovereign rights of member states and agreed to consult in a crisis and offer mutual support. However, in reality the USSR dominated the Warsaw Pact and often made military decisions without consulting its allies. The alliance was always based in Moscow and always had a Soviet commander-in-chief. Members were bound not to intervene in each other's affairs, but this was ignored when convenient, for example when the USSR invaded Hungary in 1956. The Brezhnev Doctrine of 1968 explicitly allowed intervention in member states if necessitated by the 'interests of socialism'. The Warsaw Pact was finally dissolved in June 1991.

Fig. 9 *Khrushchev with his ally, the Cuban leader Fidel Castro, in 1963*

Cross-reference

For an explanation of Khrushchev's downfall, see pages 70–72.

Activity

Research topic

This chapter is primarily about the impact of events in Communist states on the USSR rather than an analysis of these other regimes. However, you might find it useful to research exactly what happened in Hungary in 1956 to so upset the Soviets.

Did you know?

Most people know that the Berlin Wall was built to prevent East Germans escaping to the West. However, they often assume it was built by the Russians. In fact it was built by the hard-line East German Communist regime, although supported by the USSR.

De-Stalinisation and the Eastern bloc

From the beginning of Khrushchev's leadership there was the potential for major difficulties in Soviet–Eastern European relations. Eastern European leaders and their Communist parties did not hold power because of popularity within their countries: their power rested ultimately on the 'threat' of Soviet force in the background. Any suggestion that the USSR was 'going soft' would be a major threat to the power and prestige of those leaders, since opponents of the regimes would see this as an opportunity to gain freedom. The danger signs were present early on. For example, Soviet insistence on taking massive economic reparations from East Germany after 1945 helped to create the poor economic performance which contributed to the East German workers' demonstrations of June 1953. These threatened the East German Communist regime until Soviet tanks rescued it by military intervention.

Even Stalin had shrunk from imposing some Soviet policies such as collectivisation of agriculture on the Communist-controlled but strongly Catholic Poland. After Stalin's death, the independently minded Polish leader Gomulka started his own 'Thaw', releasing political prisoners. There were riots in 1956, and once again, Soviet forces had to restore order in a satellite state.

The biggest threat, however, came in Hungary in 1956. The Hungarian Communists attempted a 'Thaw' in 1956. Khrushchev allowed the reformist Imre Nagy to take power in Hungary. However, demonstrations for more reforms and Hungary's decision to leave the Warsaw Pact pushed Khrushchev into full-scale intervention. The Hungarians fought back and were brutally crushed by Warsaw Pact forces. A new hard-line regime was imposed in Hungary.

There was also the danger of conflict over Berlin. The building of the Berlin Wall in August 1961 inflamed relations with the West.

Soviet influence in Eastern Europe was particularly threatened in 1956, because of de-Stalinisation within the USSR. This encouraged ordinary people and reform-minded Communists in the satellite states to think that they had a green light to reform their own political and economic systems. This had never been Khrushchev's intention. Although the Communist regimes recovered their authority, events had appeared to fulfil the fears of Khrushchev's opponents at home. They believed that any 'liberal' concessions within the USSR would create problems for the USSR's relations with its allies. The USSR was concerned to maintain friendly states as a buffer against what was seen as an aggressive, powerful Western coalition led by the United States. Khrushchev's critics were probably right in that his policy of eliminating terror in the USSR and his appeal to peaceful coexistence appeared to give an ideological justification to reformers in Eastern Europe. They might simply resent Soviet rule or want to pursue a policy of genuine 'socialist reconstruction' within their own countries. This was not Khrushchev's intention, but was why his Party colleagues regarded him as 'hare-brained' or impulsive.

The result therefore was not only a reassertion of Communist control in Eastern Europe. Further reform within the USSR was also discouraged. Khrushchev was removed from power and his successors were determined not to adopt policies which might be seen as encouraging reforms in Eastern Europe. Such reforms might at best reduce the reliability of satellite states as allies, and at worst result in loss of Communist control in countries where that control did not rest on popular consent. In addition, changes in Eastern Europe might also raise dangerous expectations of reform in the USSR.

Interpretations of Khrushchev's overall impact

There is no one interpretation of Khrushchev's impact on the USSR. The following historians' analyses all contain elements of truth, although some interpretations may seem more sympathetic than others.

> The Khrushchev period was one of hope and despair. Great enthusiasm was engendered in the early years, but eventually despair set in as the problem of modernising the Soviet Union became intractable. Perhaps Khrushchev demanded and expected too much of the population … If he had a fault it was his optimism which led him into hasty reforms. They in turn required more reforms to rectify their shortcomings … His denunciation of Stalin … weakened his position at home and abroad … and destroyed for ever the infallibility of Soviet leadership of the communist movement. When he departed the scene in 1964 he was more popular abroad than at home.

 4   *McCauley, M., **Khrushchev and Khrushchevism**, 1987*

> [Khrushchev] lacked Stalin's basic caution, so much closer to Russian traditional policies, and embarked confidently upon adventurous courses with attractive options without seeing clearly where they might lead him. When the risks became too great, he had to beat hasty retreats, usually skilfully conducted, but finally trying too far the nerves and patience of his colleagues. Nor did he acquire the confident support of the Soviet population, despite all he had done to free them from Stalin's tyranny … However, he did bring some fresh air into Stalin's hot-house Soviet Union, did make life less dangerous and unpredictable and somewhat more comfortable for most people in the Soviet Union.

 5   *Roberts, F. in McCauley, M. (ed.), **Khrushchev and Khrushchevism**, 1987*

> During his tenure the Soviet Union ceased to be totalitarian; his rule can be better characterised as authoritarian. Ultimately his failures showed that the problems he recognised were inherent in the system that he wanted to save.

 6   *Kenez, P., **A History of the Soviet Union from the Beginning to the End**, 1999*

Activity

Thinking point

As individuals or in groups:

- list any differences or similarities in the interpretations of Khrushchev in the sources opposite

- select evidence to back up or refute these interpretations.

Another task might be to research any other interpretations of Khrushchev's achievements as Soviet leader you can find.

Learning outcomes

Through your study of this section you should have a good understanding of how Khrushchev emerged as leader of the USSR, why he embarked on reform in the USSR and what impact those reforms had. You should understand the motives for, and impact of, de-Stalinisation. You should understand the effects of Khrushchev's policies on the economy and on areas such as culture and law within the USSR. You should also have a good understanding of the impact of changes in the USSR's relations with the rest of the Communist world on developments within the USSR and Khrushchev's reputation in particular.

To what extent was Khrushchev's downfall due to difficulties in the USSR's relationship with the Eastern European Bloc of Communist states? *(45 marks)*

AQA
Examiner's tip

This question focuses on the fall of Khruschev and asks you to consider the degree to which Soviet policies in Eastern Europe affected this. You will need to analyse what happened in Eastern Europe during Khruschev's time in power, including, for example, the effect of the Hungarian rising, and assess the degree to which such developments affected Khrushchev's own position.

In order to explain Khrushchev's downfall, you will need to look at a wide range of other factors and balance these against the importance of Eastern European events. You also need to be aware that the question is focused on Khrushchev's downfall and not simply on the problems which he faced. Ultimately you must make a considered judgement as to what you believe to have been the most important reason and how the various reasons you have presented interlink. You must also ensure that you support your arguments with precise evidence.

5 The leadership of Brezhnev and the era of conservatism

In this chapter you will learn about:

- how Brezhnev came to power and exercised leadership within the USSR

- the political, economic and social policies introduced by the Brezhnev regime and their impact

- why the Brezhnev period is regarded as an era of conservatism.

Fig. 1 *Khrushchev and his eventual successor, Brezhnev, speaking by phone to orbiting cosmonauts*

Brezhnev called together Communist cosmonauts and announced that they were to take part in a space programme which would overtake the Americans, by landing on the sun.

'But Comrade Brezhnev,' the cosmonauts exclaimed, 'We'll be burned up!'

'Do you think I'm a fool!' snapped Brezhnev. 'You'll be landing at night!'

1   *A Soviet joke*

The leadership of Brezhnev

Brezhnev's early career

Leonid Brezhnev's rise to power was a lengthy process, typical of most prominent Party members. From Stalin onwards, the usual pattern was for ambitious politicians gradually to work their way up the

Party organisation at local, regional and eventually Republican levels. Successful politicians usually had sponsors who had already made it up the ladder: such patronage could be as important as ability and loyalty in rising to the top. Luck in simply surviving was also important for those like Khrushchev and Brezhnev whose careers developed during Stalin's purges. Brezhnev's most important patron was Khrushchev, although this did not stop him eventually becoming one of the prime movers in Khrushchev's dismissal in 1964.

Brezhnev was from a suitably proletarian background, born in 1906 to a steelworker father. In 1923 he joined the Komsomol, eventually becoming a full Party member in 1931. As well as enjoying Khrushchev's patronage, Brezhnev was aided in his progress by the gaps in the hierarchy opened up by Stalin's purges of the 1930s. He worked closely with Khrushchev between 1938 and 1947, and so was involved in Khrushchev's purging of the Ukraine Party. During the war Brezhnev was a political commissar attached to the Eighteenth Army, with the task of ensuring that the army obeyed Party directives. He later exploited his links with the military when engineering Khrushchev's dismissal. Khrushchev valued his support for a long time, because he was dependable, hardworking and loyal. Yet at the same time, like other political operators, Brezhnev cultivated his own group of supporters. They were known as the 'Dnieper Mafia', reflecting the fact that they came from the same region and stuck together. They were promoted along with their Party boss, Brezhnev.

In 1950 Brezhnev was put in charge of the Party in Moldavia, a sensitive area since it had only just been annexed from Romania after the war. He did what was expected, wiping out local opposition to the Party. He also ruthlessly collectivised agriculture in the new province, liquidating the kulaks or rich peasants in the process.

Brezhnev's success brought him to the attention of Stalin himself, so that he was promoted to the Central Committee, the Secretariat and eventually the Politburo, followed by a high position in the Defence Ministry. Brezhnev was briefly demoted in the uncertain period following Stalin's death, but Khrushchev put him in charge of the Virgin Lands programme. In 1956 he was reinstated in the Secretariat and Politburo. As Khrushchev came under increasing criticism, Brezhnev, who was acting as his deputy, began to distance himself from his former patron, and even began to attack his policies.

■ Exploring the detail
The kulaks

Kulaks were richer peasants, who had farmed profitably and sometimes employed other labourers. They were among the victims of Stalin's collectivisation campaign. Kulaks were regarded as class enemies by the Communists, because they profited from private enterprise and were more likely than poor peasants to oppose collectivisation, since they had most to lose. However, 'kulak' was sometimes a label attached to any 'enemy' of the regime in the 1930s in the countryside. During the early 1930s, thousands of kulaks were killed or deported, sometimes to labour camps. When the Soviets annexed a new area, it was natural for them to revive the campaign against the kulaks, which is what Brezhnev did in Moldavia.

Fig. 2 *Leonid Brezhnev: after Stalin, he was the longest-serving Soviet leader*

The challenge for Brezhnev

While Brezhnev's behaviour might suggest ambition rather than loyalty, it seems that he made his way to the top precisely because he was regarded by most colleagues as moderate and a man of the centre. As such, he might be expected to avoid both the excesses of Stalin and the unpredictability of Khrushchev. This might also suggest that he had no particular drive or obvious skills. Yet Brezhnev was to be in power longer than any Soviet leader other than Stalin. Analyses of Brezhnev sometimes focus on his later years when his mind and body became increasingly enfeebled. But he was regarded by many as a sound political operator in his earlier career. He was also regarded as an unassuming, conscientious politician who preferred consensus rather than arguments. Like anyone who rose through the ranks under Stalin, Brezhnev was no political innocent. However, it was the 'safe' image which stood out, and this was also the image projected abroad. Arguably he was too safe, given the USSR's situation. A key question was to be this: if there were a number of major issues facing the USSR, particularly economic issues, would Brezhnev have the intelligence or drive to address them? Or would he take stock of what had happened to Khrushchev and plump for caution? Unpredictability could be dangerous. However, an overdose of caution carried its own risks: it could drift into a complacency which might result in long-term damage both to the USSR as a world power and to the credibility of the Party.

■ **A closer look**

A 'grey' leader?

Brezhnev's public image was one of dullness which merged, towards the end of his life, into near senility. The Soviet dissident historian Roy Medvedev dismissed Brezhnev as a virtual puppet, vain and stupid. Brezhnev did not impose his personality on his regime like Stalin or Khrushchev had done. He was the butt of countless jokes: people liked to contrast what they saw as his mediocrity with the personality cult created for him, particularly from 1977 onwards. Brezhnev may have been self-conscious about his humble beginnings: he wanted to be taken seriously as an intellectual as well as a politician. Several ghosted books appeared, supposedly written by him. One, *Lost Land*, talked up Brezhnev's role in the 1943 military campaign . He was decorated even more than Stalin. In 1976 Brezhnev was proclaimed the 'universally acclaimed leader' and created a marshal in the armed forces. In 1977 he took on the president's role as well as being Party leader. He had four Orders of Lenin, a Victory medal, the Lenin Peace prize and the coveted title 'Hero of the Soviet Union'. He was even awarded the Lenin prize for his memoirs, although they were written by someone else and grossly exaggerated his wartime exploits. Brezhnev ended up with more medals than Stalin and Khrushchev combined, and more military medals than Marshal Zhukov. In 1981 he was hailed at the 26th Party Congress as an 'outstanding political leader and statesman … an ardent fighter for peace and Communism'.

The private Brezhnev was actually much less 'grey' than people realised. He loved the trappings of power, such as his country estate outside Moscow. Here he entertained colleagues and foreign guests, and drove fast in his fleet of Zil cars. He listened to the US 'Voice of America' radio programme to find out what foreign commentators were saying about developments in the Kremlin. He used to arm-wrestle his colleagues, including Gorbachev, and beat American President Nixon in such a contest when visiting the USA in 1973. When his doctor advised him to give up smoking for his health, Brezhnev supposedly ordered his chauffeur to drive around Moscow with the car windows tightly shut, and with his chauffeur smoking furiously so that Brezhnev could enjoy the fumes.

As the propaganda extolling his achievements became more and more excessive, Brezhnev may have begun to believe it himself. His son and other relatives were promoted to high positions in state and Party. Brezhnev's daughter, Galina, became notorious for corruption. The growing gap between the image of the wise leader and the reality of growing complacency became a major concern. The later Brezhnev era was marked by the apparent refusal of the leadership to acknowledge the serious and growing problems that plagued the Soviet economy and society. There were also concerns about his foreign policy, such as the invasion of Czechoslovakia in 1968. Eventually, for some former believers, these concerns even brought the whole philosophy of Marxism-Leninism, as interpreted by the Party, into disrepute.

The consolidation of power

After Khrushchev's dismissal, the Central Committee decided that one man should never be able to concentrate so much power in his own hands again. The posts of Party leader and prime minister were henceforth to be separate, and in theory equal. In practice this did not happen, since Brezhnev managed to win dominance over Prime Minister Alexei Kosygin. Kosygin had been appointed on 15 October 1964, the day after Brezhnev was made Party leader. The collective leadership lasted about four years before Kosygin slipped into relative obscurity.

Fig. 3 *Brezhnev and Kosygin in 1976. Kosygin, more reform-minded than Brezhnev, gradually slipped into the background*

Key profile

Key profile

Alexei Kosygin

Kosygin (1904–80) was a former Leningrad textile worker, promoted during Stalin's Terror by Zhdanov to become chairman of the Leningrad Soviet in 1938. Kosygin had an impressive political apprenticeship: he was appointed as a deputy prime minister at 36, prime minister of the Russian Federation at 39, and appointed to the Politburo at 42. He was also minister of light industry and became chairman of Gosplan in 1958. Kosygin took Khrushchev's place as chairman of the Council of Ministers in 1964. He was able and knowledgeable, and had a reformist approach to the economy. He was personally on good terms with his apparent rival Brezhnev, but was pushed out of the limelight. He probably lacked the drive and inclination to indulge in the political in-fighting which was usually necessary to get to and stay at the very top of Soviet politics.

Brezhnev had two priorities in 1964: first, to reassure his political and military colleagues that the unpredictability of the Khrushchev years was at an end; and secondly, to cement his position in power. Strengthening his position was a priority, because there is evidence that some of Brezhnev's colleagues saw him only as a temporary, transitional appointment. Nevertheless, he achieved both objectives remarkably smoothly, although the task of resolving economic and social problems was much more onerous.

There were two key parts to Brezhnev's consolidation of power up to 1968:

- In November 1964, the Central Committee Plenum overturned Khrushchev's reforms of the Party. This was immediately reassuring for those wanting stability and a guarantee of their continuing privileges. The Party organisation reverted to its pre-Khrushchev territorial divisions. At whatever level, from region up to Republic, the relevant Party boss had control over everything. In 1965 the decentralised ministries were abolished and the division of the Party into agricultural and industrial wings was ended.

- Possible rivals were eased out. In particular, Alexander Shelepin, a ruthlessly ambitious politician who had probably masterminded the coup against Khrushchev, was sidelined. He was moved from the potentially powerful Committee of Party-State Control to head the trade unions. This was a comedown for a man who reputedly had been promised the post of first secretary until Brezhnev beat him to it.

Brezhnev's political, economic and social policies: the era of conservatism

The Politburo and Central Committee

Like all Soviet leaders, Brezhnev made changes to the administration to strengthen his position. However, he criticised Khrushchev for 'the unjustified transferring and replacing of personnel'. Therefore relatively few changes were made at the lower levels of administration. In contrast, he promoted his supporters to the Politburo (the Presidium reverted to the old title of Politburo in 1966). By 1981 eight full Politburo members were Brezhnev's protégés, and four of these were members of the 'Dnieper mafia' who had been with him since the 1940s. Between 1960 and 1978 the average age of Politburo members rose from 58 to 68: when elderly

Key chronology

The Brezhnev era

1964	Brezhnev selected as first secretary and Kosygin as prime minister
	Khrushchev's Party reforms revoked
1965	Kosygin's economic reforms agreed
1966	Stalin partly rehabilitated
	Politburo reintroduced
	Brezhnev appointed general secretary
1971	Ninth Five-year Plan
1976	Tenth Five-year Plan
1977	Brezhnev Constitution introduced
	Brezhnev made head of state
1981	Guidelines agreed for Eleventh Five-year Plan
1982	Death of Brezhnev

Cross-reference

For Afghanistan, see pages 111–112.

Exploring the detail

BAM

The Baikal–Amur railway project (BAM) was one of the prestige projects of the Brezhnev era. It was designed to open up Siberia, which contained vast riches of untapped natural resources. The railway was completed to Amur in 1979, avoiding the detour of the Trans-Siberian railway around Lake Baikal, the largest lake in the world. BAM was the subject of considerable propaganda, and was a very expensive project in an inhospitable region, but it did not produce all the hoped-for benefits.

members retired, they were often replaced by other elderly politicians. The average age of Central Committee members and the Council of Ministers was also high by 1982, at 63 and 65 respectively. There was a distinct lack of dynamism, but some of the appointments were carefully chosen. For example, one of Brezhnev's friends was given the resurrected post of minister of internal affairs in order to secure the support of the police and the judiciary. Yuri Andropov was made head of the KGB in 1967 and also promoted to the Politburo. This was to ensure Party control over the potentially powerful security services. Marshal Grechko, another Brezhnev man, was given the Ministry of Defence in 1967.

The Central Committee increased in size considerably. By 1981 it had 470 members. However, it met only 12 times between 1970 and 1985 and therefore had relatively little influence over policy.

Fig. 4 *Brezhnev meeting the West German Chancellor Willi Brandt*

The Politburo in Brezhnev's era met more frequently than before, although some key decisions, like that to invade Afghanistan, were made by a small inner group within the Politburo. This group came to include two future leaders, Andropov and Chernenko. Sometimes decisions were taken within the Central Committee or Secretariat. Brezhnev had his supporters in both bodies. At other times decisions might be made in the Defence Council, chaired by Brezhnev, before they even reached the Politburo to be rubber-stamped there. Consequently the most influential politicians were those like Brezhnev himself, Suslov and Ustinov, who belonged to other organisations besides the Politburo. Sometimes Brezhnev took little personal part in decision-making: for example, arms control policy was largely managed by Defence Ministers Andrei Grechko and Dimitri Ustinov and their technical advisers. When Brezhnev was involved, the emphasis was on consensus, without the slanging matches which had sometimes characterised Khrushchev's meetings. Meetings sometimes involved disagreements between different interest groups, championing the cause of sectors like heavy industry or defence. However, Brezhnev was less inclined than his predecessors to override the advice of experts. This was not always a wise policy, since sometimes projects were agreed that were costly and counter-productive, notably the massive BAM (Baikal–Amur railway) project.

The Nomenklatura

The policy of maintaining stability of personnel at most levels, and ensuring that when there were changes at the top they were not accompanied by purges, was called the 'stability of cadres'. It was reinforced by the Nomenklatura system. This was essentially a long and carefully compiled list of reliable Party personnel. Estimates of its size usually vary between 3 and 5 million, less than 2 per cent of the population. When positions in the Party and state apparatus needed filling, people did not apply: instead the authorities promoted individuals from the list, which was constantly replenished. Party members knew that if they did not rock the boat they stood a chance of promotion. However, promotion was a rigorous process. At each stage of moving through the Party or changing jobs, testimonials were written about the individual's reliability and political 'maturity'. The local KGB branch also compiled a detailed report and carried out security screening. Promotion also usually depended on the candidate having a sponsor at the next level up in the Party.

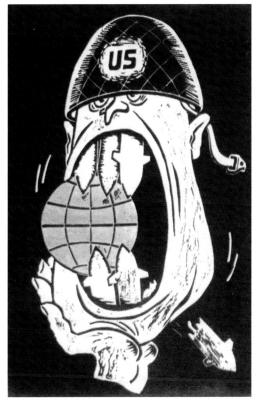

Fig. 5 *Soviet anti-American cartoon from the Cold War*

The Party

Once promotion within the Party was gained, loyalty was further assured by access to privileges reserved for Party members who had reached a particular level: dachas, better medical facilities and access to special well-stocked shops. Most full-time Party members were apparently reassured by Brezhnev's conservative approach. The only leading Party members who became frustrated were those like Boris Yeltsin and Mikhail Gorbachev who wanted some genuine reform. They were later joined by a new breed of younger Party members who wanted a more dynamic approach to change, but always within the system.

 Activity

Source analysis

What message is Figure 5 trying to convey?

Did you know?

The special shops for senior Party members contained foreign imports never available to the general population. Soviet hotels also sold luxury goods to foreign visitors in special shops from which locals were excluded. Payment always had to be made in foreign currencies in order that the Soviet state could build up its foreign reserves.

The Party

Not only did the numbers in the Communist Party change, but the character of the membership also changed in the Brezhnev period. There was a change in members' backgrounds, with a higher proportion of well-educated citizens joining the Party, and they were increasingly specialists, reflecting the increased sophistication of society. Some of the better educated people may have joined because they wanted to secure a good career rather than joining out of ideological commitment, although they would never have acknowledged this publicly. However, a trend developed in the 1970s whereby children of the Party elite sometimes did not follow their parents into a full-time Party career, seeing better prospects in professional careers instead. There may well have been career frustration, since Brezhnev's reluctance to change the top personnel made it difficult for ambitious younger people to make it to the top.

Developments in the Party at large mirrored the lack of drive at the top. Under Khrushchev there had been a sustained growth in Party membership. Under Brezhnev, stricter admission requirements and a lack of enthusiasm meant that the growth in membership fell from almost 7 per cent in 1965 to less than 2 per cent by 1973.

Fig. 6 *Brezhnev, without his hand up, at a Party Congress*

Thereafter the growth rate stabilised at an average of about 2 per cent a year. The ideological appeal of membership seemed to be losing its grip. The KGB reported an increase in corruption among Party members. However, the leadership showed no ambition to address what might have been regarded as falling standards. Rather, this was accepted almost as a fact of life, and the finger could be pointed at Brezhnev himself for the way he promoted his family. Not all Party members shared this cynicism or complacency, however. This may explain why some younger Party members were prepared to support Gorbachev's reforms in the 1980s. But the majority of Party members conformed to the existing way of doing things. Hence one historian described the Brezhnev Party as 'a refuge for nostalgics unable to accept the challenge facing all organisations in a changing world: adapt or perish' (Keep, John, *Last of the Empires*, 1996).

Further consolidation

Brezhnev oozed stability and even complacency as he grew older. The myth was sustained that it was a collective leadership, but performances like his dull eight-hour speech to the Party Congress in 1966 made it clear that he was *the* leader even then; and Congress called him by the old Stalinist title of general secretary rather than first secretary. In the 1970s his position was reinforced by a personality cult.

Brezhnev's position as leader was never seriously under threat. Only towards the end of his life in the early 1980s was there any intrigue against him by those seeking the succession. Brezhnev did not have charisma but he knew how to build a solid base of support, and many of those appointed in 1964 were still in post in 1982. Brezhnev did not even have an obvious deputy or successor. His political skill has possibly been under-rated: he tried with some success to satisfy both moderate reformers as well as conservatives.

Towards the end of his life, Soviet TV editors had great difficulty in editing Brezhnev's speeches for television reports, because he made so many mistakes and pauses that it was difficult to make it seem like a coherent performance.

Brezhnev even partly rehabilitated Stalin's reputation in 1966 and 1967: he talked of Stalin's era as being one of considerable achievement, marred only by some 'unfortunate and temporary errors', ignoring the reality that the results had not been 'temporary' for most of Stalin's victims. Yet at the same time as these pronouncements, Brezhnev managed to give people the confidence that there would be no return to the excesses of the Stalin era.

Brezhnev's economic and social policies

After his death in 1982 a common criticism made of Brezhnev was that he had presided over a regime of complacency and mismanagement. This had allowed the economy to slow down and stagnate, possibly even making the eventual collapse of the USSR inevitable. Certainly serious economic problems were developing during Brezhnev's rule. However, he did not invent the flaws in the Stalinist command economy such as poor quality goods, the neglect of key areas such as agriculture, the excess of waste and a reluctance to innovate with new technology or methods of economic administration. When Brezhnev came to power it would have been unrealistic to expect major changes. For all its faults, the Soviet economy had succeeded in mounting an impressive recovery from the devastation of the Second World War, and therefore it was difficult to criticise the system. The economy had outstripped growth rates in the developed capitalist West, admittedly starting from a much lower base in the 1930s and the USSR had shown some impressive successes in particular sectors, notably aspects of space and defence technology. Khrushchev's fate was a recent reminder of the danger of tinkering with economic reform unless positive results could be immediately guaranteed.

There was not a complete ban on reform, but most Soviet politicians and administrators hoped to address defects within the confines of the state-controlled and state-directed economy which appeared to have served the USSR well in a previous generation.

The Kosygin reforms

The reversal of Khrushchev's reforms was not carried out purely because of self-interested opposition from vested interests. After all, these reforms had not been particularly effective. Kosygin was not a reactionary and had his own programme of reform, introduced in 1965. He tried to encourage innovation and responsibility by giving enterprise managers more incentives and independence. He also encouraged them to take account of costs and profits, rather than just throw whatever resources were available at the targets. Kosygin asked managers to set sales targets, and he reduced red tape by cutting the number of plan indicators which enterprises had to follow. However, this tinkering was not effective. Despite the intentions, the dead weight of the centrally planned economy restricted progress. For example, there were inevitable clashes and compromises between those managers who were prepared to innovate and conservative bureaucrats who had their own responsibility for ensuring that quantitative plan targets were met and wanted to stick with what they knew. Many of the administrators and managers were simply too unenthusiastic or afraid to attempt innovation and the central authorities refused to give up any of their power. The old dilemmas persisted. For example, managers did not want to halt production while technological changes were introduced if they were to be penalised for not meeting a short-term target; work bonuses were still linked to the fulfilment of targets based on quantity, not quality. Consumer wishes were still low on the list of priorities.

Prices were decided centrally and bore no relation to what should have been relevant indicators such as costs or profits, demand or even need. Consequently there was no incentive for enterprises to reduce costs. The prices for some important products like coal were arbitrarily set too low, with the result that these important industries operated at a loss, whereas oil and gas were profitable. Light industry generally ran at a loss.

Enterprises which performed poorly were rarely penalised. Workers in such enterprises were not sacked, and had little incentive to work hard. Employers often kept more workers on their books than they could use, because they might be needed in the future. This led to the popular saying, 'We pretend to work and they pretend to pay us.' Attempts to reduce the number of employees or boost productivity might simply result in the enterprise being set higher targets.

Kosygin's moderate reforms were abandoned by 1970 and marked his departure from centre stage. It was not just Kosygin's ideas that did not take root. There were some younger economists who had proposed major changes: for example, the idea of enterprises having the power to set their own plans and then negotiate them with Gosplan. The economists included a Ukrainian professor, Evsey Liberman, who advocated decentralised planning and also taking account of the profit motive and the laws of supply and demand. Another economist, Vasili Nemchinov, called for more independence for enterprise managers. Their ideas were treated as heresy and too radical in the 1960s, although they came back into fashion in some quarters in the Gorbachev era.

Agricultural reform

The Brezhnev regime recognised that agricultural underperformance and rural poverty posed a major problem for the economy. The problem was being made worse by the movement of the younger, potentially more productive peasants to the towns, where conditions were better. Peasants were treated like second-class citizens. Discriminatory measures against them were now reversed and there were other reforms:

■ Peasants were for the first time given internal passports, allowing them to move home and become eligible for the same social security benefits as urban workers. This reduced, but did not eliminate, the gap in the standard of living between town and countryside. Consumer goods were still less likely to be available in the countryside.

■ There was rationalisation of the administration of farming: farms were given slightly fewer plan targets to meet.

■ There were fewer restrictions on how peasants could use their private plots.

■ There was an end to the experiments of the Khrushchev era.

■ Towards the end of Brezhnev's rule, there was an attempt to integrate farms more closely with associated rural industries like food processing. There were also attempts to link income more closely to results, with groups of peasants now working together in small brigades. These measures were based on Brezhnev's earlier experiences in Moldavia. However, the experiments did not significantly boost output.

■ There was increased investment in agriculture. In 1976–80 it received over 26 per cent of total state investment compared to 20 per cent in 1961–65. Overall state investment in agriculture tripled during the Brezhnev era, but there was a poorer return on the investment.

Activity

Revision activity

Summarise Kosygin's reforms. Write down at least three reasons why they failed.

The results of all these efforts were mixed. There was a rapid rise in output, and in the 1970s the USSR became the world's largest wheat producer. However, the gains then slowed and the returns in relation to investment input declined. The reforms had an impact on ordinary consumers in the towns: Soviet citizens were now earning more, but the resulting increase in demand meant there were often shortages in food shops, which were controlled by the State. Meanwhile prices in the collective farm markets run by peasants more than doubled. The government was reluctant to risk unpopularity by raising prices as a means of regulating demand. The result was an increasing gap between the supply and demand for food, and consequently an increased dependence on foreign imports, particularly of wheat.

Activity

Group discussion

In groups, discuss why agriculture had been a perpetual problem in the USSR and decide how effective Brezhnev's policies were in bridging the gap between agriculture and industry.

Fig. 7 *Brezhnev with US President Jimmy Carter*

A closer look

Humour in the Brezhnev years

Humour was a serious business in the USSR. It was one of the few ways that frustrated citizens could give a real indication of how they felt about many aspects of their lives. Sometimes the humour was very political, and many of the jokes circulating about Brezhnev had a political slant. It was rumoured that Brezhnev, when told about the second joke below, took it as a compliment because he thought it meant that the Soviet people loved him.

1   Kosygin is talking to Brezhnev.

'Why don't you want to open up the borders?' asks Kosygin.

'I would,' replies Brezhnev, 'Only I'm afraid everybody would rush out. We would be the only two left.'

Kosygin looks at Brezhnev in astonishment.

'You and who else?'

2   This joke satirises Brezhnev's love of the trappings of power but also makes an ironic point:

Brezhnev's mother was visiting her son.

Brezhnev showed her around his house. 'This is my car and this is my swimming pool.' He then showed her some photographs. 'And this is my second house. And this is my villa on the Black Sea. And this is my yacht.'

His mother gasps.

'You do live very well, Leonid. But I am nervous for you. What if the Bolsheviks come back?'

3   This joke satirises three Soviet leaders, including Brezhnev's complacency in the face of mounting problems:

Stalin, Khrushchev and Brezhnev are travelling on a train.

The train breaks down.

'Fix it!' orders Stalin.

The train is repaired but still it will not move.

'Shoot everyone!' orders Stalin.

Everyone is shot but still the train will not move.

Stalin dies.

'Rehabilitate everyone!' orders Khrushchev.

Everyone is rehabilitated, but still the train will not move.

Khrushchev is sacked.

'Close the curtain!' orders Brezhnev, 'and pretend we're moving.'

4   This joke is typical of Soviet jokes about the 'system' and problems in everyday Soviet life:

An Englishman, a Frenchman and a Russian were arguing about the nationality of Adam and Eve.

'They must have been English,' argued the Englishman. 'Only an English gentleman would share his last apple with a lady.'

The Frenchman disagreed. 'They must have been French. They were so passionately in love.'

'They could only have been Russian,' asserted the Russian. 'Who else would walk around naked, having nothing but one apple to eat between them, and think that they were in paradise?'

Activity

Challenge your thinking

Consider the jokes. Do they give a realistic picture of Brezhnev's USSR? How useful are jokes as evidence to a historian?

Many Soviet citizens were imprisoned under Stalin for what were deemed to be anti-Soviet jokes or 'oral propaganda'. Khrushchev had them released. However, there was concern about the tide of criticism which emerged after the 1956 speech, and many people who were heard to make jokes or insults against the regime were arrested and sometimes spent long periods in prison. As Brezhnev's period in power lengthened, the regime became much less inclined to prosecute people for telling jokes, preferring to concentrate on those they regarded as the real dissidents in the USSR – the intellectuals who made more sustained attacks on the system.

Industrial reform and Developed Socialism

Brezhnev and socialism

Khrushchev had made grossly exaggerated claims that the Soviet industrial economy was catching up with the USA and was on the verge of taking the USSR from the stage of socialism to Communism. His pronouncements had rebounded upon him and led to a more cautious assessment by his successors. On the other hand, the Soviet propaganda machine could not be too downbeat. Brezhnev's response therefore was to proclaim the doctrine of 'Developed Socialism' in 1977. He declared that it was not yet possible 'to launch the direct transition to Communism' despite the fact that the Soviet economy rested 'on a powerful, advanced industry' and on 'a large-scale, highly mechanised agriculture'. He asserted that there had been 'the gradual obliteration of any essential distinctions between town and country, between mental and physical labour, and adoption by all working people of the ideological and political positions of the working class.'

Given these optimistic pronouncements of his own, Brezhnev did not feel the need to advocate major industrial reform. In any case, there were clear limits on what reforms could be discussed. In 1972 the regime, recognising the importance of scientific and technical research in the modern world, accepted the concept of a 15-year programme which would have specific technical and scientific goals, linked to economic progress. However, despite increasing recognition that the old Five-year Plans were a blunt instrument for developing an advanced economy, Gosplan would not tolerate a rival planning agency. An even bigger stumbling block to radical reform was the official refusal to accept the possibility of an economy based on market forces rather than goals determined by the State. When the regime decided it was politically impossible to publish economic statistics which pointed to declining growth under the planned economy, the Central Statistical Administration simply cut down on the amount of statistics produced.

Economic progress?

It was disappointing for the regime that the indications of industrial and technological advance were not more promising. Oil had been discovered in western Siberia in 1964 along with huge deposits of other mineral resources. The problem was difficult access to this inhospitable area, despite the fact that by 1983, 357 million tons of oil had been extracted from Siberia, which was 60 per cent of annual Soviet oil production. The Tenth and Eleventh Five-year Plans (1976–80 and 1981–85) put a high priority on developing the vast reserves of gas and coal. Between 1974 and 1984, 30 billion roubles were spent on over 3,000 kilometres of the Baikal-Amur (BAM) railway to exploit the reserves. In addition, an expensive 3,500-mile pipeline was built to Siberia in order to carry gas to the west.

There was also investment in southern and Asian regions of the USSR such as Turkestan. No account was taken of environmental concerns. So, for example, the diversion of rivers for irrigation schemes led to the drying-up of the huge Aral Sea. There was continued disparity between the rates of economic growth in different Republics. The Russian Federation invested less per head of population than most other Republics.

Real scientific progress was largely confined to the defence and space industries, deemed necessary by the defence and political establishment but a great drain on resources. Civilian sectors which were rapidly developing in the capitalist world, particularly computer technology, were largely neglected. Even basic technology such as typewriters, personal computers and photocopying machines were regarded with suspicion as

 Cross-reference

For more detail on Soviet economic performance during this period, see Chapter 7.

Exploring the detail

The Aral Sea

The Aral Sea was exploited in order to irrigate cotton producing areas in Uzbekistan. The consequence was that in the 20 years after 1960 the Sea contracted by one-third and its level dropped by 12 metres, leaving behind a salt desert. The sea is in danger of completely disappearing. The local fishing industry was destroyed, and the local population suffered outbreaks of typhoid and hepatitis.

Did you know?

The labour-intensive Soviet workforce operated at half the level of efficiency of its American counterpart.

they threatened the State's tight control over the spread of information, so vital to authoritarian societies.

The targets set by the Ninth Five-year Plan were not met, including that of consumer goods production overtaking industrial output. Insufficient resources were diverted from other projects.

Fig. 8 *Brezhnev giving an interview to Soviet and foreign journalists*

The Tenth and Eleventh Plans recognised the problems and reduced the emphasis on increasing productive capacity, favouring greater efficiency and quality instead. However, the decline in gross national product continued, with growth at its lowest by the early 1980s. The economy was suffering from similar problems to those of the Khrushchev period, but they were intensifying. Production costs had risen without corresponding increases in output or efficiency. Ministers continued to interfere and tinker, but refused to bite the bullet of considering a major restructuring. They could not bring themselves to move the economy away from the Stalinist model under which Brezhnev and his other ageing colleagues had grown up. When, in 1979, the Deputy Prime Minister Vladimir Kirillin dared to call for radical industrial restructuring to avert a financial and economic crisis, he was immediately sacked and copies of his speech were suppressed.

Brezhnev's social policies

The rationale for change – the 1977 Brezhnev Constitution

The USSR until 1977 was governed, at least in theory, under Stalin's 1936 Constitution. This had guaranteed a number of civil rights, all of which were blatantly ignored by Stalin's regime. Brezhnev wished to make his own mark in a lasting way. The sixtieth anniversary of the 1917 Revolution seemed a good opportunity to put a gloss of legality on his regime and demonstrate modern socialist thinking. He was also conscious that Khrushchev had promised that Communism would arrive in the USSR by 1980. Because the Party realised that this would not happen, the new era of Developed Socialism had to be clearly defined. A draft Constitution was sent out for public discussion, and 150 amendments were made in response to 400,000 suggestions.

The final Constitution declared the USSR to be 'a mature socialist society', in which the 'dictatorship of the proletariat' had been achieved. The role of the Party was given a more prominent part in the Constitution than in 1936 (now Article 6 as opposed to Article 126 in 1936). The Communist Party was declared to be 'the leading and guiding force in Soviet society and the nucleus of the political system, of all State and public organisations'. The Party 'exists for the people and serves the people … The Communist Party, armed with Marxism-Leninism, determines the general perspectives of the development of society and the line of domestic and foreign policy of the USSR.' It was clearly laid out that the Party had the role of supervising all enterprises and institutions.

There were guarantees of freedom of speech, assembly, religion, the press and individual conscience – rights which had never existed in practice in the USSR – with the important proviso that the rights of individual citizens 'must not injure the interests of society and the state and the rights of other citizens'. There was provision for popular referenda, and officials who prosecuted citizens for making criticisms could be themselves indicted. The peasants' right to keep their private plots was confirmed in the Constitution.

Brezhnev spelt out his own philosophy in the *World Marxist Review* in December 1977. While declaring that democracy was both a natural and essential part of socialism, it 'is not something that is fixed and static in its forms, functions and manifestations. It develops as society develops as a whole.' He appealed to Lenin's authority to explain what socialist democracy meant: Lenin had observed that 'for the first time in the history of civilised society, the mass of the population will rise to take an **independent** part, not only in voting and elections, **but also in the everyday administration of the State'**.

Each Republic adopted the new Constitution. It was assumed that a new 'Soviet people' would eventually emerge. In anticipation of this, some Party members wanted to abolish the principle of federalism, under which, in theory, all the Republics were equal. There was no reference in the Soviet Constitution to what the official language would be, and consequently there were fears in some Republics that their own languages would disappear. There were demonstrations in some Republics – serious ones in Georgia. The outcry was successful in extracting a promise that the Republican languages would also be recognised as official.

Constitutional realities

For all the guarantees of individual rights, critics of the regime regarded the Constitution as worthless, since only the State could decide what the interests of society were. The State could always quash any appeal to individual rights on the basis that such an appeal was against the national or some other interest. In any case, individual rights were 'inseparable from the performance by the citizen of his obligations' – which again were determined by the State alone. One of those obligations was conscription into the armed forces. Despite the promise of religious freedom, the fact that the Constitution prohibited 'the incitement of hostility and hatred in connection with religious beliefs' gave the Party free rein to interfere in religious practices.

 Activity

Revision exercise

Make a comparison between Khrushchev and Brezhnev in terms of their backgrounds, how they consolidated their power and their methods of rule. Consider whether there were more similarities or differences.

 Activity

Individual or group exercise

Make a list of at least six points in the 1977 Constitution. For each one, decide whether its terms were applied in practice.

A few years after his [Brezhnev's] death a new leader would breathe life into it by introducing the notion of separation of powers [the idea that the power to make laws and to administer them must be kept separate], so taking a major step towards democracy and the rule of law. This could not of itself create constitutional government, but it did at least reduce the weight of the fictitious element in the political order.

2   *Keep, J., **Last of the Empires**, 1996*

Although most of the Constitution appeared to non-Communists as a propaganda exercise, it did allow for the possibility of later amendments. This was important, as outlined by J. Keep in Source 2.

Social change during the Brezhnev era: the major trends

Fig. 9 *President Podgorny with Communist youth members*

There was considerable social change in the USSR during the 1960s and 1970s. For example, although the USSR was already a predominantly urban society by the beginning of the 1960s, the urban population continued to rise significantly between 1964 and 1982. The proportion of Soviet citizens living in towns rose from 53 per cent to 64 per cent. Over 300 towns in the Russian Federation were dependent on only one industry, and sometimes the workforce was almost exclusively female, so there was a very high rate of male unemployment in these towns, much higher than the national unemployment average of 13 per cent.

There were significant educational advances. The proportion of adults with higher secondary or further educational qualifications steadily grew. The USSR actually began to produce more specialists in fields such as engineering than it needed, and it became difficult for many people to advance to a level which matched their qualifications. Blue-collar workers often earned more than white-collar professionals like doctors and teachers.

Negative trends, however, appeared in some key areas. Life expectancy began to fall, due to factors such as a big rise in alcohol consumption and the consequences of environmental pollution. The birth rate in European Russia fell below the level necessary to sustain the population in the long run, whereas the populations in Republics with large numbers of Muslims rose rapidly. For example, in the 10 years after 1970 the Russian population grew by 6.5 per cent, while the Tajik population grew by 35.7 per cent. There was relatively little labour mobility across regions, and so surplus labour in Central Asia was not used to solve the labour shortage in European Russia. One reason for the low birth rate in some areas was the shortage of men, a legacy from the war. Many women, particularly in the countryside, were unlikely ever to find a husband without moving elsewhere. In

Did you know?

The problem of alcoholism and associated absenteeism was so great that by the 1980s, not only had the mortality rate risen, in contrast to other parts of the developed world, but up to 20 per cent of the Soviet working population was absent from work every Monday.

Cross-reference

To refresh your memory of the geography of the Soviet Republics, see the map on page 4.

reality, anyone with any sort of ambition living in a village tried to move elsewhere, even if it was to Siberia, where wages were higher. Siberia experienced one of the highest levels of both immigration and emigration. There was always a shortage of agricultural labour despite the fact that the disparity in income between town and countryside was considerably reduced.

Living and working conditions

There was a gradual increase in the overall standard of living during Brezhnev's rule. In Khrushchev's time, 40 per cent of Soviet citizens lived in shared or communal apartments; by 1985 this proportion had dropped to 15–18 per cent. In 1967 the five-day working week became the norm, and holidays were increased from 12 to 15 working days. The minimum wage was increased, and real wages, that is, what people could actually buy, increased by about 50 per cent under Brezhnev. The consumption of meat, fish and vegetables increased by 50 per cent.

Popular attitudes are difficult to judge in a society which did not allow a free flow of public opinion. However, there is some evidence of a broad level of satisfaction with material conditions among significant numbers of people. Those Soviet citizens who emigrated often later expressed satisfaction with the job security, level of social security and educational provision in their previous existence. Their actual complaints focused on the pervasive propaganda, the limits on cultural, religious and intellectual freedom, and the petty restrictions and rigidity of their previous lives in the USSR.

Exploring the detail
Wages in the USSR

There were considerable disparities in wages in the USSR. In 1968 the minimum wage was 60 roubles a month. A skilled worker or professional such as a doctor or teacher would usually earn about twice that amount. The manager of a large industrial enterprise might earn up to 600 roubles. Government ministers and leading Party officials might earn up to 800 roubles, but more importantly, they had access to special privileges which were just as valuable as cash. The disparities in incomes between different groups were far narrower than in capitalist countries, including post-Communist Russia. However, the figures do not take account of the massive impact which the 'black' or 'unofficial' economy had on people's standard of living and access to goods and services.

'Pass it through these wonderful cast-iron railings': a satire on corruption and poor-quality products

'Spreading the sea broadly' – a satire on bureaucracy and red tape

Fig. 10 Two satirical Soviet cartoons from the 1980s

The picture of gradual improvement and broad satisfaction is complex and is also subject to significant qualification. While living standards improved overall, there were demonstrations in several cities caused by local food shortages, indicating significant problems.

There were considerable disparities between different regions of the USSR. The highest economic growth rates were in Belorussia and Moldavia; the lowest in Azerbaijan, Turkmenistan, Uzbekistan, Kirgizia and Tadzhikistan. The Baltic Republics did well. For example, collective farm workers in Estonia bucked the trend elsewhere, earning double the average for the USSR as a whole. Inhabitants in the Baltic Republics were increasingly more likely to live longer than other Soviet citizens. Babies in Turkmenistan were five times more likely to die than in Latvia. One of the few areas in which the Muslim regions scored well regarded alcohol abuse: this was not a problem in the Central Asian Republics but was a major concern in the European Republics.

There were the negative trends outlined earlier. There were high divorce rates, due partly to cramped housing conditions and the increasing dissatisfaction of women in particular with their domestic role. However, the major factor cited in divorce cases was alcohol abuse, which comprised a staggering 40–50 per cent of all divorce pleas. In urban areas of European Russia, one marriage in two ended in divorce. There were consequently increasing numbers of single-parent families and growing concerns about youth issues such as 'hooliganism' or 'delinquency'. Illegitimacy was high. There was an ageing population, a rise in infant mortality, and a drop in life expectancy, particularly for men – because men were more likely than women to die from alcohol poisoning, accidents or stress-related issues in contrast to the rest of the developed world. Alcohol consumption steadily grew, and alcohol-related deaths were common, especially as the result of home-brewed spirits. These concerns put pressure on social services and did not help an economy already showing signs of strain. This was compounded by a decline in the proportion of the State budget spent on health care, while the proportion spent on defence remained high. Doctors and nurses were reported as lacking motivation and sensitivity and being prone to taking bribes. Sometimes it was necessary to bribe a hospital even to gain admission. Hospitals were notoriously poorly equipped and badly run. Statistics were kept secret, but there was almost certainly a rise in the rate of serious diseases such as cancer and hepatitis.

The impact of all these social concerns is difficult to quantify, because the regime was often coy about revealing exact details. It even pretended that some 'problems' such as drug abuse did not exist in the USSR, because it was claimed they were caused by the inequalities of capitalism which no longer existed in the socialist world.

Gender: the socialist woman

Although women shared in the material gains of the population at large during the Brezhnev era, overall they had a rough deal compared to men. This was not a new situation: although the 1917 Revolution led to equality of the sexes on paper, in many respects women were second-class citizens in the developing socialist state. This was despite the invaluable contribution they made. The 1930s industrialisation could not have succeeded without the massive influx of women into

Activity

Group or individual activity

List five ways in which life improved for Soviet citizens, and five ways in which it did not improve, during the Brezhnev era.

Overall, consider whether Brezhnev's rule was beneficial for Soviet citizens.

the industrial workforce. Soviet war production between 1941 and 1945 would have been fatally undermined without the contribution of women workers. Women helped the Soviet economy to rebuild after the war, while women kept agriculture going in rural areas which in many cases were virtually denuded of fit male workers. In the 1970s, women formed 45 per cent of the industrial workforce. Compared to men, they were disproportionately confined to less skilled jobs and earned less than men, although they were better educated. Laws protecting women from excessively physically demanding tasks were often ignored. A much higher percentage of women than men was employed in manual tasks or construction. Women also dominated several professions: they constituted 99 per cent of typists and nurses, 74 per cent of doctors and 72 per cent of schoolteachers. These were among the lowest paid professions. Unsurprisingly, large numbers of women complained about their situation, but the authorities ignored the absence of 'socialist equality'.

The 1970 census revealed that 70 per cent of Soviet women had full-time jobs outside the home. But few women ever reached the top, especially in politics. After 1945 only one woman held a top political post: Katerine Furtseva was a Politburo member and minister of culture between 1957 and 1960. Soviet women complained that despite their massive contribution to the national economy, they had to shoulder the burden of housework, because Soviet man was notoriously reluctant to contribute to household chores. In the short story *One Week is Like Any Other* by Natalya Baranskaya, published in the prestigious literary magazine *Novy Mir* in 1969, the heroine is filling in a questionnaire about the use of leisure time. She muses:

Fig. 11 *A Soviet cartoon satirising the 'modern woman'*

> Ah, leisure, leisure. It's rather an awkward word … It's something alien – leisure. Personally, I'm attracted to sports – to running.
> I run here. I run there. With bundles of shopping in each arm, I run up. I run down. Into the tram, into the bus, into the subway and out. We don't have any stores in our district. We have been living there more than a year, but they are still not built.

3

Surveys in the 1970s showed that women shoppers (three-quarters of the total number of shoppers) each spent on average the equivalent of 21 eight-hour days a year seeking the supplies they needed in shops. Most Soviet women carried a small string bag just in case they suddenly came across a queue, which if they joined it might mean something unexpected in a shop that they or their friends could make use of. Women spent 27 hours a week on housework, while men spent fewer than 12. Women had one hour less a day than men for necessary activities like eating and sleeping. The blatant inequalities were a major factor in the high divorce rate. They also explain why many women, especially if they were educated, became increasingly reluctant to marry in the first place.

Fig. 12 The Stadium, *a painting showing young female athletes watched by an older female generation*

After all, Developed Socialism did not appear to have transformed many men from their traditional role as unreconstituted male chauvinists, a situation made worse by an increasing fondness for the bottle.

The golden years of Developed Socialism or an era of complacency and conservatism?

Sometimes the evidence of progress and the degree of popular satisfaction or dissatisfaction is conflicting. This is partly because of the difficulties of getting accurate statistics, partly because of disparities between geographical regions and different groups of people, and partly because people's expectations were probably changing, and this could reflect how they responded to what was around them. However, despite the debates among historians and sociologists, many agree that there was a paradox during the Brezhnev era. This was that just as economic growth was slowing dangerously, many Soviet citizens were enjoying a higher standard of living during the 1970s than they had done before Brezhnev or they would enjoy again after him, in the unpredictable years of the 1980s.

Summary questions

1 To what extent did Brezhnev attempt to reform the Soviet economy and society?

2 To what extent did living and working conditions in the USSR improve during the Brezhnev era?

Attitudes towards the Brezhnev regime

Fig. 1 *Soviet troops in Afghanistan*

In this chapter you will learn about:

▓ the Soviet people's attitudes towards the Brezhnev regime

▓ how the Brezhnev regime dealt with dissidents and Nationality issues.

Q: Can you name a short word that rouses women, that our people love and little boys write on lavatory walls?

A: The Party!

Q: If everything is going so well in the country, then why are things so bad?

A: That's the **dialectical unity of opposites**.

| 1 | *Two Soviet riddles* |

▓ The repression of dissidence

Under Stalin there had been very little opposition to the regime inside the USSR. It was simply too dangerous. Khrushchev's denunciation of Stalin had destroyed the notion of Stalin's invincibility. The next step was for some individuals to question other aspects of the Soviet regime. Thereby dissidence was born.

■ Key terms

Dialectical unity of opposites: dialectic materialism was the cornerstone of Marxist theory. Dialectic (from the Greek for 'debate') was the art of discovering truth by unmasking the contradictions in the arguments of your opponent. Marxists adapted this to the wider idea that all human and natural development is the result of a perpetual struggle between contradictions. In political and social terms, this meant that previous history had been determined by a struggle for supremacy between different social classes. Marxists, including the Russian Communists, believed they were living in an era of struggle between the capitalist world (in which power was exercised through the ownership of private wealth or 'capital') and the working class or proletariat, who were responsible for creating wealth in the first place. Out of this struggle would emerge socialism, representing the victory of the working class or proletariat (led by the Communist Party).

■ Did you know?

Most Soviet citizens knew that if they wanted something done, for example plumbing repairs to their flat, the bureaucracy was such it was almost inevitable that they had to offer a 'sweetener' to the workman involved, for example a small bribe such as a bottle of vodka.

Measuring public opinion in the USSR

There were no reliable opinion polls in the USSR. Probably the nearest thing to an opinion poll were the confidential reports which the KGB compiled for the leadership on people's attitudes. However, evidence of improved material conditions and the end to the oppressiveness of the Stalin era might suggest that life had improved in various ways since 1953: more and better food; higher pay; a shorter working week and more holidays; and better education. This picture was not universal: conditions in some areas of the USSR were better than in others; some citizens had more privileges than others; and there were developing social problems with difficulties in housing, availability of good public services and health issues. Society was increasingly complex.

Fig. 2 *A Soviet Gulag camp*

Many citizens grumbled about everyday shortages and the problems of queueing in shops or finding a good hospital. Yet there is no evidence of widespread public political dissatisfaction. Citizens might feel strongly about some of the directives coming from Moscow if they lived in a non-Russian Republic. If they lived in one of the Baltic states, only annexed by the USSR in 1940, they may well have resented Soviet control. There might also be artists or other intellectuals who wanted cultural freedom to pursue art for art's sake, rather than following the orthodox guidelines laid down by the Party. However, political dissent in the form of disagreement with the regime, or actual opposition to it, was very rare. The population was conditioned to accept that the regime was successfully doing what citizens generally expect from their governments: defence of their borders; ensuring a basic level of social security; and ensuring that there was plenty of work available, at least in many areas. It also maintained law and order so that the crime rate was not high by the standard of many countries, if one ignored the widespread corruption or 'black economy' which involved millions of Soviet citizens at all levels of society and in all walks of life. People may have grumbled at the rigidities in the system and the interminable Soviet bureaucracy. However, it was not simply fear and propaganda which ensured the conformity of Soviet citizens in Brezhnev's USSR.

Dissident opinions, or 'opposing views', had already begun to emerge in Khrushchev's USSR. As the regime became less totalitarian, intellectuals began to share their views more openly in a way which had been virtually impossible in Stalin's police state. Because of official criticism of some elements of Stalinism, the power of Soviet ideology was inevitably weakened, although this had not been Khrushchev's intention. It was no longer possible to pretend that everything done in the name of the State or the Party was unquestionably beyond reproach. Some daring individuals were now prepared to discuss with each other the gap between propaganda and reality.

Because the Khrushchev regime was not consistent in its approach to controlling expression of opinion, nobody was quite sure what level of 'political' discussion was possible, and what the results might be. Even such a gesture as attending the funeral of the disgraced author Pasternak would have been unthinkable in Stalin's day.

The Soviet regime faced a real dilemma: after 1956, it could no longer, even had it wished, completely suppress all 'unofficial' opinion. This would have been to return to the absolute and stifling repression of the Stalinist era. By now that was simply unthinkable for the great majority of the Party hierarchy. But equally the authoritarian regime could not envisage an 'open' society. It was because of this dilemma that Soviet policy towards dissidence was to remain inconsistent under Brezhnev.

Dissidence under the Brezhnev regime

As in so many other areas, the Brezhnev regime's cultural policy was one of cautious conservatism. It did not ignore culture, because Marxist ideology linked culture, like everything else, to the idea of class consciousness. Culture was supposed to reflect the

Fig. 3 *Dissident Andrei Sakharov at a news conference, June 1988*

interests and experience of the dominant class under socialism, that is, the working class. 'Art for art's sake' was not a recognised concept in Soviet thinking. Brezhnev did not return to the very partial liberalisation of the arts attempted by Khrushchev. His regime maintained a keen eye on developments. Nevertheless, neither did it return to the strict Stalinist controls of Zhdanov's day. The authorities tolerated some expression of differing views, but always within limits.

'**Socialist Realism**' had been the only form of cultural expression allowed in Stalin's day. Brezhnev's regime put less emphasis on this. It became possible for writers and artists to depict a wider range of subjects and emotions. It was even permissible to deal with the individual *as* an individual, rather than focus on that person's contribution to socialist society. Culture no longer had to show a heavy Marxist emphasis, as long as it did not challenge the moral values deemed by the regime as essential

Key chronology
Dissidence under Brezhnev

1966 Arrest of Sinyavsky and Daniel

1968 Warsaw Pact forces invade Czechoslovakia

1969 Solzhenitsyn expelled from Soviet Union of Writers

1970 Solzhenitsyn awarded Nobel Prize for Literature

1974 Solzhenitsyn expelled from USSR

1975 Helsinki Accords signed

Sakharov awarded Nobel Peace Prize

1976 Soviet dissidents set up Helsinki monitoring groups

Bukovsky expelled from USSR

1978 Sharansky, Orlov and Ginsburg imprisoned

1979 Soviet invasion of Afghanistan

1980 Sakharov exiled to Gorky

Moscow Olympics boycotted by 40 countries

Cross-reference

For Boris Pasternak see page 74.

For Zhdanov's Stalinist controls, see page 37.

Key terms

Socialist Realism: a concept that had developed in the 1930s. It was official policy that all art forms must focus on the socialist hero figure and show the joys of living under socialism. No negative portrayals were allowed. It was art as propaganda. Typical examples were portraits and giant sculptures of workers, smiling as they joyously worked for the socialist ideal. Photographs would be published of happy peasants gathering in a bumper harvest, even though the reality might have been very different. Art had to be simple and convey a message that all could understand. Therefore, for example, music considered too 'intellectual' and difficult to understand was banned, which caused major problems for some famous Russian composers such as Shostakovich and Prokofiev.

■ **Exploring the detail**

Soviet culture

It is true that in the early days of the Soviet regime after the Revolution, there was much artistic activity in Russia. Artists, designers and writers had been experimenting before the Revolution and saw the new era as a chance to be even more innovative. There were also innovations in film technique, particularly with the work of the director Sergei Eisenstein, although his films in the 1920s such as *October* were designed to convey the Bolshevik interpretation of recent history. However, already in the early 1920s there was a clampdown on anything deemed politically or socially controversial. In the 1930s Stalin simply enforced much more strongly a censorship which had already begun.

to society's well-being. This did not make life easy for artists. They could never be sure what the official line was, because it was arbitrary. For example, sometimes artists were allowed to put on exhibitions of avant-garde works of art or music; at other times such events might be broken up by the KGB.

Artists seeking freedom to express their artistic views were not political dissidents, because they did not necessarily have any interest in politics. It is doubtful whether there was much real political dissidence in the sense of overt resistance to the regime. There were no groups of politically inspired radicals prepared to commit acts of terror, such as the political assassinations once carried out by extremist groups in tsarist Russia. The individuals who became known as 'dissidents' in Brezhnev's USSR were not trying to form a political opposition. In fact, although they supported each other in the name of freedom of expression, they did not always agree among themselves on political issues. It was not easy in any case to separate moral from political concerns. In so far as the early dissidents expressed any political views, they advocated a return to Leninist principles. Some of them believed, wrongly, that Lenin's USSR had been more tolerant of intellectual and artistic freedom than the period in which they were now living.

The first dissidents

Sinyavsky and Daniel

Early on, Brezhnev's regime showed itself unwilling to tolerate what it regarded as an undermining of Soviet society. Andrei Sinyavsky and Yuri Daniel were put on trial, convicted and imprisoned in 1966 for 'anti-Soviet propaganda'. Daniel was a former Red Army soldier, whose anti-Soviet satirical writings had been published abroad between 1956 and 1963 under a pseudonym. Sinyavsky was his more well-known colleague, a literary critic and supporter of Pasternak. Both had met Khrushchev several times. The authorities now decided to take action against them, presumably to send out a message that 'de-Stalinisation' had gone far enough . There was an extensive official campaign in the media against them. The charge against Sinyavsky and Daniel had to be 'anti-Soviet propaganda', because although Stalin had had writers killed, publication of a literary text had not itself constituted a criminal offence. Daniel was given five years in a labour camp. After his release he continued to protest and was re-sentenced. He was not released until 1988. Sinyavsky was sentenced to six years in a labour camp. After his release in 1971 he moved to France. The whole affair was enough for the KGB to set up a new section in 1967 committed to the struggle against 'ideological diversions'.

The Sinyavsky/Daniel affair was particularly significant because it unleashed a backlash from other intellectuals in their support. It was the first time that dissidents had begun to take on the regime openly by criticising it for not adhering to its own principles of freedom of expression as outlined in the Constitution. The episode also had an impact on official policy. The regime clearly felt it had made a mistake in giving the two men an open trial. The result had been to provoke ridicule and criticism abroad, even from some foreign Communists, and it had given dissidents at home a rallying point.

The spread of dissidence

The dissidents who supported Sinyavsky and Daniel made a point of making contact with foreign sources, usually journalists, so that their writings could be published in the West and then relayed back to the

USSR. Already in Khrushchev's day dissidents had written letters, then hand-copied and distributed them as unofficial literature known as *samizdat* ('self-publishing'). The letters were usually smuggled abroad and published there. They were also read out by foreign radio stations, including the BBC's Russian service. An American station, Radio Liberty, broadcast *Doctor Zhivago* in its entirety to the Russian population from Munich. These activities pushed the Soviet authorities into cracking down on a developing human rights movement which had never existed before in the USSR.

The first manifestation of this had already taken place in Red Square in December 1965. Scientists and writers including Ginsburg, Sakharov and Bukovsky demonstrated by calling for the Soviet government to obey its own Constitution, which guaranteed civil rights. Banners were held up with the slogan 'Respect the Constitution'. The authorities were clearly caught by surprise. They detained and questioned the participants but soon released them. Later demonstrations, for example one in 1968 in support of Ginsburg's arrest, were much more harshly dealt with, with protesters being arrested and brought to trial. By then the regime had brought in new laws: for example, it added a new clause to the criminal code in September 1966, making it a criminal act to distribute 'false information harmful to Soviet state and society,' while another clause specified 'violations of public order'.

Did you know?

Long after their introduction in the West, only a few high-ranking administrators were allowed access to photocopying machines. They were considered dangerous, a possible means of spreading unofficial and unapproved writings. Dissidents trying to spread their message therefore often had to copy out originals laboriously by hand before distributing them.

A closer look

Some of the leading dissidents

Other than Daniel and Sinyavsky, the following were some of the leading intellectual dissidents in the Brezhnev era:

Aleksander Ginsburg was a writer championing free expression. He was arrested several times, and imprisoned in labour camps. In 1979, he was allowed to emigrate to the West.

Vladimir Bukovsky was arrested in 1963 as a student for circulating 'anti-Soviet literature'. After confinement in psychiatric hospitals for several years, he was expelled from the USSR in 1976, settling in Britain.

Andrei Sakharov was a renowned scientist prominent in developing Soviet nuclear weapons after the war. Later he opposed nuclear testing. He supported East–West cooperation and the new human rights movement, becoming a spokesman for democratic and humanitarian values. Sakharov was a particularly sensitive case, because of his international profile. He was awarded the Nobel Peace Prize in 1975, but five years later was banished to internal exile in the provincial city of Gorky. He was finally allowed to return to Moscow in 1986, and was elected to the new Congress of People's Deputies.

Alexander Solzhenitsyn along with Sakharov was possibly the most famous of the dissidents, because he too had an international reputation, ever since his *One Day in the Life of Ivan Denisovich* was published in Khrushchev's time. However, his later books, such as his *Gulag Archipelago*, a detailed history of Stalinist labour camps, were less acceptable, because he spoke out against the regime. When Solzhenitsyn demanded an end to censorship of literature, the authorities proposed expelling him from the Union of Writers, which would effectively have meant an end to freedom to publish. But Solzhenitsyn was defended by more than 80 fellow

Fig. 4 *Alexander Solzhenitsyn*

writers. After several terms of imprisonment he was tried for treason in 1974, and forcibly deported to Germany in an attempt to end widespread international protest and unwelcome publicity. Solzhenitsyn eventually settled in the USA. For much of his later life he kept a low profile in the West, probably because as well as criticising the Soviet regime, he also railed against what he saw as the evils of Western materialism and the loss of important values in Western society.

Anatoly Sharansky was prominent in the Jewish movement, which wanted freedom to emigrate. Sharansky was accused of Zionism, treason and spying for America in 1977. Sentenced to 13 years' hard labour, he was allowed to emigrate to Israel in 1986.

Anatoly Kuznetsov was a Ukrainian who upset the authorities with his controversial novel *Babi Yar*, which included criticisms of the Soviet administration. He defected to the West in 1969.

Josif Brodsky, a Jewish writer, was condemned as a 'social parasite' for writing poetry which offended the authorities. After several years of hard labour he was allowed to leave the USSR, and was awarded the Nobel Prize for Literature.

Czechoslovakia, 1968

Dissidence developed a further international dimension in 1968. The leader of Communist Czechoslovakia, Alexander Dubcek, introduced major reforms which allowed freedom of the press and other liberties that were not allowed in the USSR or other Eastern bloc states. Although Dubcek tried to reassure Brezhnev that Czechoslovakia would remain a loyal member of the Warsaw Pact, the Soviet leadership was afraid that it might leave it. This was too much to contemplate: it would weaken the Soviet-led military alliance, give a great propaganda coup to the West, and give encouragement to would-be reformers in other satellite states and possibly the USSR itself. In August 1968, Warsaw Pact forces invaded Czechoslovakia and crushed the 'Prague Spring'. The restoration of the old order was followed by the **Brezhnev Doctrine.**

Events in 1968 had a major impact within the USSR. Some courageous Soviet citizens openly protested at the Soviet action in Czechoslovakia and were arrested. The Party was instructed to reassert its authority in the arts, pure sciences and social sciences. Subjects such as history and economics were more closely vetted to ensure orthodoxy. The crisis led to the expulsion from the USSR of several leading writers, artists and scientists. Solzhenitsyn, who was awarded the Nobel Prize for Literature in 1970, decided not to travel to collect it because he feared he would be rearrested when he returned to the USSR (he was to be arrested and expelled from the USSR anyway in 1974).

The Helsinki Accords and the fight for human rights

Despite the international tension of the Cold War, heightened by events such as the Czechoslovakian crisis, meetings between the superpowers continued during the late 1960s and 1970s. The SALT (Strategic Arms Limitation Talks), aimed at arms control and eventually a reduction in nuclear weaponry, ushered in a period of détente. In the more relaxed atmosphere, an international conference was held in Helsinki in July 1975. It discussed issues of European security and cooperation between East and West Europe on a range of issues, including human rights.

■ **Key terms**

Brezhnev Doctrine: under the Brezhnev Doctrine, the USSR announced that it reserved the right to intervene in the affairs of other socialist states if it felt it was necessary to ensure the security of the 'socialist commonwealth'.

■ **Exploring the detail**

Détente

Détente, meaning a relaxation of tension, was very much on the superpower agenda between the 1960s and 1980s. Despite mutual suspicion between the superpowers, it was recognised by many in power that the continual build-up, particularly of nuclear arsenals, represented a great threat to the world. There were on–off negotiations to limit arms growth. This was arms control, limiting further growth, not proposals for actual reductions in nuclear weapons. Even so, the negotiations were fraught with difficulties. Some Soviet generals in particular were known to be hostile to the whole concept of arms agreements with the West.

Thirty-five countries attended, including the USSR. The final agreement, known as the Helsinki Accords, committed the participants to respecting 'human rights and fundamental freedoms', including freedom of thought, conscience, religion and a whole range of other civil rights.

In some respects the Accords foreshadowed what was to be included in the 1977 Brezhnev Constitution.

The Helsinki Agreements had an immediate high international profile, and the Soviet regime could not ignore them because of the inevitable scrutiny abroad. The significance within the USSR was that Soviet dissidents, and human rights activists, used the Helsinki Accords as a basis for their demand for more freedom. Once the Soviet government endorsed the Helsinki Accords in August 1975, groups of Soviet citizens formed several 'Helsinki groups' to monitor Soviet observance of the agreement. A Soviet branch of Amnesty International had already been set up two years earlier. Technically these groups were within the law, but their activities provoked harassment from the KGB, which was more active than ever in combating 'opposition'. The KGB often used progressive levels of response. Initially it often called in dissidents and verbally reasoned with them to conform. The next level could be threats. These might become reality, with dissidents losing their jobs. The final stage was likely to be prison or a labour camp. A new variant used by the KGB was to put dissidents into mental institutions such as psychiatric hospitals. Although this strategy was condemned abroad, it had the distinct advantage for the authorities that by incarcerating someone in a mental institution, they did not have to go though the normal legal procedures. Sometimes they justified this approach by claiming that anyone who was opposing the Soviet State must be mad, since the State always operated in its citizens' interests.

The inconsistencies also continued. For example, the historian Roy Medvedev was critical of aspects of the regime, calling for genuine competition between different political groups in order to breathe life into the political system. Yet he was allowed to go on writing and publishing – it was rumoured that he was protected by individuals within the Party leadership. Other writers were sometimes able to make thinly disguised attacks on the authorities: the writer Valentin Rasputin, for example, indirectly condemned the way that the regime's rural policies had destroyed traditional and worthy values in the countryside.

Sakharov, Ginsberg and a dissident scientist Yuri Orlov were among those harassed as the KGB's treatment of dissidents became more severe from 1977. By 1978 over 20 members of Helsinki groups were in prison. Orlov was given a seven-year sentence in a labour camp and Sakharov was under house arrest. There were further arrests and in September 1982 the Helsinki monitoring groups were disbanded. By then, 60 of their 80 members had been tried or jailed, and most of the remainder had emigrated or been deported. By the early 1980s the regime seemed to have succeeded in crushing overt dissidence: most prominent dissidents were in prison or exile, and there were far fewer samizdat publications in circulation. However, some historians have suggested that the real problem for the authorities was that by this time there were far more 'inactive' dissidents in the population at large than the few individuals who hit the headlines, at least abroad. These were people who were not actively following the dissident route, which could be dangerous, but they did sympathise with many of the dissidents' aims. There is certainly evidence that many scientists and

Cross-reference

For the Brezhnev Constitution, see pages 94–95.

Activity

Revision exercise

As individuals or in groups, research the background to arms control negotiations between the USA and the USSR, and the impact within the USSR.

technologists were beginning to view the regime less favourably than in the past, because it was now recognised as an impediment to economic and technological progress. It was these people who, while not contemplating radical political action, nevertheless became 'reformers within the system' and developed some of the attitudes to change later taken up officially by Gorbachev after 1985.

Religious dissent

During the later Brezhnev period, other aspects of dissidence also developed. These were often associated with religious or nationalist groups. Soviet Jews increasingly demanded the right to emigrate, either for religious reasons or because they wanted better living conditions. Periodic anti-Semitism had re-emerged in the Khrushchev years, with many Jewish institutions closed and Jewish cemeteries desecrated. Many Jewish would-be emigrants were arrested. Others, known as *refuseniks*, demonstrated in Red Square and various Russian cities. The resulting international concern led the regime to alter its stance and authorise Jewish emigration again, provided the emigrants paid an emigration tax. During the 1970s, 250,000 Jews left the USSR. There were 51,000 Jewish emigrants in 1979, the peak year. By 1982 the authorities were being much more restrictive: fewer than 3,000 Jews were allowed to emigrate in that year. This again had an international dimension: Soviet Jews became a pawn in the Cold War, since the USSR's attitude towards emigration varied according to the rate of progress, or lack of it, in its relations with the West.

There was a strong Catholic element to dissident activity in Poland and the Baltic Republics. Helsinki monitoring groups were set up in Catholic Lithuania. Catholic and fundamentalist Baptist groups were active in Ukraine, along with unofficial trade unions. Religious persecution grew in the late 1970s. Then, for the first time, Christians of several denominations joined in appealing to the Soviet authorities and the World Council of Churches for an end to State interference in Church affairs. This did not stop State persecution, which actually increased when the USSR invaded Afghanistan. There were also sporadic outbursts of discontent in those Soviet Republics which had a Muslim population. The regime reacted particularly harshly to Muslim discontent, because it feared **fundamentalism** developing within its borders, which could become even more potent if combined with nationalism.

Developments across the USSR

Brezhnev followed the previous Soviet Nationalities policy, as practised by Khrushchev. This was to give some political leeway to the Republics by allowing them to be led by members of their own nationalities. Those appointed were always subject to supervision from Moscow by the practice of installing ethnic Russian in posts just below the level of the indigenous leaders. The response to this practice was variable, since there was a temptation for these Russians to 'go native', putting the interests of 'their Republics' above those of Moscow. This was particularly the case under Brezhnev, since appointees were likely to remain in office for a long time, and in many cases they got involved in local networks of influence and corruption. Only four Republican leaders were replaced during Brezhnev's entire period as leader. Local officials developed powerful, well-oiled Party machines which were quite capable of subtly rendering directives from Moscow ineffective. This happened with decrees of which they disapproved, especially those that threatened to limit their authority.

Exploring the detail

A new burst of anti-Semitism

The long history of Russian anti-Semitism took on a new twist in 1967. In that year there was a six-day war between Israel and the neighbouring Arab states. The USSR supported the losing Arab states, to the extent of providing military hardware and advisers. The experience prompted a new wave of hostility towards the USSR's Jewish population.

Activity

Research task

Research the background of anti-Semitism in Soviet Russia. Why did emigration become a major issue after the Second World War?

Key terms

Fundamentalism: fundamentalists, whether Christian or Islamic, were considered a threat by the Soviet authorities, because unlike more 'moderate' religious believers, they had a fundamental belief that their religion was more important even than their duty to the State. This went totally against Soviet ideology that all citizens must regard loyalty to the Soviet workers' State, as defined by the regime, as the absolute priority.

Cross-reference

The developing issue of the relationship between the various subject nationalities and the Russian Federation is covered in more depth in Chapter 10.

Some particular trends in the relationship between Moscow and the Republics developed during the Brezhnev period:

- All-Union institutions became progressively more Russified under Brezhnev. There was an increasing proportion of Russians in the Central Committee and the Politburo (10 out of 14 full members in the 1981 Politburo compared to 6 out of 11 in 1966). The Secretariat was exclusively Russian. Non-Russian members of the Politburo were usually Republican leaders, based outside Moscow and not always involved in Politburo decisions, which in any case were increasingly delegated to small Politburo sub-committees. This development increased the tendency of non-Russian leaders to identify more with their own Republics than with all-Union issues.

- Brezhnev's regime was conscious of major differences between the Republics, particularly in levels of economic growth, and did try to address them. More investment was put into less developed Republics, particularly Kazakhstan. However, the results were mixed:

  - There was some reduction in the disparities of wealth in the 1970s, but they had widened again by the 1980s.
  - Some economic policies damaged Republican economics, noticeably the regime's attempt to force the Central Asian Republics to focus their economies on one product, cotton.
  - Soviet policies had a devastating environmental impact on some of the Republics, notably the Aral Sea.
  - Soviet policy was inconsistent, since there is also evidence that despite more investment in Asia, development overall was concentrated in the Russian Federation and the western Republics. For example the Russian Federation absorbed 62.4 per cent of total capital investment in 1980, a similar proportion to 1960. Therefore it is not surprising that the disparities widened.

Cross-reference

For more about the environmental destruction of the Aral Sea, see page 93.

Brezhnev's Nationalities policy

Historians have disagreed about the motives behind Brezhnev's Nationalities policy, if indeed he had one, and their impact:

- One interpretation is that there was almost a deliberate policy of Russification of the Republics. Evidence for this might be the increasing proportion of Russians in the leadership, as described above.

- Another interpretation is that so much of what happened in the Republics was typical of other aspects of the regime: it was more a case of inactivity or 'letting sleeping dogs lie' so that developments occurred without much forethought or planning from Moscow. This passivity may have been because Brezhnev preferred to shy away from confrontation. His regime ignored the evidence of local corruption and abuses of power. On occasions when there were serious incidents, such as national demonstrations by Georgians, Armenians, Uzbeks and Lithuanians, protesting at perceived threats to their languages or other national rights, the authorities in Moscow tended to back down.

The impact of Brezhnev's Nationalities policy

There is also debate about the impact of Brezhnev's Nationalities policy. Some analysts have suggested that Brezhnev's mixture of repression, complacency and concession may have preserved the USSR longer than might otherwise have been the case. However, most consider that the regime was simply storing up trouble for the future.

The regime did show some concern about the growth of nationalist dissent, both in the European Republics and in Central Asia. The problem in the latter was compounded, in Moscow's eyes, by the rapid growth in the local indigenous populations. Ironically, when separatist nationalist movements became a major issue in the late 1980s, they were to be much more of a threat in the Baltic states, Ukraine and Transcaucasia (the Caucasus region, which included the Soviet Republics of Georgia, Armenia and Azerbaijan) than in the Asian Republics. This was partly because of fiercer resistance in the former to policies such as promoting Russian at the expense of indigenous languages; and partly because these Republics had historic traditions of national independence. If the regime was concerned about the growth of Republican dissidence, its policies in the very last years of Brezhnev's rule were not very subtle. The Olympic Games in 1980 coincided with the launch of an aggressive campaign of 'Soviet nationalism'. The heroic exploits of the Second World War were highlighted and the propaganda machine partially rehabilitated Stalin. The strength of the Soviet State, standing up to its Cold War enemies, was contrasted with the weakness of the old tsarist State. There was no attempt to publicly embrace the contribution made by various national or minority groups to Soviet achievements.

A closer look

The Stalin cult

The cult of Stalin never really died in the USSR, or even in post-Soviet Russia. In 2008, a national television poll in Russia asked viewers to vote for the greatest ever Russian. In first place came Alexander Nevsky, a 13th-century hero who defeated the invading Teutonic Knights, and was held up as a great Russian patriot who saved the motherland. In second place came Peter Stolypin, Tsar Nicholas II's prime minister until his assassination in 1911. Stalin came third in the poll. In one sense this was surprising, given that Stalin was not even Russian. However, in another sense it was predictable, since many Russian citizens still look back fondly at someone they regard as a strong leader, who led Russia to victory in the Second World War. Prime Minister Vladimir Putin echoed the plaudits for Stalin, admitting that he had made some mistakes, such as the purges, but also claiming that 'In other countries, even worse things happened.' Part of the reason for Stalin's positive reputation is based simply on a comparison with more recent Soviet leaders. Nobody really believed that Brezhnev was a Soviet hero; while Gorbachev was dismissed by many Russians as a misguided weakling who was responsible for the break-up of the USSR, in contrast to Stalin, who they praised as a true protector of Russian interests.

Stalin never lost his cult status in Georgia, his homeland. Even though evidence of Stalin such as portraits and statues was removed after 1956 in other areas of the USSR, his existence was still acknowledged in Georgia. Georgian taxi drivers frequently displayed pictures of Stalin on their dashboards!

Activity

Challenge your thinking

Was there a 'nationalities problem' in Brezhnev's USSR? If so, how competently was it dealt with?

If there was a nationalities problem, Brezhnev did not solve it. However, one historian has suggested that, since the USSR was ultimately held together by force, Brezhnev cannot be blamed for failing to solve an insoluble problem:

The USSR was a multinational empire … Whilst most of its citizens accepted its legitimacy and few sympathised with the aims of radical nationalists at this time, tensions among ethnic groups were widespread and the ethnic diversity of the country remained, as it had been since the nineteenth century, a potential threat to its cohesion … the Brezhnev policy mix had much to recommend it, at least to an authoritarian elite committed to retaining power and holding the state together. For all its apparent contradictions and ambiguities, it represented a reasonable strategy for coping with a problem that did not admit of any ultimate solution.

2   *Tompson, W., **The Soviet Union under Brezhnev**, 2003*

Opposition to the war in Afghanistan

Fig. 5 *Yuri Andropov, one of the key figures behind the Soviet invasion of Afghanistan, with US Vice-President George H. W. Bush*

Events in Afghanistan provided a further opportunity for those who were critical of the Soviet regime to press for change. Afghanistan was strategically very significant to the USSR, mainly because it was close to Turkestan. The Soviets were afraid of Islamic fundamentalism infiltrating the USSR and influencing its large Islamic population. In 1978 a pro-Russian revolutionary movement overthrew the Afghan Republic. The new government immediately came under attack from a combination of Afghan nationalists and the Islamic Mujaheddin, who soon controlled large areas of rural Afghanistan. In December 1979 Soviet forces invaded Afghanistan in support of the government against the rebels. There was a storm of international protest, both from Islamic neighbours like Pakistan and Iran, and also from the Western powers. One result was a boycott of the 1980 Moscow Olympics by the USA and several other countries and an American embargo on exports of grain and technology to the USSR. The invasion also ended the SALT II arms control negotiations.

This international response was in itself serious for the USSR. However, there were other very serious consequences. Soviet military intervention proved to be a failure. Over one million Soviet soldiers were sent into

Fig. 6 *A Soviet cartoon highlighting the US funding of the Mujaheddin war against the Soviets in Afghanistan*

Fig. 7 *Official opening of the 1980 Moscow Olympics*

Afghanistan, armed with modern weapons, but they failed to defeat the Mujaheddin guerrillas. The war resulted in over 50,000 Soviet casualties. The costs of the war added to the regime's economic problems.

As the war dragged on, it proved impossible even for the Soviet propaganda campaign to hide the truth from its own population. There were too many dead soldiers returned to their families in the USSR, and too many conscripts came back demoralised and with psychological problems. The Afghan War also badly damaged Soviet relations with its one-time allies in the non-aligned world. These were countries which had previously supported the USSR in the Cold War against the capitalist West. Yet the war persisted until the last Red Army forces were pulled out of Afghanistan in 1989.

The significance of dissidence within Brezhnev's USSR

There has been debate about the impact of dissidence in its various forms within the USSR. The argument that dissidence was significant tends to focus on the fact that it was in the period from the 1960s to the 1980s that it became an increasing factor in Soviet life and took up more of the authorities' attention. Until then, the impact of the police state had been such that no public expression of dissent had been feasible. What happened during the Brezhnev years was that dissidents began to speak out, either literally or in print, and they began to show sympathy or support for each other. Although dissidents did not claim to be seeking the overthrow of the regime, many intellectuals increasingly shared concerns about the restriction of free expression of opinion, claiming that all they wanted was a guarantee of freedoms already promised in the Constitution. They were beginning to use Soviet law against the regime that had issued it. These ideas became more significant as it was clear that the USSR could no longer isolate itself from the outside world, and that the country was facing increasing problems. Even groups of creative people such as scientists, while they would not have classified themselves as dissidents, showed increasing frustration. The breadth of dissident activity widened to include a range of issues concerning creative freedoms, the nationalities, human rights, religious toleration and workers' rights. Another development was the increasing link made between dissidents and foreign contacts. It was possible for some discussion of issues outside official channels, in areas like sociology, although it always had to be within prescribed limits. It was possible for emerging politicians like Gorbachev to find some arguments to back up ideas for reform. However, it is not clear that dissident activity was responsible for these developments.

There is an argument that dissidence did not significantly weaken the regime, and that its importance can be overstated. There is no evidence that the majority of the Soviet population sympathised with dissidents. Indeed, they were often regarded as at best ungrateful troublemakers, at worst unpatriotic traitors. The regime was often successful in presenting dissidents as belonging to privileged factions, divorced from the concerns of everyday citizens. An article in *Izvestia* (one of the major Soviet newspapers) in 1966, focusing on Daniel and Sinyavsky, summed up the official view:

> Sinyavsky and Daniel grew up in the Soviet Union. They enjoyed all the blessings of Socialism. Everything that had been won by our elder brothers and fathers in the flaming years of the Revolution and the Civil War, and the difficult period of the First Five-year Plan, was at their service ... They replaced honesty with unprincipledness. From petty meanness to betrayal ... Essentially, these are shots fired in the back of a people fighting for peace on earth and for universal happiness ... Time will pass, and no one will even remember them ... After all, history has time and time again confirmed that slander, however thick and venomous it be, inevitably evaporates under the warm breath of truth.

3   *Daniels, R., A Documentary History of Communism Volume 1, 1987*

The regime had successfully reduced the amount of dissident activity by 1982. There were certainly fewer dissidents in prison, and fewer of their publications in circulation.

A balanced assessment of the impact of the dissidents comes from one historian, Peter Kenez:

> It is impossible to deny that a Sakharov or a Solzhenitsyn found few supporters among ordinary citizens. At the same time, it would be a mistake to write off the role of the dissidents altogether. They did change the character of the Soviet Union. Even loyal members of the party, indeed even high-ranking officials, read Pasternak and Solzhenitsyn and others, and the fact that the unsayable was said made an impression.

4   *Kenez, P., A History of the Soviet Union from the Beginning to the End, 1999*

Activity

Group debate

'Dissent in the USSR during the Brezhnev era was a growing threat to the stability of the Soviet regime.' Consider the arguments for and against this statement. Which side of the argument do you find most convincing?

Fig. 8 *Soviet troops leaving Afghanistan*

Summary questions

1 Why did dissidence become an increasing concern for the Soviet authorities under Brezhnev?

2 How successfully did the Brezhnev regime deal with the threat of internal opposition within the USSR?

7 Economic stagnation under Brezhnev

Fig. 1 *The USSR celebrates the 1980 Olympics in Moscow*

Q: Who took the first step towards building Communism in the USSR – scientists or laymen?

A: Laymen. Scientists would have tried it out first on dogs.

Q: Is it true that the Soviet Union is superior to the capitalist West in everything?

A: Of course it's true! For example, a Soviet dwarf is two inches taller than a capitalist dwarf.

1

Two Soviet jokes

■ Economic stagnation

Brezhnev's economic policies have already been described and analysed with reference to their impact on working and living standards in the USSR. Three tables in this chapter give more detail of what happened to industry and agriculture during the Brezhnev era.

Table 1 *Agricultural output, 1966–80*

	Annual averages		
	1966–70	1971–75	1976–80
Gross agricultural output (billion roubles)	80.5	91.0	99.9
Grain harvest (million tons)	167.5	181.6	205
Cotton (million tons)	6.1	7.7	8.9
Sugar beet (million tons)	81.1	76.0	88.4
Potatoes (million tons)	94.8	89.6	84
Meat (million tons)	11.6	14.0	14.8
Milk (million tons)	80.6	87.4	92.6

From Soviet sources; reproduced in Nove, A., ***An Economic History of the USSR***, 1988

Activity

Statistical analysis

As individuals or in groups, analyse the statistics in Table 1 and decide how much progress was made in Soviet agriculture between 1966 and 1970.

The reasons for economic stagnation

Table 1 above and Tables 2 and 3 on page 118 suggest some achievements both in agriculture and industry. However, it is also clear that overall economic growth rates were declining, to a level which became critical during the 1980s. Even during the 1970s the Soviet economy had ceased to close the gap with the USA and fallen behind Western European levels. There were several reasons for this:

■ Although the Soviet economy was labour-intensive, because it was not technologically efficient, the working population in many areas of industry stopped increasing, due to a decline in birth rates outside Central Asia.

■ Military production does not feature in many of the statistics, but it took a significant proportion of quality resources and was a strain on the economy.

■ Part of the decline in industrial growth was due to increased investment in agriculture, which was necessary, but meant that less was available for industry.

■ The central economic planning system continued to suffer from the faults which had always plagued it.

■ The economy still suffered from too much outdated technology and machinery except in prestige sectors like defence.

■ The Stalinist obsession with growth continued, which meant that other important economic indicators like costs and quality were given a very low priority.

■ Some vital economic activities were neglected, largely because it was not easy to measure their contribution quantitatively in the way that factory products could be – it meant, for example, that service industries and the transport infrastructure were too often neglected.

■ Environmental concerns were largely ignored.

Did you know?

Many civilian enterprises also contained secret sections devoted to military production, and the resulting products were not recorded in the official output figures. Soviet military expenditure was therefore almost certainly greater than the figures usually quoted.

- The central planning system was increasingly unable to cope with an economy which, for all its faults, was more complex than in Stalin's day.

- The technological gap with more advanced capitalist economies, which had narrowed by the 1960s, began to widen again by the 1980s.

- The regime was able to ignore some of the warning signs, because it could point to rising living standards, while true facts of economic performance were hidden – for example, sometimes the apparent rise in production was due not to real increases in output, but to higher prices, which fed the information on which statistics were based.

- Targets were geared to short-term gains rather than necessary long-term developments – due mainly to the tyranny of planning requirements.

- There were too few opportunities for meaningful discussion of possible economic alternatives in an atmosphere of conservatism and the desire to maintain the status quo.

Soviet problems were not unique – there was a global recession during the early 1970s, caused partly by a significant rise in the international price and rationing of oil.

The USSR was poorly equipped to meet an emerging economic crisis from the mid-1970s, as the effects of shortages of labour, investment funds and energy funds restricted options for the planners, just as economic growth rates were significantly slowing. The USSR was probably less affected by the 1970s oil crisis than the capitalist West. However, the Eleventh Five-year Plan shifted the emphasis on energy production from coal and oil towards gas and nuclear power.

The fundamentals of the Soviet economy remained in place, and there was no attempt at substantial economic reform until the Gorbachev era. In certain respects the economic system by the 1980s had become even more irrational: although managers could make more decisions, ministers continued to interfere in enterprises. The regime was not willing to conclude that a fundamental restructuring of ideas, strategy and organisation was necessary to halt or reverse the decline in growth, which had serious consequences for a superpower trying to compete with the capitalist West. The tinkering with the system continued: the administrators, waiting for Brezhnev to die, were reluctant to make long-term decisions. The Soviet economy, once the showpiece of socialist achievement, was creaking with old age well before Brezhnev's death in 1982.

Fig. 2 *A drilling platform on the Black Sea near Baku*

 Activity

Group exercise

In groups, discuss five factors from the list on pages 116–17 and decide which are the most important and which the least important. Compare your choices with those of other groups and justify them.

Did you know?

There were massive price rises in oil following the 1973 Middle East War. The USSR was the world's greatest oil producer, and so was not only self-sufficient in oil but exported it . Oil made up two-thirds of the value of Soviet exports. However, the production of oil and coal levelled off by 1980, and the costs of extraction were rising.

Fig. 3 *A cartoon from Brezhnev's USSR satirising backwardness in the economy*

 Activity

Source analysis

What message is being conveyed by this cartoon?

Table 2 *Industrial output, 1965–80*

	8th Plan 1965–70		9th Plan 1971–75		10th Plan 1976–80	
	1970 Plan	1970 actual	1975 Plan	1975 actual	1980 Plan	1980 actual
Industrial production (1965 index = 100)	148.5	150	147	143	137	124
Producers' goods	150.5	151	146.3	146	140	126
Consumers' goods	144.5	149	148.6	137	131	121
Electricity (billion Kwhs)	840	740	1065	1039	1380	1290
Oil (million tons)	350	353	505	491	640	604
Coal (million tons)	670	624	694.9	701	800	719
Steel (million tons)	126	116	146.4	141	168	155

Adapted from Soviet sources in Nove, A., **An Economic History of the USSR***, 1988*

Table 3 *Soviet growth rates, 1960–85*

	Soviet estimates	American estimates	Khanin's estimates*
1960–65	6.5%	4.8%	4.4%
1965–70	7.7%	4.9%	4.1%
1970–75	5.7%	3.0%	3.2%
1975–80	4.2%	1.9%	1.0%
1980–85	3.5%	1.8%	0.6%

*Khanin was a leading Russian economist whose alternative estimates of Soviet growth were crucial in influencing Soviet debates on economic policy in the late 1980s.
Statistics adapted from Harrison, M., **Economic Growth and Slowdown***, reproduced in Tompson, W.,* **The Soviet Union under Brezhnev***, 2003.*

Activity

Statistical analysis

Use Tables 2 and 3 to answer the following questions:

1 What does Table 2 tell you about the industrial priorities of the Brezhnev regime? Did those priorities change during this period?

2 To what extent were industrial targets met?

3 Were there any significant differences between the three Five-year Plans in (a) intentions and (b) results?

4 Which sectors of industry were most and least successful?

5 What other information would you need to assess the success of failure of Soviet industrial performance in this period?

6 What does Table 3 reveal about Soviet economic growth during the Brezhnev period?

7 Why do you think there are discrepancies in the estimates for growth in Table 3? Does this matter?

Fig. 4 *A Leningrad industrial scene*

Corruption: the 'black' or 'second economy'

There had always been corruption in Soviet life and especially the economy. Managers of enterprises had frequently altered production figures, lied about the number of workers on the payroll, and made unofficial deals to acquire the necessary raw materials – in short, whatever was necessary in a desperate bid to meet their targets. Many Soviet citizens resorted to bribery as a way of life in a society plagued by shortages and a bureaucracy which made it difficult to 'get things done'. The level of corruption, both at a low and high level, became more and more pronounced during the Brezhnev years. This was partly because as the standard of living rose, people had more cash, but there was often not enough on which to spend it, and saving money was not very profitable. Access to goods and services in such a system was all-important. Consequently the regime had an ambivalent attitude. On the surface, corruption was condemned as antisocial and certainly anti-socialist. Yet unofficially it was tolerated, because the Second economy helped to iron out the deficiencies which clearly existed in the 'official' planned economy. Without the black market, many Soviet citizens would probably have been much more dissatisfied with their lives.

Fig. 5 *'Now Eidorov, don't return without spare parts! The state farm will take care of your family until you return.' A satire on problems in Soviet agriculture*

Activity

Source analysis

What is the message conveyed by Figure 5?

A closer look

The extent of corruption

Some cases of corruption reached to the very top. A long-running scandal in the cotton industry was not unearthed until 1984, when government ministers from Kazakhstan, Turkmenistan, Azerbaijan and Uzbekistan were arrested. For many years their Republics had received billions of roubles in payments from Moscow for shipments of cotton which had never been made. In this case no prosecutions followed, because the leader of the whole operation was the Uzbek Party leader, Sharaf Rashidov. The Party did not want to allow itself to be discredited by prosecuting such a high-ranking political leader. Over the years Rashidov had bribed important people, including the deputy director of Gosplan and Brezhnev himself, who had been supplied with several European luxury sports cars and hunting lodges, presumably without asking any questions. Brezhnev's more puritanical successor Andropov did move against leading criminals, some of whom were eventually arrested. It was revealed that there was a regularised system of bribes for particular favours: an example would be for election as a Soviet deputy and for Party decorations. It appeared that Rashidov himself had regularly travelled around Uzbekistan in a special train, stopping off so that he and his wife could be showered with expensive gifts. However, although there were convictions, even Andropov could not bring the powerful Rashidov to justice. It also became apparent that throughout the USSR there were factories supposedly meeting their targets and receiving State resources to do so, even though the factories never actually existed. Instead their 'directors' diverted the resources over several years into secret workshops where the products that were manufactured were sold on the black market.

When abuses were known, the local authorities were often reluctant to act, because the criminals had powerful contacts who would do what was necessary to protect their interests. For years Yuri Sokolov, director of Moscow's leading food store, had been accepting bribes. His contacts reached to the highest levels, including Galina Brezhneva, the leader's daughter, and other members of Brezhnev's family. Sokolov was eventually arrested, revealed a lot of evidence about widespread corruption, and was shot in 1984. There were strong suspicions that Andropov only moved against such cases because he wanted to discredit Brezhnev, or his memory, as a means of cementing his own leadership ambitions.

The legacy of corruption

The underground 'mafia' was active in the USSR from the 1960s, engaged in blackmail, corruption, protectionism and kidnappings. There was to be no serious attempt to clamp down on this activity until 1983 and 1984 when over 1,000 death sentences were handed out. Tens of thousands of officials and Party members were sacked. However, the phenomenon of widespread corruption did not disappear. The mafia, which was to be so dominant in post-Communist Russia after 1991, did not suddenly appear from nowhere: it already had several years of apprenticeship under its belt, often with the complicity of the Soviet security services and high-ranking Party leaders and functionaries. It was relatively easy for those in privileged positions to protect their families, even to the extent of ensuring that individuals accused of serious crimes could escape trial and conviction by simple expedients such as having them sent for a short time to an institution for 'mental instability'.

The precise extent of corruption will probably never be known. Estimates of the black market and second economy, including property stolen from the State, run to over 100 billion roubles annually during Brezhnev's years. Less publicised aspects of the second economy were equally rampant. Typical examples included workers who did 'private' jobs or teachers tutoring privately during their official work time, often for mutual favours, without any exchange of money. This was illegal, but almost universal. A bribe might persuade a shop assistant to reserve you something in short supply. Illegally brewed and sold vodka probably amounted to nearly half of total spirits consumption. Various Russian and Western estimates put the value of the second economy as at least 20 per cent of gross national product and up to 40 per cent of total personal income.

The relative lack of state action against the second economy during the Brezhnev era was not just due to complacency or corruption by the authorities themselves. There was an implicit recognition that this unofficial activity actually enabled the Soviet economy to function. Large-scale corruption to line the pockets of individuals was one thing. But the widespread low level unofficial dealings were necessary for many 'ordinary'

■ **Activity**

Revision exercise

Consider the extent to which corruption was a significant part of the Soviet economy. Could the Soviet economy have functioned without the 'second economy'? Did the extent of corruption actually matter?

Fig. 6 *Consumer shortages: empty refrigerated cases in a Moscow food store, 1982*

citizens to survive in an economic system which was overcentralised and could not guarantee consistently to meet citizens' needs. Only a change of system would enable a reduction of illegal or semi-legal activity to the lower levels more typical of market-based capitalist economies – economies which themselves have been unable to eliminate the phenomenon.

■ The costs of the arms race

By the 1980s, up to 25 per cent of the Soviet economy was devoted to military spending. Relations between the USSR and the West reached a low point with the building of the Berlin Wall in 1961 and the Cuban missile crisis in 1962. Khrushchev backed down in the Cuban crisis and removed Soviet missiles from Cuba. However, the USSR took the decision that it could not afford to back down again: although it was already a formidable military power because of its land forces in Europe, the USSR embarked on a policy of global expansion, expanding their navy and also their nuclear capability in an attempt to gain parity with the USA. Kosygin argued for better East–West relations mainly because of the economic burden which vast military spending had on the Soviet economy. Brezhnev, like Khrushchev, favoured 'peaceful coexistence', and hence the USSR pursued détente, the relaxation of international tension in the 1970s. This period was marked by the 1972 SALT I Strategic Arms Limitation Treaty, the 1972 Anti-Ballistic Missile Treaty, the 1973 Nuclear Non-Aggression Agreement, the 1975 Helsinki Agreement and the SALT II negotiations between 1976 and 1979.

Fig. 7 *A parade of Soviet intercontinental ballistic missiles in Red Square*

However, this decade also saw arguments within the Soviet political and military establishments about détente and the status of defence. The USSR certainly did not drop its guard in this period and military spending continued apace. The USSR also took opportunities to increase its global influence, acquiring bases in Angola, Mozambique, South Yemen and Ethiopia, as well as supporting revolutionary movements elsewhere. Soviet military spending was at the American level by 1970, and then grew in real terms by up to 5 per cent a year while American spending declined. Détente was ended by the Soviet invasion of Afghanistan in 1979 and the repression of the Solidarity free trade union movement in Poland (1980–81).

By 1980 the USSR was the greatest nuclear and military power in the world, but dependent on a sluggish economy in which growth was declining. The USSR was poorer than the USA, but was spending over twice as much in proportion to its wealth on defence. The USSR was in danger of both overextending its commitments and seriously damaging its economy. Hence, after Brezhnev's death, there was a serious attempt to resurrect détente.

Assessments of Brezhnev

Most interpretations of the Brezhnev era tend to be negative. Brezhnev has often been accused of presiding over a period of complacency and stagnation, which allowed the USSR's economic growth to decline. The resulting problems made it very difficult and possibly even impossible for his successors to reverse the trend. Many commentators, particularly Russians, have had little respect for him. Typical was the view of the Russian historian Dmitri Volkogonov (*The Rise and Fall of the Soviet Empire*, 1998), who concluded that Brezhnev symbolised the decline of the USSR, because he was incapable even of giving any meaning to Communist ideology in the way that his predecessors had managed, for all their faults. Ideology had simply lost its meaning to much of the Soviet population by 1982.

Most negative assessments of Brezhnev focus on the following factors:

- His conservatism, evident from the start of his leadership, drifted into inaction and a lack of will to impose necessary reforms on the economy and the administration.

- His rule largely destroyed the consensus that had built up in the USSR whereby most citizens accepted that Soviet rule had achieved some creditable successes. This was most felt in the economy, where the Party's claim to legitimacy and its monopoly of power rested on its ability to manage the economy. That claim was increasingly in doubt.

- Brezhnev's regime was unable to sustain ambitious foreign and defence policies, because they were costly and the attempt at détente had failed by the early 1980s. The high level of defence spending was probably unsustainable.

- Major abuses of the system, such as corruption and patronage, continued and even increased during these years. Popular contempt for the Party probably increased, and any hold of Communist ideology over citizens was correspondingly weakened. Initiatives such as the 1977 Constitution were largely propaganda exercises.

- Despite the limited de-Stalinisation that had occurred before Brezhnev, the gains were not extended and in some cases were reversed – resulting, for example, in the rise in dissidence.

- Emerging, potentially very damaging issues, such as the relationship between the Republics and the treatment of the nationalities, were largely ignored or swept under the carpet.

- Overall, Brezhnev was unimaginative and complacent and simply stored up problems for the future. For example, the policy of 'stability of cadres' ensured that many at the top of the leadership were simply too old, frail or set in their ways to manage the country effectively.

- By the early 1980s, leading politicians were too preoccupied with determining Brezhnev's successor to deal with the country's real problems.

On the other hand, it is possible to qualify some of the harsher judgements on Brezhnev, especially with a longer-term perspective. For all the faults of the regime, Brezhnev did not try to revert to Stalinism. He tried to establish consensus, and to some extent succeeded. Dissidents during his rule were very few and had no public support. By encouraging an atmosphere of order and tranquillity, he gave the USSR what was needed after the unpredictability of the Khrushchev years. The regime oversaw a period of increased popular consumption, major housebuilding, education and health programmes and other welfare improvements. Also, although it ultimately failed, the Brezhnev regime did try to establish better relations with the West.

The problems which existed in the USSR, particularly its difficulties in sustaining economic growth and modernising the economy, did not arise during the Brezhnev years. They were already embedded, and his predecessors could also be blamed for not effectively grasping the nettle of change. The charge that Brezhnev lacked imagination is true. However, practically all would-be reformers within the USSR could not see beyond trying to reform the system within the existing framework. They were not trying to destroy it. The same charge could be levelled against Gorbachev, who began his reform programme without a clear plan and believing that reform could be implemented with the Communist Party maintaining its monopoly of power. Any radical reform, such as free-market economics, would have been absolute heresy for the Communist Party and there is no guarantee that it would have worked, particularly since nobody in the USSR had had experience of such a system. Such an attempt at reform might have led to an even earlier collapse of the USSR. Societies often come under most strain precisely when they do begin to reform, bringing all sorts of hopes, fears and strains out into the open; hopes which in particular are difficult to fulfil or to control.

There is also a danger of hindsight. Just because the USSR was broken up in 1991, it does not mean that it had to happen, or that Brezhnev was responsible. It was also, for example, difficult to predict in the 1960s and 1970s that nationalist issues would escalate as rapidly as they did in the 1980s. Could the Soviet system have survived an energetic attempt to reform it? As late as the mid-1970s many Western and Soviet observers, while aware that there were economic and social strains and problems in areas such as détente, were not thinking in terms of a major decline or crisis. By that date there was clear evidence of considerable gains, for example in living standards and the USSR's growing international influence.

Most balanced assessments accept that Brezhnev and his regime cannot be blamed for all the USSR's problems, but at the same time point to the fact that Brezhnev was unwilling or unable in the first place to seriously address those problems which were already in the system.

Activity

Challenge your thinking

Hold a class debate on the topic 'Brezhnev's impact on the USSR was fundamentally negative.' Decide which of your group will write speeches to support this view and which will write against it. Deliver your speeches and ask questions of one another. Take a vote to decide which side seemed the most convincing.

Fig. 8 *Soviet mobile SS20 intermediate-range missile launchers, 1980s*

Did Developed Socialism work?

Brezhnev's regime was not just about preservation and complacency. 'Developed Socialism' was an attempt to show how Soviet socialism differed from other socialist countries. While avoiding Khrushchev-style utopian pronouncements about full-blown Communism, Developed Socialism was seen as a means of celebrating successes and showing how there could be further progress within a mature system. Socialism was to be regarded as a prolonged period in its own right, not just a halfway house between capitalism and Communism, and was to be characterised by more popular participation in politics and social advances which took advantage of modern developments in science and other disciplines. More specialists would be used in decision-making. Unfortunately the reality did not match the aspirations, partly because the decision-makers were not as enthusiastic about the concepts as the idealists who wrote about Developed Socialism. Consequently, for example, the few attempts at reform in industry such as encouraging more innovation only resulted in managers having to worry about more Plan indicators. Ultimately, the regime was reduced to optimistic slogans which could not hide the fact that the State and the Party were all-powerful, and ultimately the individual still existed primarily for the good of the State. Only the State could determine what rights and freedoms people had. The authorities running the State had no intention of extending those rights and freedoms in such a way as to release creative potential at the cost of reducing their own power.

Learning outcomes

Through your study of this section you should have a good understanding of the nature of Brezhnev's rule within the USSR, including political developments and the economic issues which affected the Soviet economy in the Brezhnev period. You should also have a good understanding of how the regime dealt with the phenomenon of dissidence and how significant the dissident movement and the development of trends such as nationalism were. You should also have some understanding of economic stagnation under Brezhnev and the contribution of the arms race to economic problems. You should now be in a position to make a balanced overall assessment of the Brezhnev era in Soviet history.

AQA Examination-style question

To what extent did the Brezhnev regime succeed in silencing opposition to its policies? *(45 marks)*

Examiner's tip

This question requires you to consider several aspects:

■ what Brezhnev's policies actually were

■ what is meant by 'opposition'

■ what types of opposition there were at this time

■ whether the regime succeeded in silencing this opposition.

You might well focus on the activities of the dissidents, but do remember different groups who found themselves in conflict with the regime, such as intellectuals, religious groups and workers. You will need to consider the aims of the opposition: were these people trying to dismantle the system or just reform certain parts of it? As in any essay answer, you need to marshal the evidence carefully, be balanced in your approach where possible, but also ensure that you address the actual question and make a judgement.

Fig. 1 *Konstantin Chernenko, on the left, being presented with the Order of Lenin by Marshal Ustinov*

In this chapter you will learn about:

- how the USSR was governed by the regimes of Andropov and Chernenko

- how Gorbachev came to power in the USSR and the challenges facing the USSR in the 1980s.

When Brezhnev took power, Khrushchev handed him three envelopes, telling Brezhnev to open one when there was a crisis.

When Brezhnev opened one, a note inside read: 'Blame me for everything, and carry on.'

When the second crisis arrived, Brezhnev opened the second envelope. The note inside read, 'Reshuffle the Politburo and carry on.'

When the third and final crisis arrived, Brezhnev was desperate to find a solution, so he opened the third envelope. The contents read, 'Start writing three envelopes.'

1   *A Soviet joke*

Many people felt that the treatment of Brezhnev was a deliberate attempt by the ambitious Yuri Andropov to finish him off. A joke from the time had Brezhnev's last words as 'Leave the plug alone, Yuri.'

■ Key chronology

From Brezhnev to Gorbachev

1982
November Death of Brezhnev
Andropov elected
general secretary
1983
September Shooting down of
South Korean airliner
KAL 007
1984
February Death of Andropov
Election of Chernenko
as general secretary
1985
March Death of Chernenko
Gorbachev elected
general secretary

■ Exploring the detail

Andropov in Hungary

Andropov's experience in Hungary was important, since he was not only involved in the events of 1956, but he studied carefully what happened in Hungary afterwards. Andropov noted with interest subsequent Hungarian economic experiments, which led to fewer centralised controls than in other socialist states, and more initiative granted to enterprise managers. This influenced Andropov's own attitudes towards reform many years later, when there were concerns about overcentralisation of the Soviet economy and other weaknesses. Andropov also maintained contacts with Soviet personnel in several countries, which gave him a slightly broader perspective on the world than some of his colleagues. However, Andropov was too much a creature of the Stalinist system to believe in radical reform, so that when he was briefly in power in the 1980s, his limited economic policies never had a chance of getting to grips with the real problems facing the USSR.

■ The leadership of Yuri Andropov

The end of Brezhnev

Brezhnev's health seriously declined in the late 1970s, and he never really recovered from serious strokes in 1975 and 1977, one of which left him clinically dead before he was revived. His dominance inevitably began to falter. The Politburo shrank in size as the old guard finally died off: Kosygin in 1980 and Mikhail Suslov, regarded as the guardian of Soviet ideology, in 1982. Brezhnev was increasingly absent from the centre of events in Moscow. Decision-making was delegated in his absence to other Politburo members, and to Brezhnev's private office, run by Konstantin Chernenko. A struggle for power was going on behind the scenes. In early November 1982 Brezhnev was made to stand for hours in sub-zero temperatures on top of the Lenin Mausoleum in Red Square, for the annual commemoration of the Revolution. He had a final stroke and died in his sleep on 10 November.

The rise of Yuri Andropov

Brezhnev favoured Chernenko as his successor, despite the fact that he was over 70. Chernenko had shadowed Brezhnev's various posts and was a member of both the Secretariat and the Politburo, as were his rivals Andropov and Andrei Kirilenko, who was the Central Committee secretary. Kirilenko was in charge of personnel and therefore responsible for the promotion of many senior Party members. However, although Kirilenko had been a major contender, he was incapacitated by a heart attack in May 1982 and died before the end of the year. Andropov increasingly spoke on a range of issues and made implicit criticisms of the old regime. He also launched a campaign against corruption, which was in part an attack on Brezhnev and his family's record of flagrant abuse of the law. By implication this was also an attack on his rival Chernenko, who was closely associated with Brezhnev. If so, it worked, because when Brezhnev finally died, Andropov's accession to power was relatively smooth. Andropov was appointed general secretary almost immediately. The Politburo met before the Central Committee did, and although Prime Minister Tikhonov nominated Chernenko for the leadership, Marshal Ustinov announced that a decision had already been taken in favour of Andropov. It was a bloodless coup, backed by the KGB and the military.

Andropov was the son of a railwayman from the North Caucasus, and left school in 1930 at the age of 16. He worked on shipyards on the Upper Volga. After a spell as a Komsomol leader in the North Caucasus and in Yaroslavl, he served in the Second World War in Karelia, near the Finnish border. After the war Andropov had a successful Party career in Karelia. Marked out for promotion, he was brought to Moscow in 1951 to work for the Secretariat and then began a diplomatic career as Soviet ambassador to Hungary between 1954 and 1957. This was an important experience for him. Although he witnessed the brutal Soviet suppression of the 1956 Hungarian Rising, he recommended the appointment of a relatively moderate Hungarian leader after 1956.

Andropov joined the Central Committee in 1957, was promoted after the fall of Khrushchev and became head of the KGB in 1967. He created the Fifth Directorate of the KGB in 1968. Its task was to suppress all forms of dissidence, whether political, cultural, religious or nationalist. However, not only did Andropov have a more varied career background than several other prominent Communists, he was also a new breed of KGB leader: he did not believe that the KGB was a law unto itself, and emphasised the importance both of Party control of the KGB and its adherence to legal procedures. He declared that he did not believe in repression for its own sake: he would much prefer to persuade dissidents that their activities harmed the State. As head of the KGB Andropov received more accurate, propaganda-free reports of events at home and abroad, and was possibly therefore more knowledgeable than previous Soviet leaders. He was certainly a realist and not taken in by the regime's own propaganda. Nevertheless he was still an orthodox believer. While interested in reform, he maintained that the USSR must be on its guard in its ideological confrontation with the Western world. He was ruthless when he thought it necessary: it was he who ordered Sakharov's exile to Gorky in 1980, and it was rumoured that he had ordered an assassination attempt on Pope John Paul II in May 1981.

There is little doubt that Andropov had developed leadership ambitions before Brezhnev's death. He gave up his KGB role in May 1982, probably because traditionally it had been accepted that no head of the KGB could become general secretary. He was supported by the veteran Foreign Minister Gromyko and Defence Minister Ustinov. Andropov continued to use his recent KGB influence to undermine both Brezhnev and Chernenko.

Andropov's rule: efficiency and discipline

> After Brezhnev's death the Party met to choose his successor. After Andropov's unanimous election as general secretary, Andropov announced: 'Very well, Comrades, now that you have voted, you may lower your arms and move away from the wall.'

2   *A Soviet joke*

Andropov was intelligent, but he was also demanding. He was certainly different from Brezhnev in that he was genuinely concerned to carry out reforms. However, they had to be within the parameters of the orthodox Soviet system. In this sense Andropov was following in the footsteps of Khrushchev, although without the same quirks and unpredictability.

Andropov started his leadership vigorously, although he did not make himself president for another eight months, probably to avoid opposition from the remaining Breznevites. Andropov's watchwords were efficiency and discipline. He began with a campaign to remove Brezhnev's close supporters and to inject new life into the ailing Soviet economy. One-fifth of regional Party secretaries were replaced, including seven out of 20 in Kazakhstan (one of Brezhnev's power bases), along with some of Brezhnev's ministers and one-third of the departmental heads of the Central Committee. Andropov had to act because some of Brezhnev's and Chernenko's supporters were still in leading positions and rumours were circulating that Brezhnev had nominated Chernenko as his successor in his will. Many provincial Party chiefs were still Brezhnev appointees.

Andropov promoted his own younger protégés. Nikolai Ryzhkov was made Central Committee secretary responsible for a new economic programme. Grigori Romanov was put in charge of heavy industry. Mikhail Gorbachev was the only representative of the younger political generation in the Politburo, with specific responsibility for agriculture. Andropov was also supported by Gromyko, who provided continuity

Did you know?

KGB reports, when available, are among the best sources of information for what was actually going on inside the USSR. Unlike much other Soviet information, these reports, written for senior figures, were less obsessed with Soviet propaganda and said more about what people were actually thinking and doing.

Exploring the detail

Andropov's 'liberal' reputation

Relatively little was known about Andropov the man. He was regarded as personally modest and with intellectual leanings, interested in art and music. The Western press, intrigued at the rise of someone who, to foreigners, appeared something of an unknown, presented Andropov almost as a secret liberal, with a love of Western jazz and modern art. This image was reinforced by Soviet propaganda for foreign consumption and foreign policy purposes. Andropov's personal tragedy was that he was dogged by ill-health almost from the start of his leadership and therefore could not make a long-term impact, although he did pave the way for a younger reformer in the person of Gorbachev.

with the past but could not be regarded as a threat to Andropov's authority because he had no power base inside the Party.

Key profile

Nikolai Ryzhkov

Born in 1929 in the Urals and originally a mine worker, Ryzhkov (1929 –) qualified as an engineer in 1959. In 1979 he became deputy chairman of Gosplan, before joining the Politburo in 1985. Ryzhkov became Gorbachev's prime minister, and at first supported perestroika until he felt it was too radical. He opposed attempts to move the USSR quickly towards a market economy based on private enterprise. Although elected to the USSR Congress of People's Deputies in 1989, and coming second to Yeltsin in the 1991 Russian presidential elections, Ryzhkov was forced by ill-health to leave the limelight.

Andropov also launched a drive to increase efficiency in the workplace, mainly by rounding up absentee workers and encouraging enterprise managers to be more flexible. The KGB scoured shops, hospitals and cinemas, looking for citizens who should have been at work. There was a clear rationale for this: Andropov knew from an official report in 1982 that for every 100 Soviet citizens of work age, 30 were absent at any one time for 'personal reasons'.

In January 1984 Andropov began a 'limited industrial experiment' modelled partly on Kosygin's 1965 measures and partly on the Hungarian practices he had observed since 1956. Factory managers were given more power to make decisions, including those concerning production and the use of profits. Surplus labour would be reabsorbed elsewhere. Wages and bonuses were more closely linked to production and sales. More emphasis was put on prices. Competition was promoted by breaking up some large monopolies into smaller units.

Andropov's message was stark: 'There are no miracles', and 'Without discipline, we cannot advance quickly.' *Pravda*, an official press organ of the Party, was used to attack failings in the economic system, and suggested that sectors such as transport must show greater productivity if they were to receive substantial state funding. In November 1982, in a forceful speech to the Central Committee, Andropov outlined a series of problems which needed addressing:

- 'lack of coordination in the development of raw materials'
- managers of enterprises who talked about reform but did nothing
- 'the force of inertia and old habits' still prevalent at work
- the need to 'accelerate work to improve the entire sphere of economic management' and tackle 'poor work, sluggishness and irresponsibility'
- the need for 'a more resolute struggle against all violations of Party, State and labour discipline'.

In November 1983 Andropov told a conference of Party veterans: 'We have not been vigorous enough … We not infrequently resort to half measures and have been unable to overcome accumulated inertia … We must now make up for what we have lost.'

Andropov: Cold War warrior

Fig. 2 *Andropov celebrating the sixtieth anniversary of the USSR*

Andropov failed to improve relations with the USA, despite dropping hints that the Soviets wanted a resumption of détente. He declared that the USSR would not disarm unilaterally, declaring 'We are not a naive people.' Progress was unlikely while US President Reagan was pursuing his '**Star Wars**' policy. Proposals to reduce the number of Soviet missiles in Europe foundered, partly because NATO deployed its own missiles in Europe. The Afghanistan war was still in progress. Andropov made his own blunders. In September 1983 he sent Gromyko to West Germany where he publicly supported the left-wing Social Democrats in the German general election. This only strengthened the vote of their more conservative opponents. At the end of August 1983 there was a major crisis when Soviet warplanes shot down Korean Airlines passenger plane KAL 007, killing 269 passengers, including several Americans. The plane was en route from New York to Seoul, but was 700 kilometres off course, flying in Soviet air space over a militarily sensitive area, and ignoring several warnings to turn back. There were unconfirmed rumours that the plane was engaged in spying. Andropov was on holiday at the time, and the decision to shoot down the plane was taken at the local military level, in accordance with prescribed procedures. Nevertheless there was a huge international outcry, partly because the Kremlin first denied knowledge of the event, then denied shooting down the plane, and only later finally admitted it.

The impact of Andropov's policies

Andropov's regime showed little evidence of being able successfully to address the problems existing at the time of Brezhnev's death:

- Brezhnev's policy of détente lay in tatters, and Andropov had not made a positive mark on Soviet foreign policy. However, because his policy included the strengthening of the Soviet defence base, Andropov was supported by the defence lobby, led by Ustinov and Romanov, the latter in charge of heavy industry.
- Andropov, for all the talk of discipline and efficiency, continued to face resistance to proposed changes from those entrenched in the old ways.

Key terms

Star Wars: one of US President Reagan's pet projects, a policy designed to put defensive nuclear weapons in space. The theory was that these weapons would be able to shoot down any enemy missiles fired at the USA before they could do any damage. This policy was strongly opposed by the USSR: there were doubts about its viability and its costs, and above all it was seen as very provocative by the USSR and calculated to ruin chances of détente.

Ominously, in August 1983 the head of Gosplan, who had been in post for 20 years, told Andropov that any economic experiments must proceed 'cautiously'.

■ The efforts at reform were not a systematic programme. There was much exhortation and damage limitation, with the police rounding up 'slackers', but nothing with the scope or imagination which would have rectified underlying economic problems, even without the apathy and resistance that Andropov encountered. There was an improvement in industrial production in 1983, which saw the highest productivity since 1978. However, the impetus for reform then slackened.

■ Andropov himself was not optimistic. In 1983 he consciously backtracked on the optimism of his predecessors, writing that the USSR was only at the beginning of the stage of Developed Socialism.

■ Andropov was in power for too short a time, and he was seriously ill for much of that time, so there was little opportunity to make an impact.

■ Andropov sometimes spoke of the need for the Soviet people to learn lessons from beyond their borders. However, when one scratched beneath the surface, Andropov revealed some old-fashioned Soviet attitudes. He practised strict limits on expression of opinions at home. When a group of young Communist intellectuals, labelled the 'Russian New Left', argued that the USSR had acquired a new ruling class, they were arrested. There was still harassment of dissidents, Jewish emigration was halted, and direct telephone dialling facilities with the outside world were stopped. Andropov also continued the Brezhnev line of trying to 'fuse' different national groups into one Soviet people, although he did admit that the previous policy towards the nationalities had included 'mistakes'.

Andropov: an assessment

Andropov was trying to clean up the Soviet system, not overturn it. He changed nothing fundamental. However, he did at least encourage some discussion of future reform, and allowed minutes of important Party meetings to be published for the first time. He offered some hope, and promoted some able politicians such as Gorbachev, with newer ideas and more time in which to deliver them. Andropov had refused to develop a personality cult, remaining a private person. He was more aware than previous Soviet leaders of the true state of affairs in the USSR.

Andropov was too ill to attend the traditional Red Square parade in November 1983, although his portrait was carried on floats. What was described as a cold was in fact a serious heart and kidney condition. From his hospital bed, he continued to make changes in administrative personnel and called for reform. However, he fell into a coma and died in February 1984 after less than 15 months in office.

■ The leadership of Konstantin Chernenko

Even before Andropov's death the succession was being discussed. Gorbachev and Romanov were canvassed as representatives of the younger generation. Some Soviet officials claimed privately that Andropov had nominated Gorbachev as his successor. Gorbachev was already influential, having been given the task of managing internal Party elections late in 1983. However, there were still sufficient Brezhnevites

Activity

Revision exercise

How successfully did Andropov address the USSR's problems?

for their claims not to be ignored, and Brezhnev's favourite, Konstantin Chernenko, was appointed general secretary, although the election was contested. Gorbachev had formed a temporary alliance with Romanov, a protégé of Kosygin and Suslov. It is possible that Gorbachev expected the leadership, but time was on his side, and he may have agreed to Chernenko's elevation in return for an understanding that he would eventually succeed the 72-year-old man, the oldest person ever to become Soviet leader.

Key profile

Konstantin Chernenko

Chernenko (1911–85) was born in a Siberian village in 1911. He had served as a border guard on the Chinese border and later become a regional party secretary. During Stalin's Terror, in 1937 Chernenko was employed in the Dnepropetrovsk NKVD (the forerunner of the KGB). It was then that he began his association with Brezhnev. His wartime record was modest, consisting mainly of supervising evacuees and labour camps in Siberia. In 1948 Brezhnev put him in charge of propaganda in Moldavia. When Brezhnev went to Moscow in 1956, he took Chernenko with him to work in the propaganda section of the Central Committee. He later ran Brezhnev's private office and became his minder and his holiday and drinking companion. They were good friends, giving rise to a Soviet joke that 'Brezhnev has been dead for quite some time, but Chernenko hasn't told him.'

Fig. 3 *General Secretary Konstantin Chernenko*

A closer look

Joking about Chernenko

Many Soviet citizens found Chernenko's rule to be too depressing even to joke about. One of the few Soviet jokes about Chernenko went like this:

When Chernenko died he went to hell, where Lucifer gave him a choice of three punishments.

Chernenko was taken to one area where Lenin was perpetually drowning in a massive waterfall.

'Would you like this punishment?' asked Lucifer.

'No, No!' exclaimed Chernenko, 'Show me something else.'

Lucifer took him to another area where Stalin was perpetually burning on a bed of hot coals. Chernenko was horrified.

Lucifer then took him to a meadow where birds were singing, the sky was blue and flowers blossomed. In the middle of the meadow was a large vat in which Khrushchev, Brezhnev and Andropov were standing waist deep in excrement.

Chernenko thought, 'This looks quite tolerable,' and joined his former comrades in the vat.

Soon afterwards another devil appeared and announced, 'That's it! Your annual five-minute break is over! Everybody back to the handstand!'

The relative lack of Soviet jokes about Chernenko compared to other leaders partly reflects his low profile and the fact that he was not an obvious choice as leader, except that he had been a close and loyal associate of Brezhnev. He had acted as Andropov's deputy and his power had risen as Andropov's health declined, despite the fact that he had little independent support in his own right. The older generation was not concerned with Chernenko's lack of charisma or profile: he was a guarantee that the cautious, conservative approach, for which many Party loyalists still yearned, would continue, even though Chernenko's term as leader could not realistically be expected to be lengthy given his age and poor health.

Chernenko quickly gathered the titles of general secretary, president and commander-in-chief. Yet his time as leader, barely a year, was the shortest of any Soviet leader. Chernenko's handicaps were obvious from the start. The old guard of politicians who surrounded him was not particularly enthusiastic about him personally, but had supported him only as a symbol of stability. His emphysema, a debilitating lung disease, left him breathless and prone to stumble during speeches. When he became leader a Soviet joke ran: 'Why does Chernenko have three microphones in front of him when he makes a speech? Two of them supply him with oxygen.' He often missed out sections of his prepared speeches and could be inaudible. He certainly contrasted poorly with Gorbachev's confident public appearances. The Soviet propaganda machine struggled but failed to build up Chernenko's image, and Soviets joked that 'You can't have a personality cult without a personality.'

Chernenko's policies

Chernenko's acceptance speech to the Central Committee as leader reinforced his policy of caution. He talked about the need to avoid mistakes and 'wishful thinking', and repeated the proverb, 'Look before you leap.' During his 13 months in office only four new ministers were appointed.

Chernenko did not really have a coherent policy, although he presided over a Party Commission which was considering a new programme for the Party. He held to the view that peaceful competition would eventually lead to the triumph of socialism over capitalism, but wisely, unlike Khrushchev, he did not put a date on the coming victory. He dropped

Andropov's anti-corruption campaign, and the Party was reassured that its privileges would not be eroded. He emphasised the importance of educational advances, tightened censorship and continued Andropov's hard line against dissidents. He was reasonably conciliatory on the nationalities issue, emphasising that Republican concerns should be acknowledged. In agriculture, Chernenko reverted to a policy similar to Khrushchev's of increasing the amount of land under cultivation. This was to be done principally by irrigation and drainage schemes which involved redirecting the flow of some Siberian rivers towards the Caucasus and Central Asia. Gorbachev opposed this policy, preferring to concentrate on intensifying production on existing land. Chernenko continued parts of Andropov's industrial reform programme, including a scheme whereby some workers were paid by results. However, there were no fundamental industrial reforms.

In foreign policy Chernenko sought to resurrect détente. This was difficult, given the American stand on Star Wars, continuing Soviet intervention in Afghanistan, and a Soviet boycott of the Los Angeles Olympics in retaliation for the US boycott of the 1980 Moscow Olympics. There was also strong disagreement within the Soviet establishment about détente. It was opposed by the military, which feared for its influence and had a low opinion of Chernenko. This was because in 1981 and 1982 he had denied the possibility of a winnable nuclear war and had suggested that more priority be given to agriculture and consumer goods than to military production.

Activity

Thinking point

Was Chernenko any more than a stop-gap leader?

Chernenko was in hospital for two months from August 1984, seriously ill. Gorbachev and Ustinov ran what became effectively a collective government. Gorbachev ran economic affairs, while Ustinov and Gromyko managed foreign affairs. Despite their experience, a crisis developed between the military and political leaderships. The military disagreed with Ustinov's defence policy, and wanted high-technology, expensive missiles. The Chief of Staff and Deputy Minister of Defence, Marshal Ogarkov, was sacked. This was partly for contradicting the official Kremlin line in declaring that the USSR could win a nuclear war, but mostly for being ambitious. This raised old Soviet fears about military men with with dictatorial ambitions. Ogarkov's fall was a boost for Gorbachev. He was already advocating spending less money on defence and more on consumer goods, whereas his rival Romanov supported high levels of defence spending and a hard-line approach towards the West. Nevertheless, the hard-liners still had considerable influence, shown by a 12 per cent increase in the defence budget.

Did you know?

Fear of strong military personalities was a persistent theme in Soviet history. It went back to distrust of Trotsky as leader of the Red Army after 1917, and Stalin's jealousy and suspicion of the able Marshal Zhukov.

By early 1985 Chernenko's health was failing fast and the Politburo was preoccupied yet again with the succession, a fact unusually made public by *Pravda*. Chernenko died on 10 March 1985. The Politburo, which had shrunk to 10 members, was almost evenly split between the old guard and the more youthful reformers. Gromyko, seconded by KGB chief Victor Chebrikov, supported the reforming faction, represented by the relatively youthful Gorbachev. This was probably crucial in securing Gorbachev's elevation. It led to one of the first Soviet jokes about Gorbachev: 'What support does Gorbachev have in the Kremlin? None – he walks unaided.'

The rise of Mikhail Gorbachev

Gorbachev was born in 1931 to a comfortably off peasant family in the fertile Stavropol province of the North Caucasus. One of his grandfathers had founded a collective farm and was imprisoned during Stalin's Terror.

Gorbachev's father was wounded fighting for the Red Army in the Second World War. His son stayed in the village during its occupation by the Nazis.

After the war, instead of becoming a farmer, Gorbachev went to study law at Moscow University. He had several school medals and an impeccable peasant-worker background. He met his wife Raisa at university, at a ballroom dancing class. Gorbachev joined the Party, enjoyed studying and worked on the summer harvest back on his family's collective. He was known as a committed student. It was later claimed that he campaigned for Jews to be expelled from the university.

Gorbachev graduated in 1955 and worked in the public prosecutor's office in Stavropol, which opened his eyes to the corruption prevalent at the lower level of the Party. He worked for the Komsomol and began to work his way up through the Party, while completing a second degree in agronomy in 1967. In 1970 he became Party chief for Stavropol, with a reputation for honesty, hard work and discipline. Now, as a member of the elite, he met leading figures like Suslov and Andropov, who visited Stavropol to be treated for a kidney complaint. Andropov found Gorbachev to be an intelligent companion and got him appointed in 1988 as general committee secretary for agriculture, based in Moscow. At 47 Gorbachev was the youngest member of the leadership and was a full member of the Politburo by 1980. This was remarkably rapid progress during the Brezhnev era. When he became leader, a member of the Central Committee compared Gorbachev favourably with his three predecessors: 'After one leader who was half dead, another who was half alive, and another who could hardly speak, the youthful, energetic Gorbachev was very welcome.'

Gorbachev the cautious reformer

Gorbachev was too young to have been involved in Stalin's political manoeuvres. His rise was due partly to his skill in exploiting the political system, and partly due to the fact that he had powerful patrons looking for new blood to address key issues, especially economic ones, in the political flux following Brezhnev's death.

There was a tendency later in the West to depict Gorbachev as a radical reformer from his early days, but the reality was very different. His political apprenticeship, apart from his rapid rise, was orthodox – otherwise he would not have risen through the system. Gorbachev was not a liberal, and held orthodox opinions even in the later Brezhnev period, for example in his support for the Afghanistan war and the regime's stance on dissidents. His views were not markedly different from those of his colleagues. Gorbachev echoed Khrushchev and Andropov in their desire to make the Soviet system more efficient. He had personal experience from Stavropol of how encouraging initiative by paying workers by results and giving them a share of profits could be successful – despite the fact that such initiatives had been discredited in some people's eyes by a series of bad harvests. Gorbachev wanted to catch up with the West economically and technologically, not introduce Western-style democracy or capitalism.

When he accepted the leadership, Gorbachev told the Central Committee that the USSR would make a 'decisive turn' in economic progress only through a 'perfection of the economic system'. When criticised in London for the Soviet record on human rights, he retorted: 'You govern your society and leave us to govern ours.' In his funeral speech for Chernenko in Red Square, Gorbachev declared that the USSR

Did you know?

Gorbachev was the first Soviet leader to be born after the 1917 Revolution and to be brought up entirely in the Soviet era.

Did you know?

Gorbachev impressed foreign politicians who had been used to difficult relationships with Soviet leaders. After discussions with Gorbachev, the British Prime Minister margaret Thatcher declared, 'This is a man I can do business with.'

would prevail by 'force of example in all fields of life' while the regime must crack down on 'anything which contradicts socialist norms'. It was the language of cautious change, to be carried out only within carefully defined boundaries.

Problems facing the USSR by the 1980s

The USSR faced many problems by the 1980s. On becoming leader Gorbachev faced major issues covering both domestic and foreign policy, issues which were linked. The most pressing problem was probably the economy. Years of declining economic growth and economic stagnation could not be ignored. However, to restructure the economy radically was beyond the imagination of most politicians. The idea of the State-controlled, socialist economy was sacrosanct: after all, it was one of the features that differentiated the USSR from capitalist states. The economy had seen great achievements in the past. Moreover, it was closely bound up with the political structure. Any major restructuring of the economy would have major political implications, because the Party controlled the economy just like all other aspects of Soviet life. There would be opposition to change both from those ideologically opposed to it, and from those who wanted to preserve the existing system because it provided them with power and privileges. To encourage people to take risks, to innovate and to be accountable was a difficult thing to do in a society in which people were used to being told what to do by the Party and the State.

The USSR was also struggling to maintain its superpower status. Gorbachev would have to deal with the drain on resources caused by attempts to maintain parity and influence with the USA. He had to deal with difficulties caused by negotiations over détente and arms control, and the USSR was internationally unpopular because of its involvement in Afghanistan, an unsuccessful war which was another drain on resources. There were also social problems as in any modern society, and potentially difficult issues in relations between some of the Soviet Republics.

Gorbachev hoped to address these problems within existing structures. It would be a major challenge, but the alternative would have been to sit back and possibly allow the USSR to drift into terminal decline.

Fig. 4 *Mikhail Gorbachev, the last Soviet leader*

Summary questions

1. How successfully did Andropov and Chernenko deal with the economic legacy left by Brezhnev?

2. Why was Gorbachev promoted to the Soviet leadership?

9

Gorbachev's reforms

Fig. 1 *Gorbachev explaining his reforms to Russian workers near Moscow*

In this chapter you will learn about:

- Gorbachev's aims on becoming leader of the USSR
- the ideas behind glasnost and perestroika, opposition to them and the effects of these policies.

Q: What is a Soviet historian?

A: Someone who can accurately predict the past.

1

Soviet joke

The motives for, and impact of, Gorbachev's reforms

Gorbachev's aims

Gorbachev did not become leader in 1985 with a radical agenda. He recognised the need for economic reform in particular, but believed that reforms should take place within the existing political and social system, led as always by the Communist Party. He had, in effect, been running the USSR for three months before Chernenko's death and the transition to the leadership was therefore fairly smooth. However, like all Soviet leaders Gorbachev had to consolidate his position as general secretary. He had enemies in the Politburo, particularly his rival Grigori Romanov and Victor Grishkin, the 70-year-old Moscow Party boss. He also had allies, notably Gromyko, who asserted that 'Mikhail Sergeevich has a nice smile, but he also has iron teeth.' To ensure his position, Gorbachev needed to promote his own supporters. Several government ministers were replaced by their deputies.

Three of Gorbachev's main supporters were promoted to full Politburo membership in April 1985: Yegor Ligachev, who was given responsibility for ideology, Nikolai Ryzhkov (made prime minister in September 1985) and Victor Chebrikov, head of the KGB. Ligachev was soon seen as an obstacle to reform and was sacked. Alexander Yakovlev was brought into the Politburo in 1987.

Key profile

Alexander Yakovlev

Alexander Yakovlev (1923–2005) had foreign experience, having been ambassador to Canada. His significance was that he was a committed reformer, the most liberal member of the Politburo, and seen as the father of glasnost and the theorist behind perestroika. He worked closely with Gorbachev and was his senior adviser by 1991.

Local Party meetings were held at which some officials were criticised for corruption and inefficiency, while at senior level Gorbachev's rival Romanov was sacked in July 1985. Towards the end of 1985 Grishkin was replaced as head of the Moscow Party by Boris Yeltsin. Other promotions were unexpected. Gromyko agreed to retire after 30 years as foreign minister. His replacement as foreign minister was Eduard Shevardnadze.

Key profile

Eduard Shevardnadze

Shevardnadze (1928–) was relatively unknown outside his native Georgia, where he had made his name by attacking widespread corruption in the local Party organisation. He was a strong supporter of Gorbachev but his appointment as foreign minister was a surprise because he had no diplomatic experience. He stayed loyal to Gorbachev until after the break-up of the USSR in 1991 when he became head of state of the independent Georgia.

Gorbachev announced that the Party leadership and presidency would no longer be combined, while he would concentrate on the Party and the economy. By 1987 he had the support of three-quarters of the Politburo, and he also made new military appointments to strengthen his ties with the services. New diplomatic appointments abroad were made.

The impact of these changes was dramatic. Between 1986 and 1989 all 14 Republican first secretaries were replaced, along with two-thirds of all secretaries of Party organisations from regional up to Republican level. This could be a sensitive process. Kazakhs rioted in 1986 when the Kazakh Party leader was replaced by a Russian. Seventy per cent of Party

Key chronology
Gorbachev to Yeltsin

1985 Gorbachev elected general secretary
Ryzhkov becomes prime minister

1986 Perestroika and glasnost adopted as Party policy
Chernobyl nuclear power station disaster
Yeltsin elected to the Politburo

1987 Supreme Soviet approves the restructuring of the national economy
Law on State Enterprises passed

1988 Troop withdrawals from Afghanistan begin
Law on Cooperatives
Rehabilitation of some of Stalin's prominent purge victims

1989 Cuts in military budget announced
Elections to the congress of People's Deputies
Gorbachev elected chairman of the USSR Supreme Soviet

1990 The Soviet Communist Party issues new policies
Elections in Russia and some of the Republics
Law on property passed, legally allowing private ownership
Congress appoints Gorbachev as USSR president

1991 Yeltsin elected president of Russia

officials at district and city level were replaced. Of Gorbachev's Central Committee 52 per cent were new and often inexperienced. Overall, by 1991, the leadership was considerably younger and better educated than in Brezhnev's day.

■ **Key profile**

Grigori Romanov

Romanov (1923–2008) ran the Leningrad Party organisation after 1970. He was Gorbachev's early rival, supporting Chernenko in 1984. He was sacked in July 1985 and his reputation trashed. Described as an unsavoury character, his orgies and alcoholism were highlighted (in contrast to Gorbachev the teetotaller). Stories were spread about his having borrowed a priceless Catherine the Great dinner service from the Leningrad Hermitage Museum to celebrate his daughter's wedding, after which he smashed the dishes in the customary Russian peasant fashion. He also created a scandal by entertaining his mistress, a Leningrad pop singer, in a box at the opera reserved for Politburo members.

Most historians agree that had Romanov, a tough but unimaginative administrator, succeeded to the leadership instead of Gorbachev, events in Soviet history after 1985 might have taken a different turn.

Gorbachev's leadership style

Gorbachev's style as leader was very different from that of his predecessors. He was confident and self-assured, yet modest, when in public or appearing on television.

■ **Did you know?**

Gorbachev had some similarities with Khrushchev. Both enjoyed talking to ordinary people, and adopted the Western political fashion of 'walkabouts'. Gorbachev knew how to stage-manage events such as visiting the house of a working-class couple, as well as visiting hospitals, schools and factories. These events were given blanket coverage in the media.

Fig. 2 *Gorbachev and his wife Raisa on a walkabout*

Gorbachev was skilled enough to appear relaxed and spontaneous, listening to people and promising to take their views into account. He made his ministers and officials adopt a high profile too, appearing in the media and even answering consumers' complaints. It was a style of leadership not seen before in the USSR.

Gorbachev made frankness an asset. He declared that without this, the USSR's problems would never be resolved. He denied that 'Stalinism' was a problem: he told a foreign journalist that this was 'a notion made up by opponents of Communism and used on a large scale to smear the Soviet Union and Socialism as a whole'. However, Gorbachev did acknowledge that the Brezhnev period had been one of missed opportunities for change, when decisions that should have been made were put off. He described it as a time of 'a curious psychology: how to change things without really changing anything'.

Activity

Revision task

Compare Gorbachev's leadership style with that of Khrushchev and Brezhnev.

Glasnost and perestroika and their effects

Perestroika and opposition to it

The word 'perestroika' is usually translated as 'restructuring' and associated with the economy. It was Gorbachev's attempt to address problems in the USSR, but it provoked a range of reactions, depending on the position of various interest groups in the country.

Those most resistant to change were members of the established Party elite, which dominated government ministries and planning agencies. They were wary of substantial change because it was the system they had been brought up to believe in, and/or because they benefited from the system as a result of the privileges and rank they enjoyed. The same considerations influenced some members of the lower ranks of the Party and administration. Another overlapping group of doubters included many in the defence and heavy industry sectors, sometimes labelled the **military-industrial complex**. Not all interest groups were necessarily resistant to all change, but change to them meant preferably streamlining the existing system to make it more efficient, not radically changing priorities.

Those more receptive to change included intellectuals, scientists, technologists and various specialists. These groups had been increasing in size and, without becoming dissidents, had already begun to show impatience with the old ways. They resented the fact that they had no political influence without making a career in the Party, which they did not necessarily want to pursue; they resented restrictions on travel and censorship; and they wanted more freedom to make contacts abroad, where they knew that there were more opportunities to make money, share ideas, further their careers and take up other opportunities. These people were less concerned with Party ideology than in the past, and more concerned with the restrictions imposed on their lives.

Other groups did not necessarily support or oppose perestroika, because depending on individual circumstances, motivation or ability to adapt, there were possibilities of both gain and loss from radical change. Many people had increasingly benefited from the existing system over the

Exploring the detail

Raisa Gorbachev

Gorbachev was considerably aided by his glamorous wife, Raisa, who unlike other 'First Wives' was often at Gorbachev's side, and was noted for her style and her intelligence. Gorbachev claimed that he frequently consulted her about political decisions. Their behaviour made them personalities outside the USSR in a way that had been impossible to contemplate before, although in the long run it did not make Gorbachev popular within the USSR.

Key terms

Military-industrial complex: a very influential group of personnel in the military and heavy industry which commanded a large chunk of the country's resources. They had their own agenda, and had in the past resisted attempts to divert resources elsewhere. For example, some military chiefs opposed disarmament because it would mean a reduction in the army and therefore their own personal empire.

Did you know?

For most of the existence of the USSR, very few Soviet citizens were allowed to visit foreign countries outside the Soviet bloc, unless they were trusted Party members who were unlikely to defect.

previous generation or more: life had become easier, with better (and free) education and social services. The cost of living, including the prices of goods, transport, rents, basic utilities and taxes, was kept low, being heavily subsidised by the State. There was also full employment. People had not known any other system, and there was no certainty that the basic but guaranteed benefits would continue if, for example, the USSR adopted a capitalist system which exposed society to competition. That might mean gains for some but also the possibility of losses – in other words, there would be greater disparities between people in the quality of life. There were those, including some enterprise managers and administrators, who wanted to take those risks, but there were others who preferred the flawed but comfortable system they knew. For this reason, there was both opposition to perestroika and simply apathy. These were dilemmas for any reformers who wanted to make changes with the consent and cooperation of the population. It would be a challenge for even the most far-sighted politician, and it was far from clear in 1985 that Gorbachev had anything approaching a clear vision for the future, let alone a concrete plan.

Perestroika can broadly be divided into four periods:

1 1985 to the end of 1986 or 1987: the period of acceleration (*uskoreniye*)

2 1987–88 to the spring of 1989: radical reform from above

3 1989 to 1990–91: the period of attempted market-based reform and reaction

4 1990–91 to December 1991: the period of indecision, crisis and the break-up of the USSR.

There were both economic and political measures in each of these periods.

Phase 1: acceleration, 1985 to 1986–87

The term 'acceleration' was not new. It had been used since 1983. Gorbachev in this period believed that the problems in the Soviet economy could be addressed not by radical change but by 'accelerated growth', making the existing system work better. Although experts knew that the economy was in a bad way, Gorbachev believed over-optimistic analyses that national income was growing at 3 per cent a year, when the reality (which was recognised by some analysts) was probably a third of that. The measures adopted were little different from those tried in Andropov's day: calls for more 'discipline'; exhorting the administration to work more 'efficiently'; and using existing planning mechanisms, notably the Twelfth Five-year Plan. This Plan set targets considerably higher than those in the 1981–85 Plan, even though few of the latter's targets had been achieved. Workers were not happy about being told to work harder for the same wages. Gorbachev's own contribution was probably disastrous. The Plan was still being formulated when he came to power, and he had the Plan targets greatly increased, against advice. He sent the draft plan back to Gosplan three times before he accepted it. Gorbachev seemed to think that this would force people to work harder. However, it simply put more pressure on the economy, there was no breathing space, there were insufficient resources to meet the targets, and many people simply did not comply or lied as they had done in the past to make it appear that the targets were being met. For the next few years several economists argued unsuccessfully that the Plan needed to be amended or even scrapped.

Fig. 3 *A Soviet postage stamp celebrating the advance of perestroika, democratisation and glasnost, 1988*

Did you know?

'Discipline' sometimes meant something very basic such as the police rounding up people in the streets whom they thought should be at work, or opening alcohol shops later in the day to reduce drunkenness.

Nevertheless there were some innovations:

- The Law on Individual Labour Activity (passed in November 1986) allowed for some private enterprise in the service sector. It proved largely ineffective because of bureaucratic obstructionism, reflecting continued suspicion of private enterprise and the profit motive, always equated with 'unearned income'. This was considered antisocial and anti-socialist.

- The Politburo devoted a whole session in April 1985 to discussing the problem of alcoholism. A decree in May closed down distilleries. Gorbachev hoped that people would drink wine and beer instead. The results were disastrous. People turned to illegal home-brewing of spirits, sugar supplies ran out, and if anything alcoholism increased. No other measure made Gorbachev more unpopular. He became known as the 'lemonade' or 'mineral water' leader. The State also lost a lot of revenue, which Gorbachev did not appear to have anticipated when he began his moral crusade.

- There was a renewed campaign against corruption. Some leading ministers and officials were arrested for a range of offences such as illegally purchasing materials abroad. Some of those prosecuted were leading figures in the Republican administrations and resentment at Gorbachev's campaign helped to fuel opposition to Moscow from these Republics.

- Gorbachev wanted to regroup over 60 industrial ministries and state committees into a maximum of seven 'superministries'. In his first year he created three of these, in agriculture, machine-building and energy. He recognised the need for improvements in quality if the USSR were to compete in the world economy. Therefore he proposed more investment in high-technology engineering products as well as in agriculture.

- A Law on Joint Enterprises with foreign companies was agreed in December 1986. It did not work well, because foreign companies operated on the profit motive, unlike Soviet enterprises. There was confusion and corruption: joint investment funds were often pocketed by corrupt managers.

Did you know?

Illegal home brewing of spirits, especially vodka, took place on a massive scale in the USSR, and was responsible for widespread drunkenness, illness and a death rate which, in contrast to the Western world, was actually rising.

Gorbachev was gradually made aware that the initial measures of perestroika were having little effect. He claimed he was receiving bad economic advice, and following tours of the Republics he found that middle-ranking bureaucrats were obstructing change. There were complaints from ordinary people about continued shortages, especially of food, and higher prices. Government measures did not address the problems effectively. A law allowing for workers' collectives and elected managers in enterprises simply created confusion. How could managers use initiative in a system of central planning and allocation of resources? How could one be sure that workers would elect the best manager, rather than someone who sought popularity with the workers?

It appeared that Gorbachev and colleagues like Prime Minister Ryzhkov did not really understand economics. At this stage Gorbachev resorted to criticising administrators and officials. However, they were only part of the problem.

The results of acceleration

The results of acceleration were not promising. Gorbachev was still operating within the traditional framework. The Twelfth Five-year Plan, 1986–90, had the extraordinarily ambitious target of doubling national income by 2000, with the bulk of new investment being made in European Russia. The reality was very different. Ryzhkov reported to the Politburo in April 1987 that economic growth had declined. A fall in the price of oil had contributed to a huge trade deficit with the West. Key sectors like coal, oil and gas were running at a loss. The USSR was relying increasingly on grain imports and foreign loans. The Soviet budget deficit soared from about 3 per cent of national income in 1985 to 14 per cent by 1989. Money was increasingly worthless. Neither Ryzhkov nor Gorbachev really understood economics or could explain what perestroika actually meant.

Under the Five-year Plan, much of the new investment went into energy and agriculture, not machine-building as had been intended. This was because the former sectors were controlled by powerful ministries which used their influence to get favourable treatment. The term 'acceleration' was not used after 1988 and the government decided to make consumer goods its priority. But there was no restructuring of the economy, which consequently was not reinvigorated. Persistent imbalances and shortages helped to create popular dissatisfaction and largely ruined Gorbachev's credibility as a reformer.

Glasnost: support and opposition

The early reform measures went hand in hand with what became known as 'glasnost'. Often translated in the West as 'openness', in Russian the word also means 'publicity'. Gorbachev did not advocate complete freedom, particularly for the media. He wanted a greater willingness to explain publicly the reasoning behind decisions. This was an aspiration, not a concrete plan for reform. Gorbachev's motive for glasnost was primarily that he believed there could be no effective reform unless there was an unambiguous admission first that changes were necessary. He believed that such admissions would actually strengthen rather than weaken the regime. It should be the sign of a mature, confident people, or as *Pravda* declared, 'Timely and frank release of information is evidence of trust in people, respect for their intelligence and feelings, and their ability to assess events.' Such publicity would also promote awareness of incompetence and corruption, and assist Gorbachev's attempts to root them out.

Glasnost got off to a bad beginning because the regime dealt badly with the Chernobyl disaster, which got widespread publicity throughout the world.

■ **Exploring the detail**

The Chernobyl disaster

In April 1986 one of the nuclear reactors at Chernobyl atomic power station in Ukraine exploded. The regime was slow to react properly, and the local inhabitants were not evacuated from the area for three days, while the Soviet media was silent. Life went on much as normal until people were evacuated from a wider area a week later. Gorbachev did not appear on television and talk about the disaster until 14 May, more than two weeks after the explosion. Only in November was the damaged reactor finally sealed, after thousands of lives had been lost, including many of the servicemen and women involved in the rescue operation. The disaster was a blow to Soviet claims of progress, but it also showed the limitations of glasnost. The USSR was still operating a policy whereby such disasters, along with plane and train accidents, environmental accidents and casualties of the space programme were treated as taboo subjects.

Fig. 4 *Chernobyl, 1986: the destroyed nuclear reactor unit and the steel and concrete protection mantle put around it*

Activity

Challenge your thinking

Why were perestroika and glasnost such radical policies in the USSR?

One of the leading forces in promoting glasnost was Aleksander Yakovlev, who believed that perestroika could not succeed without it. He was responsible for the media, which was given considerable freedom. There was too much freedom as far as Gorbachev was concerned, because he still held to his socialist principles. Among the positive results of Yakovlev's policy was religious toleration: over 400,000 churches, mosques and synagogues were returned to religious use. There was also more rehabilitation of Stalin's victims.

The media did not have complete freedom: for example, publishers were still supposed to monitor output. However, it became possible to publish previously forbidden works such as Pasternak's *Doctor Zhivago*, *Lolita* by the émigré Nabokov and the works of the Marquis de Sade. Controversial political works such as Hitler's *Mein Kampf* and George Orwell's *1984* were published in the USSR for the first time. Films appeared dealing with social issues. Because restrictions on movement were relaxed, some former émigrés like the ballet dancer Mikhail Baryshnikov returned home. Interviews with Western politicians were shown on Soviet television. The press began to debate previously taboo subjects such as suicide, abortion and crime.

Did you know?

Despite extensive criticism of Stalin since the 1950s, criticism of the revered Lenin was virtually taboo until after the break-up of the USSR.

Did you know?

Until the final years of the USSR, social problems such as abortion and drug use were rarely even acknowledged publicly in the USSR, because they were officially regarded as vices of capitalist Western societies.

Fig. 5 *A Soviet cartoon about glasnost: 'We are keeping in step with the times – we are developing glasnost.' The posters read – 'Our miscalculations' – 'Defects' – 'Our shortages' – 'Our slackers'*

КРОКОДИЛ
№ 9 ● март ● 1987
ISSN 0130-2671

Glasnost provoked a mixed response:

- Intellectuals were probably the most enthusiastic supporters, because they had more, if not total, freedom than before.

- Conservatives and some Party members were among the fiercest critics, since they were used to a controlled society and believed that 'publicity' would simply invite social instability, the very thing that the Brezhnev regime had sought to avoid; also, because it proved difficult to confine political criticism just to Stalin and Brezhnev, there was less respect for the Party and its claim to legitimacy.

- The majority of people may have had mixed feelings, or none at all. They had more pressing concerns in their daily lives, such as the queues for basic necessities. Many must have found it difficult to believe that official attitudes would change overnight in a society where frank and open exchanges of views were rare.

Phase 2: Radical reform from above, 1987–88 to 1989

Reformers in the Party came to realise that tinkering with the system was not enough. As far as the reformers were concerned, the economy

Exploring the detail

The controversy about glasnost

The debate about glasnost would not go away. In March 1988 a schoolteacher, Nina Andreeva, published a newspaper article criticising attacks on former Soviet heroes like Stalin. The article was widely publicised and there was a debate in the media. Then it emerged that this incident had been organised high up in the Party by Ligachev. *Pravda* then published a rebuttal, written partly by Yakovlev. What the incident showed was not just that glasnost produced a range of responses among ordinary people, but that there were also firm disagreements about glasnost at a high level in the government.

was still too centralised, and there was a lack of accountability and meaningful reform. Calls for more discipline and a crackdown on corruption were not enough. However, there was no unanimity on how best to proceed. Gorbachev took from this the need for more popular participation and more accountability. This would require some political reform, although always under the guidance of the Party. In terms of the economy, this meant:

- reducing the power of the Party to interfere in the economy and transferring some powers from Moscow to the Republics and from the planners to factories and farms
- reducing the powers of the all-Union ministries
- a Law on State Enterprises, effective from January 1988, giving workers the chance to elect their managers and more personal incentives to improve production; enterprises had more control over their finances and decision-making, although ministries still had final control
- a new Law on **Cooperatives**, adopted in May 1988, which legalised private enterprises. Cooperatives, mostly in the service sector, were slow to develop, mainly because there were many regulations and much obstructionism. Furthermore, being outside the central planning system, these enterprises were starved of resources.

Once again, the economic results of these reforms were disappointing, so much so that by the end of 1988 there was widespread rationing of basic foodstuffs such as meat, potatoes and sugar. Even ration coupons did not guarantee the provision of goods. By 1990 levels of poverty were rising. Factories found it increasingly difficult to get what they needed from the State, and had to resort to barter with other enterprises.

Key terms

Cooperatives: small and medium-sized private businesses that could set their own wages and prices and sell directly to the Republic. In Soviet terms, this was a radical move.

Table 1 *Soviet economic growth, 1986–90* (percentage figures)

	1986–90	1986	1987	1988	1989	1990
National income produced	4.2	2.3	1.6	4.4	2.4	4.0
Industrial output	4.6	4.4	3.8	3.9	1.7	–1.2
Agricultural output	2.7	5.3	–0.6	1.7	1.3	–2.3

From Soviet sources

Activity

Individual exercise

Study the statistics in Table 1. What conclusions about the Soviet economy can you draw from them?

Phase 3: Market-based reform and reaction, 1989 to 1990–91

Economic activity was seriously affected by political changes taking place which undermined the unifying role of the Party throughout the political, economic and social system. The central planning authorities were still in place but found it increasingly difficult to assert any control. They were increasingly ignored, particularly as the Republics took measures for their own survival as nationalist tensions grew. Growing economic collapse led to major disturbances, beginning with a major coal miners' strike in the summer of 1989, repeated in 1990 and 1991. Other important groups like railway workers also struck.

Cross-reference

For developments in the Republics, see Chapter 10.

The Shatalin Plan

Shatalin and Grigory Yavlinsky were leading economists who rose to prominence under Gorbachev until he found their ideas too radical. They produced the Shatalin Plan. This was designed to carry out the transformation of the economy to a market-based structure in 500 days. The plan even recognised the importance of the black or second economy and stated that it should be legalised 'in the interests of everyone in the country'. The Plan was extremely ambitious, but it was sign of how desperate the economic situation was seen to be by many experts.

Phase 4: Indecision, crisis and the break-up of the USSR, 1990–91 to December 1991

By the summer of 1990 it was very clear that there was a major crisis in the economy. Most reformers now accepted that the tinkering was over, and only a rapid move to a full market-based economy could avoid catastrophe. Gorbachev now allied with Yeltsin to set up a team of reforming economists, headed by Stanislav Shatalin.

Gorbachev and Ryzhkov refused to accept the Shatalin Plan because it proposed decentralising economic power to the Republics, and in his usual fashion Gorbachev sought a compromise. The Shatalin Plan was rejected on 1 September 1990, and in its place the Supreme Soviet approved a compromise package in October. There would be a four-stage process over a 'relatively short time'. First, there would be the commercialisation of State enterprises, then a relaxation of State control over prices, while social security measures would protect vulnerable citizens. Then there would be changes to the housing market. Finally, the rouble would become a fully convertible currency. This was a necessary step if the USSR were to trade freely with other leading nations.

Predictably, this programme satisfied few people either on the left or the right. In January 1991 the Russian Supreme Soviet implemented a law permitting private property ownership. This effectively ended the planned economy, since private enterprises could now set up, while the Russian Federation began to take over oil, mining and gas concerns which were on its territory but were all-Union. This meant that the remaining economic base of the USSR was being destroyed.

Why the economy declined

Fig. 6 *Gorbachev with US President Reagan in the USA*

Many Soviet citizens blamed economic failure on sabotage, corruption, the siphoning off of State supplies and all the old scapegoats which had regularly surfaced ever since the early days of the USSR. Although the economy was already approaching crisis in 1985 when Gorbachev came to power, it was still working. It was perestroika which appeared to have made things worse, so that an ailing economy was approaching something close to economic collapse by 1991. Often it seemed as if the worst features of the old system were actually exaggerated, and attempted reforms just did not take root. There were a number of reasons for this.

The actual reforms were not carefully planned or thought through. The people who made the reforms, including Gorbachev, were not economists, and although they had the ideal of a modern, industrial, go-ahead society, they had no idea of how to get there. Gorbachev blamed bad advice, but when he did get advice from economists, he often ignored it. What Gorbachev wanted was probably impossible: the advantages of a market economy within the confines of a State-controlled economy.

Several administrative reorganisations created confusion and lack of coordination at several levels, and enabled enterprises to ignore demands of which they disapproved. The Party lost much of its power to force enterprises to conform. By 1990 there were several bodies responsible for economic policy but all competing with each other: Gosplan (controlled by the Council of Ministers); the State Commission on Economic Reform (set up in 1989); the USSR Supreme Soviet (which had to approve economic laws); Gorbachev's own presidential bodies, which included a socio-economic section; and individuals like Boris Yeltsin, whose Russian Federation came up with its own policies. Republican authorities increasingly blocked attempts by Moscow to implement central policies.

Arbitrary decisions were made which had drastic consequences. For example, in January 1991 Prime Minister Pavlov suddenly withdrew all high-denomination banknotes from circulation. People had too little time or opportunity to change notes and their savings became worthless overnight. Many enterprises found it difficult to deal with new laws and carried on as before, trying to meet old targets and relying on State subsidies. The government still controlled the supply of money and fixed most prices. Enterprises still lied about meeting targets and the authorities had no accurate picture of how the economy was actually doing. Enterprises which did exploit new freedoms sometimes made the situation worse by switching to making more profitable products, although these might not be what people needed. The economy was harmed by inflation and the collapse of the rouble. Many individuals and enterprises reverted to barter. The amount of revenue obtained by the Union government fell to 15 per cent of the planned level by 1991.

Production was affected by increasing unrest in the workforce. In 1990, Republics began to indulge in local protectionism, creating customs barriers against each other and disrupting trade. For example, Ukrainian mines could no longer get supplies of timber needed for pit props from Russia. The collapse of Communist regimes in Eastern Europe deprived the USSR of secure trading partners.

On top of all this, Gorbachev inherited costly projects, particularly the war in Afghanistan and a commitment to match US defence spending, and these costs could not be eliminated overnight.

The economy was neither one thing nor the other: the old central control mechanisms were being dismantled, yet the new market forces were still restricted. Many people by 1990–91 came to accept that a market economy of some sort was probably necessary. But it would have to be created in very disadvantageous circumstances. A true market economy would involve major changes such as allowing genuine competition, privatising land and property, regularising the money supply and having appropriate economic laws in place. This would mean a genuine economic revolution. Gorbachev did not have the inclination or real understanding for this, at least until it was too late. His economic policies were really a hotchpotch of initiatives which were not thought through, were characterised by indecision, often lacked support both from colleagues and from the public, and were being introduced at a time of major political instability which was leading to the break-up of the USSR's structure. It was scarcely surprising that the Soviet economy, in its final months, appeared to be heading into meltdown.

Gorbachev's beliefs

Apart from changes in personnel in key positions, in the early months of taking power Gorbachev made no major changes to the political system. This was not so much because he feared opposition, but because he did not see the need for such a change. Gorbachev believed firmly in the 1917 Revolution. He seemed to believe that this had established the principle of democratic rule, and that what had gone wrong since was excessive centralisation of power. This had reduced popular democracy, and combined with Stalin's repression and inertia under Brezhnev, had led to a 'deformed' socialism. This interpretation of Leninist rule as somehow democratic would not have been shared by many outside the USSR, but was the view of many would-be reformers in the USSR who accepted the need for reform, but still believed in the essence of the Party-led socialist state.

Political reform in the non-Russian Republics

Other Republics went for a single chamber, a directly elected Supreme Soviet, although they eventually changed to the central model. This model was to be very significant, because it gave the Republican Supreme Soviets direct control over both law-making and administration in their Republics, so it could be seen as paving the way for the break-up of the Union. This was not intended in 1988: indeed, Gorbachev intended to address the issue of relations between the Republics and the centre later. Typically he did not appreciate the problem he was storing up for the future.

■ Political developments: from authoritarianism to flawed democracy

It was becoming clear to Gorbachev by the late 1980s that elements of perestroika such as encouraging more democracy in the workplace and encouraging popular participation in local soviets were not enough. By the end of 1987 he seems to have concluded that more had to be done if he was to get the sort of democracy which would ensure the rule of law and prevent bureaucracy from stifling meaningful popular participation. He wanted to preserve the key elements of Soviet socialism – the Party, the local soviets, the planned economy – but wanted to democratise them in the sense of encouraging people to feel enfranchised and genuine participants in decision-making, as he imagined to be the case in liberal democratic societies.

Gorbachev was often accused of being naive in believing that you could transform the workings of Soviet society and politics without changing the system itself. This assumed that the fundamentally undemocratic one-Party State could sustain one-Party rule while supposedly allowing different views, because the other assumption was that all right-thinking people were seeking the same ends! Gorbachev's soul-searching resulted in a series of political initiatives. Like the economic ones, they were not particularly well thought out, and resulted in a very flawed sort of democracy. This helped to make the overall situation of the USSR even worse and contributed significantly to its break-up.

Political change

Gorbachev came to his decision on political reform in late 1988:

- There were to be legal changes to make judges and the whole system of law independent of the Party, so that all Party officials were accountable to the law.
- A new constitution would guarantee individual rights and clearly separate the powers of influential organisations like the Party, the administration, the Soviets and the judges.
- There was to be a new law-making body, the Congress of People's Deputies, directly elected by the people. It alone could amend the constitution. It elected deputies to the new Supreme Soviet (they were not directly elected by the public) and could ratify or amend its laws.
- The Supreme Soviet would become a working parliament with full-time paid deputies. They were to meet twice a year for sessions lasting several months, and basically make laws. The Soviet would ratify ministerial appointments, including the president's choice of prime minister. It could question ministers, and set up commissions and committees.
- This two-tier structure was to be adopted at all-Union level for the USSR and for the Russian Republic.
- Local soviets were to be made more accountable and more professional. They had the power to run local affairs, but were supervised by local elected deputies.

While on paper Gorbachev's reform promised a much more accountable system of government, it contained an important contradiction which he was never able to resolve in his own mind. He always wanted to maintain the leading role of the Party, which had been an article of faith from Lenin's time onwards. The Party was supposed to be leading the working class in creating the socialist state. Yet how could the Party have such a dominant role if Gorbachev was at the same time creating a democratic state in which there was a clear separation of powers between the law-makers and the administrators? How could there be real separation of powers, with the Party subordinated to the law, if the Party was involved in making the law? What happened if the Party, which was not an elected body, disagreed with decisions made by deputies elected by the Soviet people?

The new constitution was not drafted until June 1989 and was then never finished, because the problem could not be resolved without taking away the 'leading role' of the Party. Some commentators believe that this was already obvious to many people, given that all the old powers of the Party, including law-making and administration, were being taken over by other bodies. The old Party therefore seemed redundant to some. But this was not obvious to Gorbachev or other dyed-in-the-wool Party careerists. A genuine democratic system, if it contained political parties to represent ordinary people's views, had to allow for different parties. But Gorbachev always resisted the concept of a multi-party system. Gorbachev's reservations came to the fore at the Nineteenth Party Conference. Before this, the elections to the new USSR Congress of People's Deputies had been rigged. In most constituencies local electoral commissions managed the election, and these were dominated by the Communist Party, which operated in the usual way. The result was that almost 90 per cent of the elected deputies were Party members, as Gorbachev had expected and hoped, and well over half were professional, paid administrators. This aroused so much criticism that the system of electoral commissions was not used in the subsequent Republican and local elections.

Fig. 7 *A Soviet postage stamp celebrating perestroika, 1988*

The new structure

There was criticism of the fact that 750 out of the 2,500 seats in the USSR Congress of People's Deputies were reserved for the representation of specific public organisations. Sakharov's supporters got him included on the list of 23 candidates representing the Academy of Sciences. The Communist Party had 100 seats reserved for its nominees. These 100 deputies, one of whom was Gorbachev, were not elected but directly nominated by the Politburo, whose own members were on the list. It might therefore be argued that the overall electoral process was only partially democratic. The partially democratic Congress then chose the membership of the Supreme Soviet, which was therefore indirectly dominated by the Communist Party. The first Congress of People's Deputies elected Gorbachev as chairman of the Supreme Soviet.

Did you know?

When Gorbachev was elected chairman of the Supreme Soviet, he first had to undergo the embarrassing experience of facing questions about the role of his wife Raisa in influencing his decisions, since Gorbachev had previously talked publicly about how he discussed political business with her.

It was agreed at the Nineteenth Party Conference that local Party secretaries should be the chairpersons of Republican and local soviets. This happened in 1990 and again ensured that the Party was still closely bound up with the State. Another anomaly was that the Supreme Soviet had the power to make laws and supervise the country's administration. However, there was always the possibility that the Congress would amend the Supreme Soviet's laws or reject them, which meant that the parliament was unlikely to be the reforming body which it was originally intended to be. There was much confusion and argument over procedures. Neither body proved effective at law-making or as an institution capable of effectively supervising the government, especially when a presidency was set up in March 1990. Nevertheless, some of the deputies of both institutions did challenge actions both of the Party and the government. In addition, although many Party members were elected as deputies, there was no longer a guarantee that *all* Party nominees would automatically be elected, and so the Party's position was weakened. This became evident during 1989 when the Congress, which had already shown itself not fully compliant with what the Party wanted, saw the emergence of the International Group of Deputies. This group began frequently to challenge the government, the Party and the Supreme Soviet. In effect it was the first organised opposition and prompted the formation of other political groups.

Reform of the Party

In order to justify his belief in the continued domination of the Party, Gorbachev knew that the Party itself needed reforming. He wanted it to be more open, more prepared to listen to different viewpoints, less interfering and less dictatorial, all in the spirit of glasnost. Several reforms were implemented:

- Party officials and Party Conference delegates were to be genuinely elected from competing candidates within the Party.
- From 1988 a Party position could not be held for more than two consecutive terms of five years.
- The Party lost its control of economic policy.
- The Politburo was to deal only with internal Party affairs.
- Nobody was allowed to hold both a Party and State position at the highest level (although Gorbachev ignored this rule in his own case).

Significant ambiguities remained. The Party still controlled some key institutions such as the KGB and the military, and was strongly represented in others. No one could really believe that the power of the Communist Party had significantly declined. Many ordinary Party members felt confused. If Gorbachev did not really understand what democratic socialism meant in practice, neither did they. If they were elected deputies, were they supposed to be representing their electors or following a Party line? A common ideology no longer held the Party together; it lacked clear leadership and began to dissolve into factions.

Activity

Thinking point

How significant were the changes in the Communist Party? Consider the role of the Communist Party under previous leaders and compare this with the role of the Party in Gorbachev's USSR.

■ A closer look

The growth of opposition and political diversity

After five years of Gorbachev's rule, there was evidence of growing political diversity as the authority of the Communist Party was undermined. Early in 1990 the Bloc of Democratic Russia was formed. It was made up of over 50 organisations committed to reform, including free elections and the removal of the Communist Party from influential positions. When the Bloc put up candidates in the local and regional elections of March 1990 , it defeated several Communist candidates. Other parties were forming. The largest was the Democratic Party, which argued for a decentralised, democratic Russia within a voluntary union of republics. The Democratic Reform Movement, set up in 1991, included some former Gorbachev supporters such as Shevardnadze and Yakovlev. There were socialist and 'green' parties. The Soviet Communist Party of Bolsheviks claimed to have inherited the mantle of the Communist Party. On the right were the Bourgeois Democratic Party and the Christian Democrats. Despite its name, the Liberal Democratic Party, founded in 1990, was led by an extremist, Vladimir Zhirinovsky, who wanted the creation of a separate Russian state. There were also fringe parties including anarchist groups, a Humour Party and an Idiots' Party. There were over 500 parties at Republican level, most of which lacked resources or an established base. They were certainly not in a position to challenge the strong executive government, and by mid-1991 only two parties, including the Communist Party, had registered with the Ministry of Justice, as they were legally obliged to do. As one historian commented:

> Political reform, by the early 1990s, had certainly succeeded in dismantling a largely Stalinist inheritance, but it had not yet succeeded in replacing it with a viable combination of Leninism and democracy, of central-party control which yet allowed the voters to be sovereign.

 2   *White, S., **Gorbachev and After**, 1991*

The presidency

Gorbachev realised by 1990 that the constitutional experiment had not been a great success. The disagreements between the Congress of People's Deputies, the USSR Supreme Soviet and the USSR Council of Ministers, which was now effectively the government, did not make for stability. An executive presidency was therefore established in March 1990. Originally the plan was for the president to be elected, American-style, by the entire population. However, Gorbachev got himself elected by the Congress of People's Deputies. There were no other candidates, although only 71 per cent of deputies voted for him.

Gorbachev hoped that the presidency would allow a return to strong government and stop the fragmentation that was occurring in the USSR. Even the Communist Party was affected: Party membership declined after 1989 for the first time in 30 years. In 1990 3 million members (14 per cent of the total) left the Party, and many others stopped paying their subscriptions or said they intended to leave. They cited concerns such as a lack of direction and the failure of the Party to democratise itself or take full responsibility for past mistakes. Gorbachev's acquisition of the presidency did not help in the long run. His failure to submit himself for popular election dented his authority considerably.

Nevertheless the presidency seemed at first to be a powerful institution which directly went against the previous stuttering moves towards a parliamentary democracy. Gorbachev's powers included the right to veto legislation (although this could be overridden by the Supreme Soviet); to appoint the prime minister and other important government appointments (although the Supreme Soviet had to confirm these); to dissolve both the government and the USSR Supreme Soviet; and to get the Congress of People's Deputies to elect a new Soviet. He could also declare a state of emergency. A Council of the Federation was set up, made up of the heads of the Republics, and responsible for inter-Republican relations. A new Presidential Council was responsible for deciding foreign policy. In September 1990 there were further modifications. The Council of Ministers was replaced by a Cabinet, responsible to the president but headed by a prime minister. The president appointed a new Security Council, responsible for defence and internal civil order. The Presidential Council was abolished. Gorbachev used the Council of the Federation to make most important State decisions.

Fig. 8 *Cartoon depicting an indecisive Gorbachev as Humpty Dumpty, sitting on a crumbling wall*

The results of political change

The results of all these changes was further confusion. The president appeared to be powerful, since he could play off the Congress and Supreme Soviet against each other. However, the Congress was elected, and Gorbachev could not force it to comply with his wishes. The exact relationship between the president and the other bodies was not clarified. The arguments went on. What was clear, however, was that Gorbachev's apparently extensive powers could easily be turned into dictatorial powers.

It was a long way from democracy, and his opponents such as Boris Yeltsin were very critical of what Gorbachev had done. These fears were apparently confirmed by a move to the right, represented by the Law on Press Freedom passed in June 1990, five years after glasnost was introduced. The law made it a criminal offence to abuse freedom of speech and spread information that 'did not correspond with reality'.

 Activity

Group exercise

In groups:

1. Discuss how effective perestroika and glasnost had been by 1990.
2. Discuss how far Gorbachev had fulfilled his objectives by 1990.

The death of Communism?

A new programme for the Communist Party was drafted in August 1991, mainly by Gorbachev. The basic notion that the USSR was moving towards Communism seemed to have disappeared. Khrushchev's talk about the imminent arrival of Communism was not only criticised, but references to Communism had almost vanished, other than it being recognised as a 'social ideal'. There was no longer a formal commitment to the idea of a Communist system emerging from a 'restructured' Soviet society. There were previously unheard of statements about socialism having to learn from capitalism, and how major crises and conflicts could occur under socialism. The Marxist notion that the historical process could be explained by scientific laws went out the window. Socialism was described as 'no longer a stage in the transition to communism, but becomes an end in itself … and one whose prospects of being realised can only be damaged by the perpetuation of communist values'. The old Bolshevik commitment to transforming the world was abandoned, along with any belief in what was once orthodox Marxism-Leninism. There was very little in this programme that would have been out of place in the programme of a social democratic party in Western Europe. It is not surprising that 'old' Communists felt moved to mount a coup against Gorbachev in 1991, since he seemed be taking the Party, to which they had devoted their lives, down a route that went against everything they had been taught.

 Summary questions

1. What were Gorbachev's motives in introducing glasnost and perestroika?
2. How did the role of the Communist Party change during Gorbachev's leadership?

Exploring the detail

Interpretations of political developments

Historians still disagree on the significance of some of these political shifts. Some historians feel that several of the changes strengthened Gorbachev's personal authority. Others, like Martin McCauley, argue that the decline in the power of the Party after 1988 resulted in a parallel loss of authority by Gorbachev, who had to rely upon his position as head of state. Robert Service believes that Gorbachev deliberately moved the emphasis away from the Party as perestroika progressed. Others, such as the Russia historian Dmitri Volkogonov, believed that Gorbachev tried to strengthen his control of the Party in order to push through his reform programme. No one is quite certain about how far Gorbachev wanted reform to go, or how much he valued the Party by 1991. He was probably not certain himself.

10

The break-up of the USSR

In this chapter you will learn about:

- how the rise of nationalism in the Soviet Republics and the collapse of the Communist regimes in the satellite states contributed to the break-up of the USSR

- the reasons for the coup against Gorbachev in 1991

- the results of the coup and why the Soviet Union broke up

- an assessment of Gorbachev's contribution to the USSR.

Fig. 1 *Mikhail Gorbachev as Soviet president in 1991*

The old system tumbled down before the new one could begin functioning.

1

From Gorbachev's resignation speech as president in December 1991

The growing threat of nationalism

During the first years of Gorbachev's leadership, the focus of the regime had been on economic and then political reform. Although there had been some concerns about nationalist and ethnic resurgence, few predicted that it would develop so rapidly as seriously to threaten the existence of the USSR. However, with hindsight some historians have suggested that the nationalities question was a timebomb waiting to explode.

A closer look

The development of the USSR: a union of equals?

In the early days of Communist rule, Lenin's regime had promised the nationalities within the old Russian Empire the right to secede from his new State. However, by the time the USSR was created in the early 1920s, those regions had been firmly incorporated within the Soviet fold, so this right only existed on paper. Any signs of separatism were crushed as 'counter-revolutionary'. Although the USSR was a Union of equal Republics, some were more equal than others, and it was the Russian Republic that was dominant. Each Republic had its own Communist Party structure. However, it was the central Party apparatus in Moscow that made all the important decisions. While national groups remained proud of their own identities, they frequently suffered from persecution. Prominent Republican leaders were liquidated in the purges. In the early 1930s the Ukrainian people were deliberately targeted by Stalin, and during the process of forcible collectivisation millions of Ukrainians had starved, with no relief from the State. The USSR actually extended its territory under Stalin: the Baltic Republics of Latvia, Estonia and Lithuania, which had gained their independence from Russia at the end of the First World War, were forcibly annexed by Stalin in 1940. Moldavia was incorporated into the USSR at the end of the Second World War. During that war, Stalin had again shown his ruthlessness by his arbitrary treatment of groups such as the Crimean Tatars.

Cross-reference

For more about Stalin's treatment of ethnic groups in the Second World War, see pages 33–34.

The background: the nationalities under Brezhnev

Brezhnev's policy on the nationalities had been to recentralise control in Moscow, after Khrushchev's fall. This raised again the issue of Russia's relationship with the supposedly autonomous Republics. Seventeen per cent of the Soviet population was Ukrainian. Apart from the other large groups such as Uzbeks, Kazakhs and Belorussians, there were small racial groupings such as the Crimean Tatars and Volga Germans, who had suffered particularly badly during the Second World War. Brezhnev resurrected Stalin's old policy of trying to create a new 'Soviet community', aimed at reducing the differences between the Republics. The Russian language was promoted, and was an essential requirement for promotion anywhere in the USSR. The spread of non-Russian culture in literature and other forms was restricted. The main purpose was to ensure Russian dominance. However, non-Russians were still able to make their way in the Party, which was the one institution that held the USSR together. Many of these Republican sections of the Communist Party were allowed considerable leeway, which resulted often in widespread corruption, but which also ensured considerable loyalty to Moscow.

Did you know?

In 1971, only 54 per cent of the 240 million people in the USSR were ethnically Russian.

Developments under Gorbachev

Fig. 2 *A pro-Communist demonstration in Russia*

The restrictions under which the various national groups lived were similar to those experienced by Russians. Signs of growing nationalist discontent were most evident in the Baltic Republics, Ukraine and Georgia, because these Republics, much more than those in Central Asia, had a historic tradition of nationhood. The Baltic states in particular had only been annexed by the USSR in 1940. Many Russian Jews also wanted to emigrate and gain religious and political freedom. From the early 1980s, however, nationalist discontent became a much greater political factor. The anti-corruption drive under Andropov and Gorbachev upset some of the Party elites in the Republics, where such corruption was rife, often at a very high level. There was also increasing discontent with Moscow's economic policies. Then, crucially, Gorbachev's political reforms as outlined in Chapter 9 had the effect of weakening Moscow's control of the Republics, both because of changes in political institutions and because of the loss of power and influence of the Communist Party. The weakening of central control was also crucial because several of the Republics included minority ethnic groups within their borders, and local tensions simmering beneath the surface now emerged into the open, especially in the atmosphere of glasnost.

■ Did you know?

An additional complication for the nationalities question was that increasing numbers of Russians had moved to settle in some of the Republics, particularly Latvia and Estonia, which created local fears among the indigenous peoples of being submerged within a 'Greater Russia'.

■ A closer look

The fate of minorities

Some of the smaller national groups led a very precarious existence under Soviet rule. The Crimean Tatars had been deported to Central Asia by Stalin in 1944. In 1956 Khrushchev liberated them, but although he incorporated Crimea within the Ukrainian Republic, the Tatars were not allowed to return home. A national movement developed to gain their freedom, and in 1967 they were officially exonerated from accusations of treason during the Second World War. However, when some Tatars tried to resettle in Crimea they were arrested. The Tatars were still campaigning for their rights when Gorbachev came to power. A group of them demonstrated in Red Square in the summer of 1987, demanding the right to return to their homeland.

The Volga Germans, who had first been encouraged to settle in Russia in the 18th century, were persecuted by Stalin even before the Second World War for their religion and their resistance to collectivisation. When the Germans invaded the USSR in 1941, the Volga Germans (of whom one-third had already died since the late 1920s) were declared 'enemies of the State', although many were to fight in the Red Army. Most were deported to the east and forgotten until 1955, when the remaining million were granted an amnesty for what had been a non-existent offence. In 1964 the Volga Germans were declared innocent of any wrongdoing – but they still found it difficult to return to their original settlements, which had been taken over by other people.

Gorbachev, as in many other areas, did not appear to have a clear understanding of, or policy for, the nationalities, as shown by his initially hesitant response to crises which developed during his leadership.

He first became aware of the problem in December 1986, when Kazakhs rioted in their capital, Alma Ata, in protest at the replacement of the Kazakh Party leader by a Russian. But later events proved more bloody.

Key chronology

The rise of nationalism

1989

January	Moscow imposes direct rule over Nagorno-Karabakh
February	The last Soviet troops leave Afghanistan
March	Elections to the USSR Congress of People's Deputies
May	Gorbachev elected chairman of the Congress
August	Huge nationalist demonstration in the Baltic states
November	Berlin Wall comes down, symbolising the end of the Cold War
	Georgia declares sovereignty
December	Lithuanian Communist Party breaks away from Soviet CP

The move towards separatism in the Republics

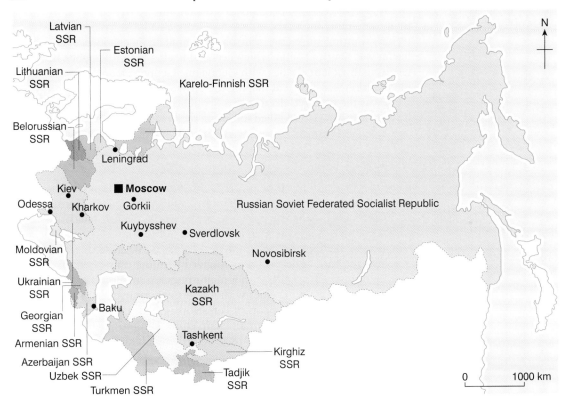

Fig. 3 *Map of the Soviet Republics, c.1989*

Nagorno-Karabakh

Nagorno-Karabakh showed exactly how dangerous nationalist tensions could be. It was an autonomous region, and although three-quarters of its population were Armenian, it had long been incorporated inside Azerbaijan. In February 1988, following demonstrations in the Armenian capital Erevan to transfer Nagorno-Karabakh to Armenia, the Nagorno-Karabakh Party organisation supported this claim. The response of the Azeri population in the disputed region was to turn on the Armenian population and massacre at least 30 people. Moscow was indecisive in its response, and further violence followed. In July 1988 Nagorno-Karabakh announced its union with Azerbaijan, although this was overturned by Moscow. The tragedy was compounded by a massive earthquake in Armenia, which killed tens of thousands of inhabitants. In January 1989 Moscow finally acted, declaring direct rule over Nagorno-Karabakh. Neither Armenians nor Azeris would accept this and violence spread, despite the dispatch of thousands of Red Army troops to affected areas.

There was no easy solution to this problem for Gorbachev, and he had other major concerns on which to focus. He has been criticised for not being decisive enough and not using force early enough or with sufficient vigour to force a solution. However, would that have worked? The whole affair was an early and graphic reminder of how historic tensions outside Russia could easily erupt once the local elites no longer danced to the central Party tune. The various component parts of the USSR were beginning to take matters into their own hands as a response to the decline in authority from the centre.

Georgia

Georgia was relatively quiet until April 1989, when there was a march in support of independence which was attacked by Soviet troops. This resulted in several deaths and calls for independence; sovereignty was declared in November 1989. The call for independence was supported by almost 99 per cent of Georgians in a referendum in March 1991. By then there were more internal conflicts, as Georgia had its own disputes with regions wanting autonomy, self-rule, or complete independence. One such region was South Ossetia, which declared itself a Union Republic in 1990, resulting in violent clashes with Georgians. Georgia claimed that Soviet intervention was aimed at helping the breakaway groups. In May 1991 there was the first free election of a Republican leader in Georgia, although he was overthrown and killed following the break-up of the Union, to be succeeded as President by ex-Soviet Foreign Minister Eduard Shevardnadze.

Ukraine

Despite a very difficult time under Stalin, when millions of Ukrainians had died, many of them from starvation, and the horrors of German occupation during the war, Ukraine by the 1970s seemed relatively stable. The Ukrainian Party was seen as hard-line but loyal to Moscow. The situation by the late 1980s became more difficult because those seeking to follow the path of perestroika disagreed with the traditionalists. The Ukrainian Party split, with a majority group in parliament, led by Leonid Kravchuk, taking sides with a reformist group called Rukh (the Popular Movement in Support of Perestroika). Nationalist protests grew, culminating in a massive human chain commemorating Ukraine's short-lived independence in 1918. The orthodox Ukrainian Party lost membership. In July 1991 Ukraine declared its own sovereignty.

Belorussia

Belorussia suffered more than any other Republic during the Second World War, with possibly a quarter of its population dying. The Communists remained strong in the Belorussian parliament, but faced increasing popular opposition by 1990, from among others the Belorussian Popular Front. The Communist leadership stood firm in the face of protests, which included major strikes calling for political changes.

The Baltic states

The Baltic states proved to be one of the major flashpoints of nationalist discontent, partly because they had never come to terms with their annexation by Moscow early in the Second World War.

A closer look

Nationalism in the Baltic states

The desire for freedom in Estonia, Latvia and Lithuania was not just fuelled by the grievance of annexation in 1940. There were also significant economic and other issues. The three Republics enjoyed a good standard of living compared to other Soviet Republics, including Russia itself, and this encouraged immigration into the Baltic Republics from Russia and other Soviet Republics. The Baltic states were also close to Western Europe and other Baltic countries, and tended to gravitate towards them rather than the Soviet hinterland.

In August 1987 Estonia, Latvia and Lithuania commemorated the signing of the Nazi-Soviet Pact of August 1939, which had secretly ceded these states to the USSR, and this was the forerunner to a series of protests by rapidly growing national movements, culminating in huge nationalist demonstrations across all three states in August 1989. In late 1988 the Estonian Supreme Soviet declared that its laws took precedence over the USSR's laws. In May 1989 a Baltic Assembly in Tallinn (the capital of Estonia) discussed joint action between the three Republics. The Lithuanian Party split, with the larger faction supporting independence. This was a step too far for Moscow, seeing Communists dividing against one another. Gorbachev visited Lithuania in January 1990 in a vain attempt to reconcile the breakaway group, but in the following month the Estonian, Lithuanian and Latvian Supreme Soviets all declared their intention of moving towards independence. The majority Sajudis Party in Lithuania took the lead by declaring immediate independence in March 1990. This move was rejected as illegal by a furious Moscow Congress and there was a prolonged state of tension. Estonia and Latvia wanted to copy Lithuania, but had to be cautious, given their large Russian minorities. Nevertheless, Gorbachev, unusually for him, resolved on strong action. In January 1991 Soviet forces invaded Lithuania. They attacked the radio and TV stations in Vilnius, the capital, killing several people, although Gorbachev claimed to know nothing about the incident! There were similar Soviet attacks in Latvia and Estonia.

The net result of these incidents was simply to fuel discontent, and the Baltic states were at the forefront of attempts by some Soviet Republics to break away from Moscow.

Controversy followed within the USSR, and Yeltsin's Russian government recognised the independence of the three Baltic states. Gorbachev's hard-line approach failed: early in 1991 referenda in the three Republics heavily supported the declaration of independence. To be fair to Gorbachev, he faced a very difficult situation. However, his prestige was irretrievably damaged, internationally as well as within the USSR. The attempt to use force had a similar impact. Yet to have accepted this as fait accompli would have encouraged other Republics to break away and it would have been the end of the USSR. Gorbachev's eventual 'solution' was to call for a USSR which would offer more autonomy to individual Republics. However, any appeal that remaining in the USSR held for several of the Republics was rapidly fading, given the USSR's major economic problems and rising nationalism.

Key chronology

The break-up begins

1990

February	Local elections begin throughout the USSR
March	The Communist Party's monopoly of power in the USSR is formally ended
	Lithuania declares its independence
	Gorbachev elected Soviet president
May	Yeltsin elected chairman of the Russian Supreme Soviet
June	Russian Supreme Soviet declares its laws take precedence over Soviet laws
July	Ukraine declares sovereignty
	Russian Republic adopts 500-day market economy programme
	Belorussia declares its sovereignty
August	Several other Republics declare sovereignty
November	USSR Supreme Soviet agrees to Gorbachev's proposal for a new Soviet Federation
	Publication of new Union draft treaty
December	Shevardnadze resigns as foreign minister
	Gorbachev's powers as president increased by Congress

Activity

Thinking point

How important was nationalism in the break-up of the USSR?

Activity

Research task

Take any one of the Soviet Republics and examine nationalist developments in that Republic in the final years of the USSR What impact did these events have on Gorbachev's policies?

The revolution in Eastern Europe

The history of the Communist satellite states of Eastern Europe is beyond the scope of this book. However, the overthrow of Communist regimes in 1989 was also significant to the USSR. Ultimately, the Communist regimes of countries like East Germany had rested on Soviet support, and even direct intervention, as had been seen in Czechoslovakia in 1968. Gorbachev's declaration in 1989 that the USSR was no longer prepared to support these regimes by force opened the floodgates, because by 1989 they had little popular support. Gorbachev's public refusal to back the hard-line East German leader Eric Honecker probably made the collapse of the Berlin Wall inevitable. However, these events did little for Gorbachev's reputation within the USSR, since they were regarded as another sign of his weakness.

The impact in the USSR of the collapse of Communism in the satellite states

The collapse of Communist regimes in Eastern Europe in 1989 had a significant impact on the eventual break-up of the USSR. These events had already convinced the Party in Moscow that it had to rethink its policies in order to survive. The fate of countries like Poland and Czechoslovakia, which had thrown off Soviet influence and Communist rule, could only inspire nationalist sentiment within the Soviet Republics. In September 1989 a Plenum was held in Moscow to review policy. It recognised the unjustness of Stalin's Nationalities policy (although it still praised Lenin's policies). The Plenum argued that the Nationalities policy needed to be redefined on a more 'voluntary' basis, and with more respect for the culture and rights of the Republics. Some of the participants expressed concerns over important issues such as the meaning of self-determination; the rights of the Republics in the face of directives from all-Union ministries; and how clashes between different ethnic groups could be resolved.

Deliberations in Moscow were overtaken by events in the Republics. Increasingly the Party elites in the Republics, especially outside Central Asia, were identifying with those Republics rather than Moscow. By 1991 Republics such as the Baltic states and Georgia were simply ignoring Soviet laws, and in other areas such as Armenia and Azerbaijan there were bloody conflicts. When Moscow did respond, as in the Baltic states, the response was patchy and certainly not part of a coherent strategy that could hope to restrain, let alone reverse, the situation. The separate Republics themselves were not united except in their desire to loosen central control from Moscow. Ironically it was the actions of the new Russian government in Moscow that pushed the various Republics, which were far from united, into a breakaway movement that ended the power of the Soviet centre and signalled the rapidly approaching end of the USSR.

The August 1991 coup and the overthrow of Gorbachev

The rise of Yeltsin

While nationalism was becoming an increasing threat to the stability of the USSR, developments in the Russian Federation were increasingly dominated by a relative newcomer to high level politics, Boris Yeltsin. Yeltsin's career was temporarily blocked when he was sacked as Moscow Party leader in November 1987. However, he retained great popular support in Moscow, and despite determined efforts by the Party to obstruct him, he was elected by the Moscow district to the Congress of People's Deputies with a huge majority. Yeltsin angered Gorbachev because of his radicalism. This was confirmed by the creation in July 1989 of the Inter-regional Group, which included Yeltsin, Sakharov and other radical deputies. The 338 members, two-thirds of whom were Russian, committed themselves to the aim of a democratic state. Yeltsin also managed to get a seat in the USSR Supreme Soviet when one of the elected members stood aside for him. The would-be democrats then formed Democratic Russia, an organisation which aimed to win support in the elections to the Russian Congress of People's Deputies due in March 1990. They also wanted radical reforms such as a new constitution and a market economy. Large rallies were held in support of reform. Radicals did well in the elections.

Fig. 4 *Yeltsin, Russian President, courting popularity*

After these elections, Gorbachev was chosen as president, while retaining the post of general secretary of the Party. This appeared to put him in a strong position. However, in May Yeltsin was elected chairman of the Supreme Soviet of the Russian Federation, and Gorbachev's power was weakened by the fact that the Communist Party was losing members and much of its drive. At the 28th Party Congress in June 1990, rifts between reformers and conservatives in the Party came out into the open. Yeltsin dramatically resigned from the Party and walked out of the Congress, in the full glare of the media. Yakovlev resigned from the Central Committee, while later in the year Shevardnadze was to resign as foreign minister. After sitting on the fence, Gorbachev promoted more conservatives, partly because he was facing an increasing struggle with the Russian Federation.

Gorbachev and Yeltsin

Gorbachev had a law passed allowing him to create a state of emergency by which he would have acquired great power. He also increased the powers of the KGB. Yeltsin demanded a new government in which he would share power with Gorbachev, who by now was his personal enemy. Gorbachev was in a difficult position, since he was still trying to hold the Union together while coming under more and more pressure from the Russian Federation, which was calling for ever more reforms. Before Gorbachev's referendum of March 1991 on the future status of the USSR, radicals from Russia, Ukraine and Belorussia formed a coalition in support of Yeltsin.

Key profile

Boris Yeltsin

Yeltsin (1931–2007) began his Party career in Sverdlovsk Province. In 1985 he joined the Central Committee, with responsibility for construction. In 1986 he joined the Politburo, and became Moscow Party secretary. He was sacked in 1987: conservatives disliked his populist style as a 'man of the people', and his reforming zeal. In the 1989 elections for the new Congress Yeltsin was triumphantly elected for Moscow, despite being opposed by the manager of the Zil limousine factory. In June 1991 he was elected president of the Russian Federation, and was on a collision course with Gorbachev.

Yeltsin amassed great power as Russia's leader. However, after 1991 many regarded him as a failure because of his handling of the post-Communist transition. Yeltsin attracted attention in the West for his flamboyant approach and lifestyle. He was notorious for hard drinking. On a state visit to Ireland, Yeltsin was unable to leave the plane on the runway because he was too drunk. His reputation probably rests on his stand against the Moscow coup. However, some commentators regard him as one of the reasons for the decline in Gorbachev's authority and the rapid break-up of the USSR.

Because the referendum produced a result of about 3 to 1 in favour of maintaining the USSR's structure, albeit an adapted one, Gorbachev declared it to have been a success. However, demonstrations and rallies continued in Moscow in support of Yeltsin, who argued that Gorbachev had too much power and should resign. Russians voted in favour of

Key chronology

The end of the USSR

1991

January	Soviet forces attack institutions in Lithuania Valentin Pavlov appointed prime minister of the USSR
March	Referendum in the USSR and Russia on the future of the USSR Warsaw Pact dissolved
April	Russian Federation grants Yeltsin extensive powers Georgia declares independence
June	Yeltsin elected president of the Russian Federation
July	Yeltsin sworn in as Russian president USSR Supreme Soviet approves Union Treaty
August	Coup against Gorbachev Estonia, Belorussia and some other Republics declare independence
September	Widespread ethnic violence in some areas, including Armenia and Azerbaijan Several Republics declare independence and sever all ties with USSR
October	KGB is dissolved Economic treaty signed by several Republics
November	Yeltsin bans Communist Party in Russia
December	Russia, Ukraine and Belorussia declare dissolution of USSR and formation of Commonwealth of Independent States (CIS) Some other former Republics join the CIS Resignation of Gorbachev as Soviet president At midnight, the USSR ceases to exist

Fig. 5 *Yeltsin (on the left), Ligachev and Gorbachev, before the August 1991 coup*

a Russian presidency, and Yeltsin announced his decision to stand. He called for cooperation with Gorbachev, on the grounds that both wanted reform. It was not a real accommodation between the two rivals: Yeltsin was aware that powerful forces, including some in the military, were calling for drastic measures such as a state of emergency and a suspension of political activity. There were also extreme reactionary groups, notable *Pamyat* (Memory), an anti-Semitic organisation totally opposed to anything that smacked of liberalism or Western-style politics. Yeltsin probably did not want Gorbachev to be forced out, because a more hard-line replacement for Gorbachev might be more difficult for him to deal with, and there seemed a real possibility of civil conflict in Russia between radicals and conservatives.

Yeltsin won the Russian presidential election with a personal vote of 57 per cent. He was the first democratically elected president in Russia. It seemed there was now a system of dual power in Russia operated by Gorbachev and Yeltsin. However, Yeltsin's intentions were clear. In July he

Fig. 6 *Russian postage stamp celebrating Boris Yeltsin's election as Russian president*

decreed that members of political parties could not be active within State organisations, including the KGB and the army. He was trying to ensure that he, and not the Communist Party, had power in Russia. In another move which angered the Party, Yeltsin signed an agreement with Lithuania, so that Russia and Lithuania recognised each other's sovereign status.

Meanwhile, as a result of Gorbachev's efforts, a new draft Union Treaty was drawn up and approved by the USSR Supreme Soviet in July. A New Democratic Movement was formed in the same month, which included well-known politicians like Yakovlev and Shevardnadze, in opposition to the Communist Party. The conservatives clearly felt that Gorbachev was not in control, and that Yeltsin was effectively asserting authority over Russia. It was important for them to act, because if they allowed the new Union Treaty to be signed, control over the Republics would almost certainly have been lost. However, as some commentators have pointed out, the conservatives should probably have plotted against Yeltsin rather than Gorbachev. They made the mistake of not realising that old institutions like the Party, which they knew and loved, were no longer the centres of power.

Did you know?

At this time there was a strange situation with the two rivals, Gorbachev and Yeltsin, both having offices in the Kremlin.

Activity

Challenge your thinking

Was Gorbachev or Yeltsin more responsible for the break-up of the Soviet Union?

The coup

The various political forces were heading for a showdown. There were people with liberal leanings in all institutions, including the KGB and the army, although these bodies were mainly dominated by conservatives. Conservative forces were weakened by the fact that they had no one obvious leader, although they were driven by a desire for self-preservation as well as belief in the ideology of Communism as they understood it. At times the conservative programme appeared to appeal to little more than law and order, but it could also be argued that liberals did not have a detailed and coherent programme either. Some conservatives determined to act because they were convinced by 1991 that the centre of political gravity was shifting from Moscow to the various Republics. The new Union Treaty would have removed the word 'Socialist' from the title. The new state would become a completely voluntary Union of Soviet Sovereign Republics. If this happened, the conservatives would lose their important power bases in the army, Party and KGB. They were also alarmed by Yeltsin's activities. Gorbachev was concerned for a different reason: if the USSR broke up, he would have no political position, since by now Yeltsin was controlling Russia.

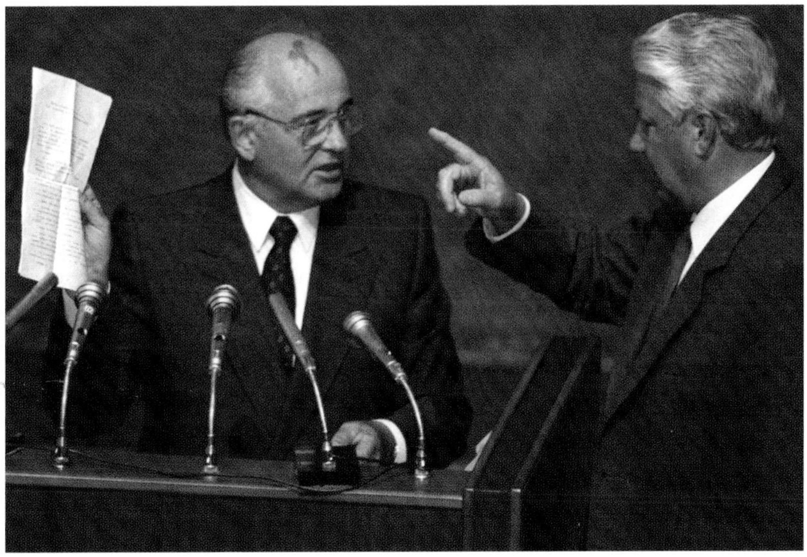

Fig. 7 *Yeltsin challenging Gorbachev in the dying days of the USSR*

On 18 August 1991 Gorbachev was on holiday in Crimea, working on a speech. A few days before, his former colleague Yakovlev warned in a television interview that a coup was being prepared by a 'Stalinist grouping' within the Communist Party. Nevertheless Gorbachev was still taken by surprise when four delegates arrived from Moscow and placed him under house arrest. They dismantled the telephones so that Gorbachev had no

Did you know?

Crimea, in Ukraine, with its Black Sea coastline, had been a popular holiday and health resort for Soviet leaders from Stalin onwards.

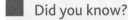

contact with the outside world. KGB troops surrounded his holiday home. Gorbachev was under intense pressure, but refused the delegates' demands either to resign or to sign a decree ordering a state of emergency.

The delegates represented a 'State Emergency Committee', a group of plotters which had assumed power in Moscow. They were eight Kremlin conservatives, led nominally by Gennadi Yanaev. However, the real power among the plotters lay with other men appointed by Gorbachev. They included Vladimir Kryuchkov, Chairman of the KGB; Dimitri Yazov, Minister of Defence; Valentin Pavlov, Prime Minister; and Boris Pugo, Minister of Internal Affairs. There were other key figures belonging to the army, the KGB, the police, the state administration and the Party hierarchy.

Key profile

General Gennadi Yanaev

Yanaev (1937–) was always an unlikely choice as leader of the coup. He first came to attention in December 1990 when Gorbachev appointed him his vice-president, as a sop to conservatives, although his appointment was opposed by several colleagues. His unsuitability was evident during the coup when he headed a press conference to announce Gorbachev's retirement for 'health reasons'. He sat drumming his fingers on the table, appearing indecisive. He was also apparently drunk. His colleague Yazov admitted that the conspirators 'have absolutely no plan.' After the coup, Yanaev was arrested but given an amnesty by the Russian parliament.

The plotters, acting as an eight-man committee, declared a state of emergency. They issued several decrees, one of which renounced the Union Treaty, including the provision that individual Republic laws should override USSR laws. Several newspapers associated with glasnost were banned. Tanks appeared at prominent sites around Moscow and armoured troops were sent into Leningrad. A naval blockade was ordered against the Baltic Republics.

The rebels knew that they needed popular support to be successful, and probably thought that there was enough dissatisfaction with the recent course of events to ensure this. However, Yeltsin called for resistance to the coup, and specifically a general strike, in a dramatic gesture which involved standing atop a tank outside the 'White House', the Russian parliament building. Yeltsin announced a presidential edict, accusing the plotters of treason under Russian law. Enough civilians helped erect barricades to prevent any further Soviet tanks entering Moscow. There was even more popular resistance to the coup in Leningrad. There were also younger elements within the army and the KGB, both officers and the rank-and-file, who were prepared to support Yeltsin. The successful resistance to the coup soon made the committee realise that it had miscalculated. Yazov and Kryuchkov wavered and then defected on 20 August. Yeltsin took over the army and made it clear that he controlled everything on Russian territory. The next day, other members of the committee fled to Central Asia.

When the Soviet parliament met, the committee's decrees were cancelled. The rebel leaders were subsequently arrested. Pugo had already committed suicide. Less than three days after the coup had been launched, a freed Gorbachev flew back to Moscow, after an audience with both a delegation of the Russian Supreme Soviet and members of the Emergency Committee which had flown out to Crimea.

Why the coup failed

The coup failed for several reasons:

- Possibly the biggest mistake of the conspirators was their failure to arrest Yeltsin. The result was that when the coup failed, it was Yeltsin who gained, not Gorbachev.

- Yeltsin was supported by men with considerable experience or prestige, such as Shevardnadze and the Mayor of Leningrad, Anatoli Sobchak, who rallied support for him both in Russia and in the outside world. Leningrad held out very strongly against the plotters.

- The conspirators did not have the support of all the armed forces, including in Moscow.

- Most lines of communication in Russia were left open. The media kept people informed about resistance to the coup.

- Many ordinary people came out on the streets of Moscow to defend the constitution – certainly enough to dissuade the leaders of the coup from attempting forcibly to suppress their opponents. The Russian military was dissuaded from trying to storm the Russian parliament building.

- The coup leaders lacked sufficient conviction, initiative or a coherent policy.

- Ironically, central authority in the USSR had already deteriorated to the point that there was little for the coup leaders to actually take over!

- Although it became fashionable later to deride Gorbachev's role in the crisis, his refusal to buckle to pressure was possibly a factor in the plotters losing their nerve.

Fig. 8 *Yeltsin defies the coup atop a Russian tank in Moscow, August 1991*

Some commentators have played down the idea that there was a lot of resistance to the coup:

■ For all the protests, many Russians stayed out of the quarrel. Although there were some strikes, for example by the miners, Yeltsin's call for a general strike went unheeded.

■ Several Republican leaders hesitated and only came out against the coup when it had obviously failed.

■ It is possible that had the plotters been more decisive and prepared to use force, the coup might have succeeded.

Had the coup not taken place, probably by that stage the USSR would have disintegrated anyway. But the coup did speed up the process because it gave a further impetus to forces in the Republics trying to break away from Moscow.

The failure of the coup was not a triumph for democracy, but a victory for Yeltsin's Russia. This victory undermined the old USSR and Yeltsin inherited what was left of its power. Russia was to be the dominant force among the newly emerging independent Republics.

■ The end of the USSR

The aftermath of the coup

The coup had demonstrated that the central authority had lost much of its power. It also showed that new political parties were too weak to protect public interests effectively. It was typical of Gorbachev by this stage that he showed he had learned too few lessons from the coup, and certainly not quickly enough. If there were ever a time for him to act decisively, it was surely now. He might even have taken over the leadership of the liberals and democrats who resisted the plotters. Even now they might have provided Gorbachev with some of the popular backing he lacked. Instead, he seemed out of touch with events, and he dithered. On his return to Moscow he spent the night in his Moscow flat instead of going to Yeltsin to thank him and the Russian parliament for securing his release. The next day he totally misjudged the popular mood by expressing his continued faith in the Communist Party at a press conference: 'I will struggle until the very end for the renewal of the Party. I remain a committed Socialist to the depths of my soul.'

To Yeltsin's fury, Gorbachev filled the government vacancies after the coup with conservatives who had not opposed the coup and may have sympathised with the plotters or even collaborated with them. He did not at this stage appear to realise how much the balance of power had shifted towards Yeltsin during his absence.

The Russian parliament held a televised session on 23 August. In dramatic scenes, Gorbachev was criticised for failing to give sufficient credit to Yeltsin for his release and for making a declaration that many in the Party were still loyal to him. An angry Yeltsin handed over minutes of a cabinet meeting which showed that every member of Gorbachev's cabinet, bar one, had supported the coup or had not spoken against it. Even Gorbachev could no longer hide from the truth and reluctantly agreed that the government should resign.

These events had great significance:

■ Although the president was now free and on paper a powerful leader, the reality was that his power had been effectively destroyed.

■ The rest of the old Soviet Communist establishment had also been effectively discredited, including those conservatives who had been resisting the reforms of the previous few years and had showed themselves to be incompetent, hesitant and lacking in ideas.

- Liberals and democrats received a boost to their morale.
- Nationalist forces in the Republics were equally boosted by the confused situation in Russia and the weakness of the central authority. Consequently the break-up of the USSR was significantly nearer. The Republics in any case had little option but to break away. Because their Communist leaders were no longer recognised by Yeltsin's Russia, their only chance of political survival in the prevailing power vacuum was to identify with the nationalist aspirations in their host Republics. Republican leaders were afraid of the possibility of being brought back in the future under the control of a revitalised Russia.

Yeltsin's prestige and power grew as his opponents' power declined. He made new appointments and on 23 August suspended the operations of the Communist Party in the Russian Federation. A few days later the Supreme Soviet decreed the same for the entire USSR. The Party's financial assets were frozen and all its buildings seized. Gorbachev had to agree to approve Yeltsin's decrees issued during the coup and accepted that the Russian government had equal status to himself.

On 24 August Gorbachev resigned as head of the Party and called for the dissolution of the Party and other measures to be taken against it similar to those already carried out by Yeltsin in Russia. On 29 August the USSR Supreme Soviet banned all activities by the Communist Party throughout the USSR because of its role in the coup.

In the prevailing uncertainty, Yeltsin was increasing his power and taking measures such as disbanding the KGB and promising the protection of Russians living outside the territory of the Russian Federation. He also took control of the Union budget.

The secession of Ukraine in December 1991 finally killed off any prospect of a loosely federated Soviet Union surviving. Yeltsin acknowledged this, since he believed that any further attempts at a new Union Treaty would be useless. The new states began forming their own armies.

The CIS

In December 1991 Russia, Ukraine and Belorussia formed the Commonwealth of Independent States (CIS). They were soon joined by several other Republics. The 1922 Treaty setting up the USSR was formally cancelled. Gorbachev was excluded from the process. The CIS was a loose organisation, with no parliament or presidency. It agreed to honour international agreements signed by the now deceased USSR. It also agreed on the principle of unitary control of nuclear weapons. More difficult to resolve were economic arrangements between the states, since these were bound up with the old Soviet command economy, issues to do with the rights of minorities, and ethnic and territorial disputes.

Exploring the detail

The response of the Republics to the coup

The response of the Republics to the coup had been varied. Some Republics, including the Baltic states, Ukraine, Armenia, Georgia and Moldavia, opposed the coup in varying degrees, not wanting conservatives to seize power in Russia. Some Republics, like Tajikistan, had supported the coup or had sat on the fence. Some minorities, and Russian settlers in the Republics, also supported it. The process by which Republics were declaring their independence was already under way. Gorbachev had little power left, but continued with his project of getting a new Union Treaty signed, although it was an increasingly irrelevant process. On 1 September 1991 Gorbachev announced agreement by ten Republics on a treaty between sovereign states. He also sought an economic agreement.

Did you know?

One of the major fears at this time, in the West as well as in the USSR, was what would happen to control of Soviet nuclear weapons situated in Republics outside Russia and increasingly beyond Russian control.

Fig. 9 *Yeltsin, the Ukrainian President Leonid Kravchuk and the Belorussian parliamentary speaker sign the agreement establishing the CIS*

Gorbachev's departure

In Russia, Yeltsin inherited some of Gorbachev's old problems. The State still dominated economic and social provision. Yeltsin faced a conservative parliament, which was difficult to control. His popularity was to be tested in 1993 when a referendum on his continued presidency gave him only 57 per cent of the popular vote. There was increasing popular disaffection, and the Communist Party was even allowed to re-form in 1993. It was to become the largest of the political parties in Russia.

Gorbachev was clearly redundant. He resigned his posts on 25 December 1991. He claimed that he had taken the USSR from totalitarianism to democracy, but still opposed the break-up of the USSR.

Gorbachev left office as possibly one of the least popular men in Russia. A new era was beginning for the new states of post-Communist Russia, and the focus, at least in Russia, was on its President, Yeltsin, rather than the last of the USSR's leaders.

An assessment of Gorbachev

Historians have on the whole not been kind to Gorbachev. While not blaming him for the long-standing problems within the USSR that had never been effectively addressed by Gorbachev's predecessors, his policies have often been held to have contributed significantly to the break-up of the USSR in 1991.

Interpretations critical of Gorbachev often focus on his unpopularity within Russia. Gorbachev had high standing in the Western world, where he was widely regarded as a charismatic leader who played a major role in ending the Cold War through his arms-control agreements with the West and his role in the collapse of Communist rule in Eastern Europe. However, he had little popular support in the USSR, and neither was he popular with many intellectuals. The prominence given to his glamorous wife Raisa was seen as unseemly by traditionalists in the USSR.

> Gorbachev was a cautious leader, and he often saw his role as one of intermediary between various factions, keeping in mind Khrushchev's removal for being too impetuous and alienating both the army and the KGB.

2   *Marples, D., The Collapse of the Soviet Union 1985–1991, 2004*

This quote is typical of a more balanced view of Gorbachev. The Russian historian Volkogonov called Gorbachev the 'last Leninist', who only came to reform late in his career, and had never shown a long-standing commitment to it. He showed a Leninist dogmatism in refusing to end the monopoly control of the Party. Robert Service was slightly kinder, agreeing that Gorbachev was an enthusiastic Leninist but also believing that he was open to radical ideas. More sympathetic historians like Archie Brown have argued that Gorbachev was a reformer from an early age, and that he was influenced by events such as the Czechoslovakian crisis of 1968, long before he came to power.

Although Gorbachev recognised that the Party was holding back reform, for far too long he kept to the belief that he could reform it sufficiently so that it could retain its legitimacy and popular support as the driving force in a new Russia. Gorbachev wanted to retain the Party as the driving force in Russia, but his reforms of the Party structure actually weakened it,

Did you know?

In what was regarded by many as a mean-spirited gesture, Yeltsin ejected Gorbachev from the Kremlin with a staff of 20, two cars and only 4,000 roubles. He earned a lot more later on the public-speaking circuit.

which was fatal. It was the Party that ultimately had held the USSR together, and its weakening created a power vacuum. None of the replacements, such as the Supreme Soviet or Gorbachev's presidency, had the authority to fill the vacuum.

Gorbachev was not decisive enough, and was therefore unable to give a lead to those people who were prepared to support him. Some historians like Catherine Merridale have argued that there were many professional people who were frustrated and keen to change things, and that the Party was not as conservative and resistant to change as often depicted. If this was the case, then Gorbachev was unsuccessful in providing a lead for these people. He certainly had no coherent programme for reform.

Gorbachev actually destabilised the USSR, resulting in the opposite situation from that which he intended, for example by replacing liberals with conservatives in 1990:

Fig. 10 *Gorbachev returning to Moscow after his brief house imprisonment during the August coup, 21 August 1991*

- He never understood the strength of nationalist feeling unleashed especially by glasnost, and he never dealt with it effectively.
- He had other personal failings: Yeltsin claimed he did not like admitting to mistakes; he was too obsessed with the past, especially Lenin.
- There was no substance to Gorbachev's policies: they were sometimes little more than slogans.
- He had notable blind spots, notably his failure to recognise the seriousness of the situation even after the 1991 coup.
- He could not come to terms with Yeltsin and refused to work with him.
- He did not work sufficiently hard at maintaining good relations with most of the Republican leaders.
- Gorbachev's policies in Eastern Europe, by withdrawing support from the Communist regimes there, simply destroyed the legitimacy of Communist rule in the USSR itself.
- He made serious errors – for example, he became too concerned with maintaining his good international reputation as a man of peace. Some have suggested that this was why he was reluctant to crack down on Republican unrest.
- Above all, he was remembered after 1991 by conservatives in Russia as the man who destroyed the Soviet Union.

The changes that he started were ultimately uncontrolled, and resulted in disintegration.

3   *Kenez, P., A History of the Soviet Union from the Beginning to the End, 1999*

Some assessments of Gorbachev have been more generous. They focus on the fact that he recognised the need for reform from the start of his regime. He could have continued with the 'Let sleeping dogs lie' policy of some of his predecessors, which would ultimately have been fatal to the USSR. He faced major problems: it is doubtful whether anyone could have resolved the nationalities question once it had emerged as a major issue. Some have suggested that he might have followed a constructive policy, such as negotiating the peaceful breakaway of the Baltic states, and thereby preserved the rest of the Union. However, it is difficult to see such a policy succeeding.

Western historians are more willing than some Russian colleagues to give Gorbachev credit for his role in ending the Cold War and freeing Eastern Europe from unpopular Communist regimes. They are also more inclined to suggest that he showed some vision and was more radical than previous reformers. This was evident in the speed of the change. He also introduced a marked change of emphasis, seen in strategies such as choosing colleagues on ability rather than because they were political cronies. It is also possible to argue that Gorbachev showed a grasp of some important factors. For example, he recognised, unlike some previous leaders, that the economy needed 'intensive' rather the 'extensive' growth – hence he emphasised the importance in economic reform of science, technology and more attention to factors such as prices. Perestroika and glasnost were brave attempts to set the agenda for necessary reform. Gorbachev also showed personal bravery at critical times, notably during the coup when he refused to cooperate with his captors. At times he showed admirable restraint: he must have been tempted to use widespread force, for example to crush nationalist unrest. However, he did not, in the interests of peace and humanity. It should also not be forgotten that other reformers like Khrushchev and Andropov had failed before Gorbachev, and that he had to operate in a difficult environment. There was a limited pool of able people from which to choose colleagues.

Those who argue that the collapse of the USSR was inevitable, or that Gorbachev hastened the collapse, are using hindsight. As late as the summer of 1991, it was not evident to many at home or abroad that the USSR was on the verge of collapse. Some critical events could not have been foreseen, for example the decisions made by Ukraine late in 1991, which were crucial in the break-up of the USSR. It might also be argued that many of their accusations made against Gorbachev could equally be levelled at Yeltsin. Yeltsin, like Gorbachev, did not have a coherent long-term policy. He simply had more ruthlessness, ambition and willpower. Yeltsin was very successful at portraying himself as a popular hero, and he had played his cards skilfully, for example working with Ukraine in 1991 after having been its opponent. He was ruthless in promoting Russian interests at the expense of the USSR, taking advantage of conditions such as economic crisis. Some see Yeltsin as having more faults than Gorbachev, and as the real destroyer of the USSR. Yeltsin's faults were magnified after the fall of the USSR, when he ruled Russia erratically and as a virtual dictator. He was to suppress parliamentary opposition in Russia forcibly in 1993 and practised as much nepotism and corruption as old Soviet leaders. He was an opportunist and a demagogue. He was praised by the historian Volkogonov, but then the latter worked for him!

In the end, it did not really matter whether Gorbachev was a flawed reformer, who lacked the necessary conviction, decisiveness or determination; or whether he was an able and pragmatic leader who failed in a task which would have defeated anyone, that of satisfying both conservatives and reformers. Whichever of these interpretations, or any other, is adopted, the reality was that it was difficult for any one man to prevent the break-up of the USSR once the outer regions of the USSR began to break away and there was so much uncertainty within the USSR itself.

Activity

Revision exercise

Each student should come up with a success and failure of Gorbachev as leader of the USSR and then compare answers with others in the group.

Also, discuss these questions:

Was the break-up of the USSR inevitable?

Does Gorbachev deserve the poor reputation he has among most Russians?

Fig. 11 *A roadside memorial, 1993, marking the death of Soviet Communism*

Learning outcomes

Through your study of this section you should be familiar with the reasons for Gorbachev's rise to power in the early 1980s and his aims for the USSR. You should have a good understanding of the impact of policies such as glasnost and perestroika and how the Soviet people reacted to them. You should also understand the political and economic problems within the USSR which eventually led to its break-up in 1991. In particular, you should have acquired a good understanding of the significance of rising nationalist discontent in the USSR, and the political developments that led to the weakening of Gorbachev's authority. You have also looked at the dissatisfaction in Russia which resulted in the August coup. You should now be in a position to make an assessment of the role of Gorbachev and other individuals in the processes which led to the end of the USSR.

AQA Examination-style questions

1   How important were nationalist tensions in the years 1929–64 in contributing to the eventual break-up of the USSR?

(45 marks)

The focus of this question is on the part played by national tensions in the break-up of the Soviet Union, but since it has a long time framework, you will need to outline those tensions (preferably thematically) before looking more closely at their contribution to the eventual break-up. In examining the Soviet Nationalities policy as established under Stalin you should explain that although, in theory, the USSR was a union of equals, the reality was that it was an empire controlled from Moscow, with the Communist Party the main institution which ensured political conformity, whatever social, cultural and economic variations there were within the various Republics. The tensions beneath the surface, particularly in the Baltic States which had more recently been incorporated in the USSR, will be of particular importance as you look at the later period under Brezhnev and Gorbachev. You will need to analyse the impact of the Gorbachev era, which by implementing reforms whilst at the same time decreasing the power of the Communist Party allowed nationalist tensions to rise in two ways: by allowing inter-ethnic tensions to surface and by encouraging separatist movements to attempt to get autonomy or even independence from the USSR. You will also need to consider other factors responsible for the break-up of the USSR, such as economic issues in order to provide an effective and balanced answer with some judgement on importance.

2   How successfully did the Communist Party maintain its leading place within the Soviet Union between Stalin's death in 1953 and the break-up of the USSR in 1991?

(45 marks)

This question is typical of those that cover a substantial part of the period 1945–91. It requires students to include some detail, but not too much. The important thing is to identify the main trends and features of the Party and explain how its role changed during this period. Since the starting point is 1953, an obvious point might be to emphasise the stranglehold which the Party had over all aspects of Soviet life at this time, then compare it with the situation in 1991 when it had been banned and effectively lost all influence. In between, students could highlight key developments such as Khrushchev's limited reform of the Party structure, which had little impact because of opposition to the changes. The continued dominance of the Party under Brezhnev might be analysed, with reference to its continued influence but apparent decline in ideological commitment. Gorbachev's attempts to maintain the importance of the Party, while eventually trying to reform it, will also feature in the answer, as will the Party's attempts to cope with the USSR's lurch towards some kind of multi-party system in the late 1980s.

Fig. 1 *A nest of dolls commemorating some of Russia's leaders from Lenin to Putin*

By 1941 Stalin had been in power for over ten years. During that time his priorities had been to industrialise and strengthen the USSR, and then strengthen the hold of the Communist Party over the country and his own hold over the Party. Part of this process involved attacking what the Party called 'national communisms'. This meant purging the leadership of the Republican Communist Parties, and promoting 'Russian' or 'Soviet' culture at the expense of indigenous cultures in the various Republics. An important part of this process was making it compulsory for the Russian language to be taught in all schools throughout the Soviet Union. This process of 'Russification' was continued during the Great Patriotic

War of 1941–45 under the guise of appealing to the spirit of Russian nationalism. This was a largely successful attempt to resurrect the very un-Marxist idea of patriotism as a weapon in mobilising the population against the invader. It meant calling on old values which had supposedly been eliminated after the 1917 Revolution as being symbolic of the old backward, class-ridden, imperialist, pre-revolutionary Russia.

Stalin did not appear to have any qualms about ignoring or suppressing indigenous cultures, since they might become the basis for the development of a national consciousness in the various Republics. Although the USSR was on paper an association of equal Republics which had voluntarily associated in the USSR, Stalin had never really believed in this model. This was perhaps ironic, given that as a Georgian he himself was an 'outsider'. He believed very much in exercising power over the USSR from the centre, that is, Moscow.

Under Stalin's successor Khrushchev there was some relaxation in the regime's approach. Some limited expression of national consciousness was permitted, so that indigenous literature and films were produced in the various Republics. The relaxation of Moscow's control was furthered by Khrushchev's policy of limited decentralisation. This allowed some of the local Republican elites to strengthen their power, both legally through their control of the local Party apparatus in their Republics and also illegally through the activities of local 'mafias'. These were involved in all sorts of underhand political and economic activities. Moscow tolerated this, provided the local elites promised stability and prevented any obvious expression of local Republican separatist or nationalist sentiments. In other words, it was perfectly acceptable to encourage Republican dance and singing groups, but not to allow any suggestion of political debate or questioning of the political system devised by the central Party apparatus in Moscow.

This situation continued under Brezhnev. The local elites in the Republics became even stronger. The Brezhnev emphasis on stability and 'not rocking the boat' in Russia was just as pronounced in the other Republics, so that the same Republican Party bosses became even more entrenched in power. Corruption grew to unprecedented levels. The Republican leaderships toed the line, and the Soviet leadership totally ignored local susceptibilities. This was evident, for example, in the way that the indigenous economies were subordinated to the dictates of the economic plans determined in Moscow. Environmental concerns were ignored, with sometimes disastrous consequences, such as the irrigation schemes in Asia which led to the catastrophic drying up of the Aral Sea. There were pressures building beneath the surface, due partly to increased Russian migration into the Republics. Furthermore, there were existing tensions within some of the Republics where there were different ethnic groups living somewhat uneasily side by side.

It was the reforms of the 1980s that brought the tensions into the open, eventually with fatal results for the USSR. Gorbachev's reforms were designed primarily to halt the decline in the Soviet economy, which had been largely ignored by his predecessor. There was no intention of introducing radical political change. Few people realised even in 1985 how nationalism would suddenly emerge as a major issue once the regime began to reform at the centre. Gorbachev certainly did not anticipate that the 'national question' was going to become as least as significant as the economic agenda in the space of two or three years.

A key turning point was probably December 1986: in that month the long-serving, corrupt Kazakh Party leader Dinmukhammed Kunaev, a personal friend of the late Brezhnev, was sacked. The sacking was seen as a snub by Kazakhs, who rioted in the streets. It was a sign of things to come, as the USSR began the unintended transition from the centralised, stable structure forged by Lenin and Stalin into a collection of separate states which faced an uncertain future. After 1991 they had to try to create something meaningful out of the chaos created by the collapse of single-party rule from Moscow and the end of economic dependency on Russia and the military security provided by the centre.

The federal structure of the USSR had never fitted comfortably into a Marxist doctrine which promoted the belief that as humankind progressed towards socialism, so national borders would become irrelevant, because the working class would put class unity above national differences. The Soviet leaders, certainly from Stalin onwards, never believed this anyway, although they paid lip-service to the ideology. This is why the USSR had remained in essence a highly centralised state. The Republican leaders had remained compliant because the regime based in Moscow had been able to ensure stability. Crisis only surfaced when economic and social problems within the USSR prompted the leadership at the centre, in the Russian Republic, to attempt reforms which were not only flawed, but unintentionally undermined the nationality policies which had appeared to work for so long.

Gorbachev's reforms meant the end of coercion and conformity. Although the first steps towards democratisation were very limited, they provided glimpses of 'people power' as the authority of the Communist Party quickly deteriorated. In the Republics, especially those with an existing sense of grievance against Moscow and a sense of national identity, this led to the creation of 'popular fronts'. These campaigned for both civil rights and political concessions. There was no tradition in the USSR of grassroots democracy or independent institutions which could represent the views of particular social or economic groups, because such institutions had never been tolerated. Consequently, once the Soviet system began to break up, clinging to one's national group seemed the best option, if not already an instinct, for many people, whether it was in Russia or any of the other Republics. In the outlying Republics, the instinct took an anti-Russian stance, even among many members of the Communist Party who identified with their 'own' people. Within Russia itself, nationalism took mainly two forms. Sometimes it was a nostalgia for Russia's imperial past, which had involved the creation of a great Russian empire in the 19th century. Sometimes it was a desire to free Russia from its cumbersome and troubled empire altogether. A variant of this was a desire of some Russians to forge an alliance with their 'Slavic cousins' in Ukraine and Belorussia, breaking away from the rest of the Union. When Gorbachev did finally acknowledge that there was a national problem, he tried to make the federal structure more flexible and acceptable in order to counter demands for greater sovereignty. This process began by developing alternative economic strategies involving some element of self-management. However, this simply encouraged some Republics, principally the Baltic states, to try to break away completely from the Soviet economic system. And because the concessions came so late, demands for economic sovereignty soon became demands for complete political separation, which Gorbachev could not accept. The leadership resisted all attempts to create military and police forces that were not controlled from Moscow. The growing differences between the Soviet centre and the Republics were strengthened by personal hostility between Gorbachev and Yeltsin, while popular support within Russia for the continuation of the USSR declined sharply. This was evident in the March 1991 referendum on the preservation of the Union, when little more than half of Russian voters opted in favour.

Nationalism alone was not the cause of the break-up of the USSR. The failure of Gorbachev to appreciate the 'national question' was serious, but not by itself necessarily fatal. The seriousness of the economic situation was equally significant, and indeed initially prompted the reform process that in turn increased nationalist discontent. Gorbachev made many errors, but there would have been a serious situation in the USSR even had a more able leader been in charge. There would probably have been a major crisis eventually, even had there been no attempt at reform in the 1980s. All the emerging examples of ethnic violence and other problems within Russia and the other Republics meant that something eventually had to give. Gorbachev and others received much criticism for their actions or lack of them. However, in spite of the violence which did occur in some areas and the uncertainty everywhere, the transition from the USSR to a new Eastern European order was smoother than it might easily have been. Many of the real challenges for the new states were still to come.

Glossary

B

Blitzkrieg: a method of warfare used by the Germans to great effect in the early years of the war. It depended on the daring use of mobile warfare, principally tanks supported by air power, to surprise the enemy, drive deeply into enemy territory, and disorient and surround enemy forces. It proved very successful in the German campaigns in Western Europe in 1940 and in the initial stages of the invasion of Russia in 1941. It then proved less effective once German forces had become enveloped in the vast spaces of the Russian interior, with their supply lines stretched and facing an enemy which refused to give in.

Brezhnev Doctrine: under the Brezhnev Doctrine, the USSR announced that it reserved the right to intervene in the affairs of other socialist states if it felt it was necessary to ensure the security of the 'socialist commonwealth'.

C

Capitalist: countries like the USA and Britain where, despite some government regulation, the economy was based on the free movement of private capital or wealth. People could own private property and dispose of their income as they wished, which meant that business responded by producing goods that people wanted to buy, and thereby also made profits for businessmen and their shareholders.

Cooperatives: small and medium-sized private businesses that could set their own wages and prices and sell directly to the Republic. In Soviet terms, this was a radical move.

Cossacks: tribes from the southern steppes of the USSR. They were renowned for their prowess as horsemen, and their homeland had only been absorbed by Russia from the late 18th century onwards. They were renowned as fierce fighters, and formed crack regiments in the Russian army.

D

Dialectic unity of opposites: dialectic materialism was the cornerstone of Marxist theory. Dialectic (from the Greek for 'debate') was the art of discovering truth by unmasking the contradictions in the arguments of your opponent. Marxists adapted this to the wider idea that all human and natural development is the result of a perpetual struggle between contradictions. In political and social terms, this meant that previous history had been determined by a struggle for supremacy between different social classes. Marxists, including the Russian Communists, believed they were living in an era of struggle between the capitalist world (in which power was exercised through the ownership of private wealth or 'capital') and the working class or proletariat, who were responsible for creating wealth in the first place. Out of this struggle would emerge socialism, representing the victory of the working class or proletariat (led by the Communist Party).

F

Fundamentalism: fundamentalists, whether Christian or Islamic, were considered a threat by the Soviet authorities, because unlike more 'moderate' religious believers, they had a fundamental belief that their religion was more important even than their duty to the State. This went totally against Soviet ideology that all citizens must regard loyalty to the Soviet workers' State, as defined by the regime, as the absolute priority.

G

Gosplan: the State Planning Agency originally created in the 1920s. It was the main agency for deciding the Five- and Seven-year Plans and allocating the resources. The plans were then broken down into shorter-term plans, and each enterprise was given targets to be met in particular months and years. Targets were sometimes revised while the plans were in progress.

Great Terror: the name often given to the period in the USSR in the middle and late 1930s when Stalin and his security services carried out mass arrests, imprisonment and executions of millions of Soviet citizens, both Party members and others, who were accused of real or imagined crimes against the State. Some prominent Party members, former colleagues or rivals of Stalin, were given public show trials before being executed for treason.

K

Komsomol: the All-Union Leninist Union of Youth, formed out of various youth groups in 1926. It was for aspiring Party members between the ages of 14 and 28. Children under 14 could join the Young Pioneers.

L

Lend-lease: a scheme employed by the wealthy USA to provide military aid to its Allies during the war on credit. After the war the USSR refused to make the payments which the USA demanded, although these payments were relatively low in relation to the supplies which the Americans had provided.

M

Military-industrial complex: a very influential group of personnel in the military and heavy industry which commanded a large chunk of the country's resources. They had their own agenda, and had in the past resisted attempts to divert resources elsewhere. For example, some military chiefs opposed disarmament because it would mean a reduction in the army and therefore their own personal empire.

NKVD: the Soviet security services, commonly referred to as the secret police. It was run by Beria. It was the forerunner of what later became the KGB, and was responsible for internal state security. It had great power, and was effectively answerable to Stalin.

Politburo: (Political Bureau) was the main decision-making body of the Party and the State, known as the Presidium between 1952 and 1966. It had a mixture of full and candidate members, usually no more than 20 in total, all leading figures in the Party. It functioned something like the British Cabinet, meeting regularly to discuss key policies, although Stalin often bypassed it, preferring to make decisions by himself or with individual colleagues.

Second Front: a term commonly used after 1941 when the bulk of land fighting was taking place on the Russo-German Front. The idea was that the British and Americans would open up a second front' by invading Western Europe, so relieving some of the pressure on the USSR, which was doing the bulk of the Allies' fighting. Stalin felt that the Allies were dragging their feet. The Normandy invasion eventually took place in June 1944. By then it was technically the third front, since Allied forces had already invaded Italy in 1943.

Socialist Realism: a concept that had developed in the 1930s. It was official policy that all art forms must focus on the socialist hero figure and show the joys of living under socialism. No negative portrayals were allowed. It was art as propaganda. Typical examples were portraits and giant sculptures of workers, smiling as they joyously worked for the socialist ideal. Photographs would be published of happy peasants gathering in a bumper harvest, even though the reality might have been very different. Art had to be simple and convey a message that all could understand. Therefore, for example, music considered too 'intellectual' and difficult to understand was banned, which caused major problems for some famous Russian composers such as Shostakovich and Prokofiev.

Star Wars: one of US President Reagan's pet projects, a policy designed to put defensive nuclear weapons in space. The theory was that these weapons would be able to shoot down any enemy missiles fired at the USA before they could do any damage. This policy was strongly opposed by the USSR: there were doubts about its viability and its costs, and above all it was seen as very provocative by the USSR and calculated to ruin chances of détente.

Total war: a modern concept meaning that war was not a struggle between professional armies, but a war in which civilians as well as soldiers were in the front line. The whole nation's resources should be directed at the war effort, mobilised by the government. Both the British and Soviet governments operated total war from the start, but the Germans did not adopt the concept until after the Battle of Stalingrad, when it was clear that there was to be no quick victory.

Ukraine: one of the largest Soviet Republics, had an unhappy history under Communism. Stalin was suspicious of what he saw as Ukrainian nationalism. In the early 1930s, his treatment of Ukrainian agriculture ensured a manmade famine that caused millions of deaths. Not surprisingly, some in Ukraine initially welcomed the Germans as liberators in 1941. Ill-feeling between Ukraine and Russia continued beyond the break-up of the USSR in 1991.

Bibliography

General accounts

Keep, J. (1996) *Last of the Empires*, Oxford University Press. One of the best, readable summaries of the 1945–91 period.

Nove, A. (1988) *An Economic History of the USSR 1917–1991*, Penguin. Still the authoritative overall account of economic development.

Bellamy, C. (2007) *Absolute War*, Macmillan. Good coverage of the Second World War experience in the USSR.

McCauley, M. (1995) *The Khrushchev Era 1954–1964*, Longman. Brief and analytical.

Filtzer, D. (1993) *The Khrushchev Era*, Macmillan. Brief and analytical.

Tompson, W. (2003) *The Soviet Union under Brezhnev*, Pearson Education. One of the few accessible books on the Brezhnev era.

Marples, D. (2004) *The Collapse of the Soviet Union 1985–1991*, Longman. Useful analysis of the main issues.

White, S. (1993) *After Gorbachev*, Cambridge University Press. Useful analysis of the Gorbachev period.

Smith, J. (2005) *The Fall of Soviet Communism*, Palgrave Macmillan. Useful summary, covering various interpretations.

Lapidus, G., Zaslavsky, V. and Goldman, P. (eds) (1992) *From Union to Commonwealth*, Cambridge University Press. Useful analyses of the impact of Gorbachev's policies on the various Soviet Republics.

Biographies

Service, R. (2005) *Stalin: A Biography*, Pan Books.

Volkogonov, D. (1996) *Stalin: Triumph and Tragedy*, Prima Publishing. A useful Russian perspective.

Taubman, W. (2005) *Khrushchev: The Man; His Era*, The Free Press. Detailed and readable.

McCauley, M. (1998) *Gorbachev*, Longman. Useful, readable biography.

Source books

Acton, E. and Stableford, T. (2007) *The Soviet Union: a Documentary History: Volume 2, 1939–1991*, University of Exeter Press.

Acknowledgements

The author and publisher are grateful to the following for permission to reproduce copyright material:

Text acknowledgements

p18, p22, p25 extracts from J. Barber and M. Harrison, *The Soviet Home Front 1941–1945*, Longman, 1991. Reprinted with permission of Pearson Education; p27 (both) extracts from Mark Harrison, *Soviet Planning in Peace and War 1938–1945*, Cambridge University Press, 1985. Reprinted with permission of Cambridge University Press; p30 extract from Oleg Rzheshevsky, *World War II: Myths and the Realities*, Progress, 1984. Reprinted with permission of the author; p31 extract from Richard Overy, *Russia's War*, Penguin Books, 1999. Copyright © IBF Films Distributions, 1997. Reprinted with permission of Penguin Group UK; p46 and p47 extracts and tables from Alec Nove, *An Economic History of the USSR*, Penguin Books, 1969. Copyright © Alex Nove, 1969, 1972, 1976, 1982, 1989, 1992. Reprinted with permission of Penguin Group UK; p49 extract from Christopher Read, *The Stalin Years*, Palgrave Macmillan, 2003, pp227–8. Reprinted with permission of Palgrave Macmillan; p60, p67, p88, p96, p171 extracts from John Keep, *Last of the Empires*, OUP, 1995. Reprinted with permission of Oxford University Press; p67 and p79 extracts from Peter Kenez, *A History of the Soviet Union from the Beginning to the End*, Cambridge University Press, 1 edition, 1999. Reprinted with permission of Cambridge University Press; p79 (both) extracts from M. McCauley (ed.), *Khrushchev and Khrushchevism*, Macmillan, 1987. Reprinted with permission of Palgrave Macmillan; p99 extract from Natalya Baranskaya, *One Week is Like Another*, 1969. Reprinted with permission of The Russian Author's Society; p111 and p118 (bottom) table and extract adapted from W. Tompson, *The Soviet Union under Brezhnev*, Pearson Education, 2003. Reprinted with permission of Pearson Education; p113 extract from R. Daniels, *A Documentary History of Communism, Volume 1*, I.B. Tauris, 1987 (with cuts). Reprinted with permission of I.B. Tauris Limited.

Photo acknowledgements

Edimedia 1.2, 1.8, 1.10, 2.2, 2.4, 3.5, 4.1, 4.4, 5.12, 6.4, 7.1, 7.7, 7.8, 9.3, 9.6, 9.7; **Getty Images** 4.6; **John Laver** Intro2, 1.7, 1.11, 1.13, 1.15, 4.2, 4.7, 5.5, 5.10a, 5.10b, 5.11, 6.6, 7.3, 7.5, 9.5; **Photo 12** 1.1, 1.12, 2.5, 3.4, 4.9, 9.4, 10.9; **Public domain** 6.1, 10.1, 10.6; **Russian Look** 1.4, 1.6, 1.9, 1.10, 1.14, 1.16, 2.1, 3.1, 3.2, 3.3, 4.5, 5.2, 5.3, 5.6, 5.7, 5.8, 5.9, 6.1, 7.6, 8.4, 9.1, 9.8, 10.2, 10.5, 10.11, Con1; **Topfoto** 3.6, 4.3, 4.8, 5.1, 5.4, 6.3, 6.5, 6.7, 6.8, 7.2, 7.4, 8.1, 8.2, 8.3, 9.2, 10.4, 10.7, 10.8, 10.10.

Photo research by Alex Goldberg and Jason Newman of Image Asset Management and uniquedimension.com.

Every effort has been made to contact the copyright holders, and we apologise if any have been overlooked. Should copyright have been unwittingly infringed in this book, the owners should contact the publishers, who will make corrections at reprint.

Index